Twayne's Filmmakers Series

Warren French
EDITOR

Lewis Milestone

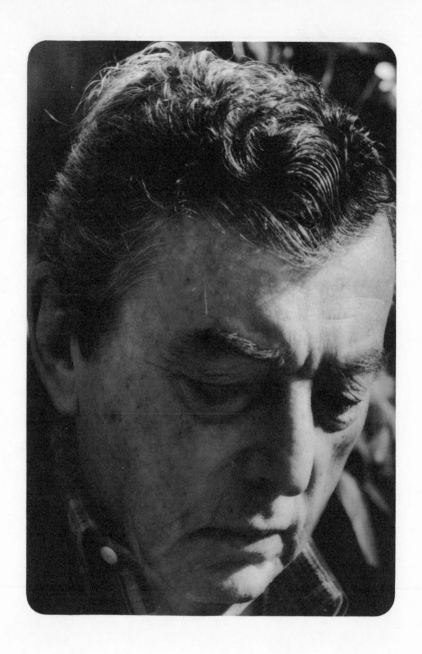

Lewis Milestone

JOSEPH R. MILLICHAP

University of Tulsa

BOSTON

Twayne Publishers

1981

Lewis Milestone

is first published in 1981 by Twayne Publishers,
A Division of G. K. Hall & Co.

Copyright © 1981 by G. K. Hall & Co.

Printed on permanent/durable acid-free paper and bound
in the United States of America

First Printing, November 1981

Library of Congress Cataloging in Publication Data

Millichap, Joseph R.
Lewis Milestone.

(Twayne's filmmakers series)
Filmography: pp. 202–214
Bibliography: pp. 200–201
Includes index.
1. Milestone, Lewis, 1895-   . I. Title. II. Series.
PN1998.A3M4575   791.43'0233'0924   81-4143
ISBN 0-8057-9281-3   AACR2

To my parents,
who took me to my first movies

Contents

About the Author

JOSEPH R. MILLICHAP, a native New Yorker, studied at St. Peters College and received his Ph.D. in English from Notre Dame University. After teaching at the Universities of North Carolina (Greensboro) and Montana, he came to the University of Tulsa, where he is now Associate Professor and Chairperson of the Faculty of English. During 1977–1978 he was Fulbright Professor of American Literature in Finland.

Dr. Millichap's primary field is American studies, particularly American fiction and film. In addition to these areas he teaches and publishes in the fields of communications, humanities, and creative writing. His scholarship includes monographs on Hamilton Basso (Twayne United States Authors Series), George Catlin, and Carson McCullers, as well as a study of American immigration and the novel. In the area of media studies, he has published articles and delivered papers on many aspects of film and television, particularly literary comparisons and genre studies. His most recent research project is a book length study of John Steinbeck and film, to be published soon.

Editor's Foreword

THE KEY to understanding the busy and distinguished, but also uneven and often stormy, career of Lewis Milestone is, I believe, a statement of the director's that Joseph Millichap stresses in launching his account: "Throughout my career I've tried not so much to express a philosophy as to restate in filmic terms my agreement with whatever the author of a story I like is trying to say." Millichap also points out the importance of Milestone's observation in an unpublished article that the director "is the one who tells the story to the audience."

Milestone is clearly not an *auteur* in any current acceptation of the term. His attitude toward his work recalls William Wyler's, as discussed in Michael Anderegg's book in this series, as well as François Truffaut's disparaging identification of contract directors as "the gentlemen who add the pictures" to scripts provided by the production company.

Lewis Milestone was not, however, a passive partner in his productions. As Millichap shows in detail, the director preferred to select his own material when he could and to collaborate actively on the script. He worked closely with all of those responsible for the look and sound of the film, and he understood from the outset of his career the importance of editing in creating a "moving" picture. His comment about "a story I like" in his statement of his aims indicates, too, a strong temperamental—if not philosophical—bias that affected his work.

His work was, in fact—as Millichap points out—notably uneven because when he applied his cinematic style to "strong literary matter," memorable films resulted; but when he was assigned weak, trivial material, the results were usually mediocre. Coupled with quarrels that led to Milestone's abandoning some projects and severing relations with some producers, this lack of consistency in his work indicates that Milestone was not simply a competent technician. He was as strongly opinionated as Alfred Hitchcock, who also usually worked with other people's stories; but he was not able to create for himself a role in filmmaking as distinctive as Hitchcock's or Cecil B. DeMille's.

A comparison of Milestone's work with William Wyler's is enlightening. Wyler, especially through his association with Sam Goldwyn, has become a much more celebrated director than Milestone; yet he had to work at times with even worse material than Milestone ever accepted. Milestone never had to try to make something of such empty material as *Her First Mate* or *The Gay Deception* or even *Counsellor at Law;* yet Wyler brought to the styling of even such froth an energy and enthusiasm that made the films lively and eye-catching. Milestone, on the other hand, failed to make even of Cole Porter's *Anything Goes* and Sacha Guitry's *Lucky Partners* vehicles as diverting as others have fashioned from these works of great comic artists.

Finally, although some of Wyler's greatest films deal with grand passions, little violence actually occurs on screen. *The Little Foxes, Jezebel, Wuthering Heights, The Best Years of Our Lives* demanded a subtle revelation of great love or hate. When Milestone dealt with such material, as in *Arch of Triumph,* he produced his least successful work. Milestone's greatest body of work is films about war—from *All Quiet on the Western Front* to *Pork Chop Hill*—and about other terrifyingly violent situations—*The General Died at Dawn, The Strange Love of Martha Ivers, Of Mice and Men.*

The point I am making is not simply that Wyler had a greater sense of humor than Milestone, but rather that Milestone had an unusual taste for violence and a sensibility that enabled him to bring often shocking material to the screen with great artistic discipline. He had the misfortune also to be working in Hollywood during the period when there was a titanic struggle by the forces of decency to keep off the screen anything that suggested that the good, true, and beautiful would not eventually triumph—a proposition with which most producers and directors were willing to agree.

Milestone's memorable work is totally alien to this dominant sensibility during his most productive years. His talent was for taking stories dealing with war and other episodes of irrational violence and imposing a narrative order upon them in order to make communicable and perhaps controllable the seemingly incommunicable passions that so often ruled the world (his affinity for John

Steinbeck's work is thus not surprising, although one wishes he might have filmed more of Steinbeck's novels, including *The Grapes of Wrath*).

Most Hollywood films, on the other hand, like the Dracula-Frankenstein school of Gothic extravaganzas, the recent wave of "catastrophe" films, and even our most beloved triumphs like *Gone With The Wind* and *Casablanca* begin with utterly fantastic or superficially sentimental situations and then exaggerate appeals to the audience's emotion to provide transient excitement. The prevailing philosophy (in the uncritical sense of that term) is that life is really routine and boring and that people come to the theater in search of transient thrills that offer no threat to our real lives. Milestone, however, preferred material that depicts life as truly horrible and worked on the premise that the function of art should be to suggest that we can indeed master menacing situations if we strictly discipline ourselves to handle them. His work is thus almost diametrically opposed to the populist "lost horizons" of Frank Capra and the pious spectacles of Cecil B. DeMille, the only two directors truly to attain *auteur* status through the Hollywood studio system during Milestone's best years.

Milestone's work is more closely related to the Expressionist films of Fritz Lang and F. W. Murnau, but it most closely resembles that of Abel Gance, who turned out a great many routine pictures like *Lucrezia Borgia* in order to support his efforts to bring his personal vision to the screen in films like *Napoleon* and *Beethoven*. Milestone lacked Gance's intense dedication to his art, but it is significant that they have been most honored for two of the greatest antiwar films, *All Quiet on the Western Front* and *J'Accuse*. Milestone's career is thus of unusual interest not just because of the permanent value of his best films, but also because of the example he provides of the failure of Hollywood's studio system to make the most of the talents of an artist whose vision transcended the narrow limits imposed upon the system by external censorship and an internal preoccupation with escapist fantasy.

W. F.

Preface

LEWIS MILESTONE remains a neglected director of the Hollywood studio period of American film history, that technical, commercial, and artistic peak which began after World War I and lasted until sometime after World War II. During these years Hollywood was preeminent in film production, setting the standards of movie entertainment and cinema art for the world. Scores of successful films and hundreds of entertaining movies were generated by a combination of creative talents within the studio system—the commercial acumen of producers, the technical expertise of production crews, the artistic gifts of writers, musicians, and stars. Yet this cinematic success was most importantly the work of the great Hollywood directors. Names like Cecil B. DeMille, Frank Capra, John Ford, Howard Hawks, Alfred Hitchcock, Orson Welles, and John Huston are known to most Americans, film buffs or not. The great directors combined business savvy, technical expertise, and artistic talent—a rare combination indeed. The reasons for this profusion of directorial talent are many and complex. The most important was the conjunction of a modern entertainment medium with the great traditions of art and humanism. From this primary impetus, the interaction of talented individuals within the great commercial structures of the studios extended the golden age of American film over three decades and more.

Arriving in Hollywood shortly after the First World War, from Russia by way of New York and the U.S. Army Signal Corps, Lewis Milestone directed his first silent feature, *Seven Sinners* in 1925; the last film he directed, the ill-starred *Mutiny on the Bounty*, was released in 1962. During the intervening period Milestone directed a film a year, another thirty-six features, six silent and the rest sound. Among them were classics such as *All Quiet on the Western Front* (1930), *The Front Page* (1931), *Rain* (1932), *The General*

Died at Dawn (1936), *Of Mice and Men* (1939), *A Walk in the Sun* (1945), *The Strange Love of Martha Ivers* (1946), and *The Red Pony* (1949). His early sound features, particularly his antiwar classic, *All Quiet on the Western Front*, proved very important in freeing film from the stage conventions transported to Hollywood with the advent of talking movies. Lewis Milestone had a long and productive, a successful and influential career as a Hollywood director, a director at the center of American film throughout its golden age.

Milestone was both the pupil and the mentor of other important Hollywood directors, from Thomas Ince to Robert Rossen. He numbered among his colleagues and friends not only the best-known directors, but the best-known producers, screenwriters, cinematographers, and stars. Both his life and his work reflect the historical development of Hollywood from 1925 to 1962. His films were often artistically and financially successful, often influential on the work of other directors. The thematic concerns, stylistic devices, and production techniques of the American film are also reflected in his movies. His antiwar film, *All Quiet on the Western Front*, taught other directors to handle sound more effectively, but his World War II movies only mirrored the propaganda of hundreds of lesser efforts; his *Of Mice and Men* is a classic of cinematic adaptation, but his *The Red Pony* merely reflects the postwar rash of kid and animal movies. As late as 1961, when the multi-million-dollar production of *Mutiny on the Bounty* was foundering, the movie moguls called Lewis Milestone out of retirement to finish the film.

Milestone's better films result from the creative cooperation which characterized the studio system at its best. Although he always exercised firm control of his projects, Milestone worked best in cooperation with sympathetic talents. The director himself has said that he did not create the subjects and themes of his works; rather he worked to realize the ideas and values of literary texts he chose to interpret for the screen. When he was blessed with a good literary property—as in *All Quiet on the Western Front* or *Of Mice and Men*—or when assisted by an able production crew and cast—as in *The General Died at Dawn* or *The Strange Love of Martha Ivers*—Milestone created fine movies. These films were enhanced by his eclectic and complex, yet efficient cinematic style, a style blended from the Expressionism which characterized the silent screen and the Realism which evolved with the advent of sound. When Milestone combined strong literary matter with his powerful cinematic style, the result was memorable cinema. When stuck with a weak literary vehicle, an indifferent production team, or studio miscasting, he often produced mediocre results. Milestone's canon proves diverse in subject, eclectic in style and mode, and uneven in artistic quality. Taken as a whole, his profuse body of work contains more successes than failures; the good films certainly outweigh the bad. Thus Milestone is one of the more important directors, both historically and artistically, in the peak years of American film.

In spite of his important contribution to American film, Milestone is most often ignored, neglected, or slighted by film historians, scholars, and critics. This neglect seems hard to explain, especially in terms of the recent revival of interest in Hollywood's studio period; perhaps it might be attributed both to the nature of Milestone's achievement and the natural tendencies of film criticism. Milestone created a profuse, eclectic, and uneven body of work which defies easy catagorization, analysis, or evaluation. The director is not an *auteur*, in the general sense of that widely used and often abused term; rather he seems to have been, like William Wyler, a cinematic interpreter of literary texts. Therefore, his canon lacks the cohesion necessary for either *auteur* criticism or for historical generalization. Also, Milestone was somewhat overpraised in the early stages of his career, and a corresponding critical reaction set in during his later years. In particular, the negative judgements of Andrew Sarris in the early 1960s set the tone of most serious criticism of his films.[1] Of course, Milestone has always had his champions, and numbers of film scholars (cited in the bibliography) have written about his work, both positively and constructively.

The present study, the first full-length work on Milestone, will continue this constructive analysis and positive assessment of both the man and his films. Essentially this study will approach Lewis Milestone as an intelligent, literate, and creative director who worked within the Hollywood studio system. He was not always successful, but when he was his efforts are among the finest produced by Hollywood during its classic period.

This study will outline Milestone's life and career, generalize on his relationship to the tradition of American film, analyze his major works, evaluate his overall achievement, and document its conclusions. Chapter 1 "The Man and the Movies," defines the important critical contexts of technology and business, of entertainment and art, of Realism and Expressionism which shape Milestone's career. Succeeding chapters then analyze and interpret all thirty-eight of the director's films in chronological order; each of the chapters is

organized around close analyses of historically or artistically important films, a dozen in all, with briefer discussions of less interesting
movies. Chapter 1 also fills in the outline of the director's early life
and work provided by the Chronology. Milestone's most influential
works—the early sound films, *All Quiet on the Western Front* (1930),
The Front Page (1931), *Rain* (1932), and *Hallelujah, I'm a Bum*
(1933)—center the discussion in Chapter 2, "The Early Sound Era."
In Chapter 3, "The Later Sound Period," discussions of the
important films *The General Died at Dawn* (1936) and *Of Mice and
Men* (1939) demonstrate Milestone's developing Liberal Realism.
Chapter 4, "The War Years," considers Milestone's return to war
movies in *Edge of Darkness* (1943), *The North Star* (1943), and *A
Walk in the Sun* (1945). The reprise of earlier work in *The Strange
Love of Martha Ivers* (1946), *The Red Pony* (1949), and *Halls of
Montezuma* (1951) is traced in Chapter 5, "The Postwar Period."
Chapter 6, "The Later Years," briefly discusses a number of films
including *Pork Chop Hill* (1959) and *Mutiny on the Bounty* (1962).
Chapter 7, "The Quiet Craftsman," offers some conclusions about
Milestone's career in Hollywood. Finally, the Notes, Bibliography,
Filmography, and Index document the analysis, interpretation, and
evaluation presented in the preceding chapters.

Acknowledgments

HOPEFULLY, this study will renew interest in Lewis Milestone's films, as well as contribute to the growing scholarship on Hollywood history. If it does so, the writer must acknowledge a number of debts, both scholarly and personal. The critical attitudes evident in this study were influenced by many students of American culture, literature, and film, including a number of teachers and students, colleagues and friends. In particular, the writer is indebted to earlier critics of Milestone's work, especially to Charles Higham, David Parker, and Kingsley Canham. The writer also used the tapes and/or transcripts of several unpublished interviews with the director, including those with Richard MacCann (USC, 1959), Dale Mackey (USC, 1959), Barry Freidkin (UCLA, 1966), and Mark Lambert (UCLA, 1968). Mr. Milestone graciously consented to several interviews and to the writer's perusal of his files and papers in May 1979. This personal contact was facilitated by the director's good friends Norman Lloyd and Lewis Gallo, who also provided interesting insights into Milestone's working methods. Assistance was also forthcoming from the American Film Institute, the Directors Guild of America, the University of California at Los Angeles Film Archive, and the Library of Congress. The writer's proposal to do a study of Milestone received encouragement and support from the Editor of this series, Professor Warren French. The University of Tulsa also afforded help in terms of grants for travel, film rental, and typing assistance. Hazel Kight and Michelle Cox typed the handwritten manuscript, no easy task, while Barbara Reinhardt typed the final copy. Long discussions of Milestone's films with the writer's colleague and friend, Tom Bohn, as well as with his wife, Paulette Millichap, produced considerable insight into the director's achievements. All of this help is gratefully acknowledged; without this generous assistance the present study would not exist.

Unless otherwise credited, all stills have been provided by *Movie Star News*, through the courtesy of Paula Klaw and David Noh.

Chronology

1895   September 30, Lewis Milestone (originally Milstein) born in Odessa, Russia, son of a successful manufacturer.

1900   Milestone's family moves to Kishinev, the capitol of Russian Bessarabia; in this small city Lewis grows up, attends local schools, and has his first experience of the theater.

1912   Enrolls in the Engineering College at Mitweide, Germany.

1913   Emigrates to the United States.

1917   Enlists in the photography section of the Army Signal Corps in New York.

1918   Becomes an editor at the film laboratory located in the Medical Museum in Washington, D.C.

1919   Discharged from the army, Milstein becomes an American citizen and changes his name to Milestone. Goes to Hollywood and serves as assistant to director Henry King.

1920–1921   Works at Sennett and Ince Studios.

1922   Moves to Fox as assistant editor.

1923   Goes to Warner Brothers as an editor, where he establishes his reputation as a "film doctor."

1924   Begins screenwriting with William A. Seiter's *Listen Lester*.

1925   Moves with Seiter to Universal Studios. Later returns to Warner's to write *Bobbed Hair* for director Alan Crosland, and to direct his own first feature, *Seven Sinners*.

1926   Directs *The Caveman* for Warner's, and *The New Klondike* for Paramount; begins *Fine Manners* for Paramount but leaves the production after a dispute with its star, Gloria Swanson.

1927   Directs *Two Arabian Knights* (Howard Hughes's Caddo Company and United Artists). The film earns Milestone the Academy Award for Best Comedy Direction in the first awards presentation by the Motion Picture Academy.

1928   Directs *The Garden of Eden* (Paramount) and *The Racket* (Caddo and United Artists).

1929   Directs *Betrayal,* his last silent film, and *New York Nights,* his first sound effort, both for United Artists.

1930   Directs *All Quiet on the Western Front* (Universal), which wins the Academy Award for Best Direction as well as Best Picture.

1931   Directs *The Front Page* for Caddo and United Artists; the film later is nominated for the Academy's Best Picture Award. Heads a list of the "Ten Best Directors" compiled by *Film Daily* from a poll of 300 movie critics.

1932   Becomes production head for United Artists and directs *Rain* for the studio.

1933   Directs *Hallelujah, I'm a Bum* (United Artists) and researches the uncompleted project *Red Square* in the Soviet Union.

1934   Directs *The Captain Hates the Sea* (Columbia) and unsuccessfully negotiates with Alexander Korda about the direction of *Things to Come*.

1935   Marries Kendall Lee Glaezner (no children). Directs *Paris in the Spring* (Paramount).

1936   Directs *Anything Goes* and *The General Died at Dawn,* both for Paramount.

1938   Sues Hal Roach,who removed him from directing *Road Show*. Roach settles out of court, agreeing to help finance the director's projected adaptation of John Steinbeck's *Of Mice and Men*.

1939   Directs *Of Mice and Men* (Hal Roach and United Artists), as well as *Night of Nights* (Paramount).

1940   Directs *Lucky Partners* (RKO) and heads his own production unit.

1941   Directs *My Life With Caroline* (RKO).

1942   Compiles the documentary *Our Russian Front* from Soviet newsreel footage, in conjunction with documentary filmmaker Joris Ivens.

1943   After working on an unrealized adaptation of *Moby Dick,* directs *Edge of Darkness* (Warner Brothers) and *The North Star* (RKO).

1944   Directs *The Purple Heart* (20th Century-Fox) and works on *A Guest in the House* for United Artists before leaving because of illness.

1945	Directs *A Walk in the Sun* (20th Century-Fox).
1946	Appears as an "unfriendly witness" before the House Unamerican Activities Commission. Directs *The Strange Love of Martha Ivers* (Paramount).
1948	Directs *Arch of Triumph* (Enterprise) and *No Minor Vices* (MGM).
1949	Directs *The Red Pony* (Republic), his first color film, in cooperation with author John Steinbeck.
1951	Directs *Halls of Montezuma* (20th Century-Fox).
1952	Directs *Kangaroo* in Australia and *Les Miserables* (20th Century-Fox).
1953	Directs *Melba* in England (United Artists) and *They Who Dare*, a British production filmed in England (Mayflower).
1954	Directs *La Vedova* (English title: *The Widow*), an international production filmed in Italy for Venturini-Express.
1957– 1958	Directs television series programs.
1959	Directs *Pork Chop Hill* (United Artists).
1960	Directs *Ocean's Eleven* (Warner Brothers).
1962	Finishes direction of *Mutiny on the Bounty*, replacing director Carol Reed, for MGM.
1963	Begins *PT 109*, for Warner Brothers, but is replaced by Leslie Martinson. Also directs television programs.
1965	Begins *La Guera Secreta* (English title: *The Dirty Game*), an international production filmed in Italy and North Africa, for American International Pictures but is replaced by Terence Young.
1968	Works on an unfinished autobiography, tentatively entitled *Milestones*.
1978	Mrs. Milestone, Kendall Lee Glaezner, dies in Los Angeles.
1979	The Director's Guild pays Pioneer Tribute to Milestone.
1980	Lewis Milestone dies in Los Angeles, September 25, after a long illness.

1

The Man and the Movies

The Director's Craft

LEWIS MILESTONE'S strengths and weaknesses as a director are inherent in his directorial philosophy, one that can be implied by his films and confirmed by his comments on them. Milestone himself recognized film direction is both a craft and an art, both a job and a vocation. Milestone possessed an immigrant's pragmatism in his dealings with the Hollywood business establishment. He was interested in material success, and though he did not compromise himself in any serious way to achieve it, he did allow pragmatic considerations to influence his choice of projects. In short, he was willing to work on many inferior films of widely varying types simply because he wanted to keep working. Milestone dismisses these failures with a shrug, both real and metaphorical. In interviews he says things like, "Then I did two insignificant musicals at Paramount." Or, "This particular pair of comedies were of the kind you did if you hoped to stay in motion pictures." Or, "What can I say about my version of *Les Miserables*? It had been done before: I hope it will never be done again." Or, of *Halls of Montezuma*, "I liked certain things in it, but it was really just a job." Or, summing up this attitude, "Everyone in the film industry—writers, directors, actors—has to compromise; you're faced with the alternative of staying out and telling everybody what a big hero you are."[1]

Milestone is probably quite accurate in his summation of the harsh alternatives faced by creative talents under the studio system. In his behalf it can be said that he tried to secure good projects, often working for a modest salary or investing his own money in order to have a chance at filming something worthwhile. Also, he did the best possible job with meager opportunities, for example, laboring to realize the beauty of the locations in the tax write-offs

A disheveled Corinne Griffith confronts polite society in The Garden of Eden *(1928) (credit: Museum of Modern Art/Film Stills Archive).*

Kangaroo and *Melba*. But other directors working under the studio system were able to thrive on a diet of programmers. A Capra or a Ford or a Huston could take an unpromising genre idea and turn it into something truly artistic and uniquely his own. In a real sense they became the artists, the authors—the *auteurs*, if the term must be used—of their films.

Because of his conception of the director's art, Milestone never quite managed to transform his material, trash or classic, in this manner. For Milestone, the director was very much the center of a production, but he was more analogous to the conductor of the orchestra than the composer of the score. For example, he has said, ". . . the director . . . in the last analysis, is the one who tells the story to the audience."[2] Notice the emphasis here; the director "tells" the story, but he does not create it. Rather, Milestone says, "Throughout my career I've tried not so much to express a philosophy as to restate in filmic terms my agreement with whatever the author of a story I like is trying to say."[3] Here Milestone expresses a theory of adaptation, not creation. At least he implies the adaptation of an interesting story; unfortunately, as he states in other places and as his movies demonstrate, he applied the same philosophy to any script. "The story is the important thing and the director has no business intruding."[4] This philosophy enabled Milestone to create some of his finest films, but it also limited his possibilities for salvaging some of the disasters he was stuck with by the studios. More than most directors of talent, Milestone was the prisoner of his literary property; if it was great he could soar with it, but if it were mediocre he could only rarely rise above it.

More importantly, Milestone's ideas about movies for money and film as art combine to weaken the creative thrust of his career. He tended to be truly creative only when he felt challenged by the artistic merit of his materials. Although he would make some effort at quality with his potboilers, for the most part he settled for quiet craft rather than passionate art. Over the course of his career this pattern of occasional artistry must have limited his creative development. Not only did he lose individual chances for exercising creativity, he also failed to develop permanent creative patterns. Aside from the war story, there is no typical Milestone situation or Milestone character or Milestone plot or Milestone setting. Even in terms of style, Milestone's efforts tend to become devices at the service of the story rather than an integral part of an artistic whole. Milestone's directorial philosophy determined the diversity of subject, eclecticism of style, and unevenness of quality in his filmic canon.

On the other hand, Milestone's attitudes also account for his directorial success. His philosophy of adaptation provided a strong foundation for the complicated business of directing a film; in other words, this devotion to his text gave the director some place to start building. In his best works it supplied inspiration; in his weaker efforts it presented a challenge. His literary bent also provided a methodology, as over the years Milestone developed a careful procedure of moving from printed page to final cut.

Milestone always proceeded in a careful, ordered manner. "After reading the book, I started to re-read it—this time with an eye to making a breakdown of the novel." This "breakdown" is then used as the basis of a preliminary screenplay. Milestone never penned his own screenplays, but he always worked closely with his screenwriter, though only occasionally claiming a screenwriting credit. He explains his usual procedure in an unpublished article:

After making a breakdown, I then write what I consider to be the main story points. I select from this essay, the spine, or super-objective of the story, avoiding, at all times, a mechanical conception to which I must rigidly adhere. In addition to setting down a conception of the story, I write impressions of the characters: their stories, before, during and after the tale I tell; their relation to each other and the objective of each character in the film, which we call the spine. I find this to be of enormous value to actors who most often shoot out of continuity and, in many cases, enter and exit from the making of the film at random points. The work on the characters and story line is done with the screen writer, who, of course, must agree if we are to succeed in telling a clear story. If the author of the novel is available, then I consult with him on these basic points.[5]

Fortunately Milestone was blessed with some top screenwriters, including Maxwell Anderson, Clifford Odets, Lillian Hellman, Robert Rossen, and John Steinbeck. The next step in Milestone's procedure was the transformation of the story in visual terms. At this point the director worked as closely with his artistic director and set designer as he had with the screenwriters earlier:

As I don't draw, I make sure that we both visualize the scene the same way. Then we try various drawings until it's perfect. Finally he does a polished drawing of it and that's it.

I can see what the scene needs on paper just as well as I would see it on the stage—better, in fact, because I'm relaxed, no one's pushing me, the

front office isn't badgering me wanting to know how many scenes I've done
so far; I'm working all by myself.

I design the whole picture like that, scene by scene, setup by setup. It
stands to reason doing it that way because it saves time during production.
If you suddenly have a new idea on the set, it might take two hours to
achieve the proper angle, and meanwhile everyone else just sits around
waiting for the technicians. It's idiotic not to prepare ahead.[6]

Milestone was not averse to improvising on the set, but the solid,
shot-by-shot preparation undoubtedly helped create the smooth
professionalism of Milestone's films, even his least interesting.

Milestone's care in production did not stop at this abstract stage
of development. If he had control of casting—as he did on most of
his films—he chose his players as carefully as a professional football
coach building a team. As producer-director Lewis Gallo, once
assistant director to Milestone, recalls, "Milestone requested photographs from the actors and began pinning them up all over the
walls. He was composing a cast; he was Toscanini looking at his
orchestra. We then began having readings."[7]

Once his cast was selected, Milestone believed in careful rehearsals, where camera positions were considered as well as lines and
blocking. He would even have his artist sketch the rehearsals,
providing another visual perspective before shooting even started.
Of course, he would also have careful planning sessions with his
cinematographers and audio people, as well as his music directors.
As Milestone always insisted, a good film results from the selection
of good literary materials, a good cast, and a good visual style.

On the shooting set, Milestone was the boss, yet he remained
approachable by everyone in the production. Records and reminiscences indicate that he conferred with all and sundry about every
detail of the picture. Evidently he was quietly reassuring, particularly to his actors and actresses, from whom he coaxed some
wonderful performances. Even a bit player would get a quiet
coaching on how to play his bit for the camera. In all, Milestone
supervised every detail of his production, exercising his craft if not
his art in the creation of a fine motion picture. As Lewis Gallo states;
"I was putting in ten to twelve hours a day, six days a week, and
Milestone worked longer and harder. I never saw a man work so
hard. Whoever said talent is the result of hard work was right."[8]
The production on which Gallo assisted Milestone was *PT 109* (the
director was eventually replaced for scrapping the Service Comedy
aspects of the script). While that film was being prepared in 1963,
Milestone was sixty-seven years old!

The Director's Style

Lewis Milestone is most highly regarded as a cinematic stylist, but as this short discussion of his working methods indicates his smooth style was the product of careful preparation and hard work. As with other aspects of his direction, Milestone derived his particular style from his literary property. As he puts it, ". . . each story dictates its own style."[9] Or, "My approach, my style is governed by the story, not the story governed by my style."[10] However, Milestone had at his disposal a style both complex and efficient, a style derived eclectically from diverse sources of silent Expressionism and sound Realism. When he was able to wed a good story to his best style he created excellent films.

Perhaps the most important source of Milestone's style is his early experience as a film technician. He was a photographer's assistant, laboring in the darkroom, even before he became a talented still photographer. In Hollywood he was splicing film as an assistant editor before he became even an assistant director. Film was always a technology to be mastered for Milestone. As he puts it, "Directors must, of necessity, be first-class mechanics as well as interpretive artists."[11] As a technician Milestone was fascinated by the possiblities of the camera. Especially in his earlier films, he seems often to experiment for the sake of experiment, exuberantly trying the limits of his medium.

The most important part of Milestone's technical background was his experience as an editor. Very early in his career, Milestone was recognized as an editing virtuoso, a film doctor who could save a movie through inspired cutting. As with screenwriting, Milestone, as director, always employed an editor but worked carefully with him through the whole editing process. His bitterest complaints are reserved for the studios which tampered with his carefully edited director's cuts. Milestone clearly realized that the interplay of continuity and cutting created the stylistic unity of a film.

But in the films we must deal with a force called continuity. Continuity is the sequence in which you tell your story. In films, continuity is the structure of your narrative and it is not only affected by plot and character but also by cutting. Cutting is the dramatization of continuity. It is accent, effect. Cutting is the single element which gives films their most unique power. You can photograph many scenes of fine value both in character and story but, until these scenes are properly cut, all one has is an assembly of film which does not add up to any dramatic effect whatsoever.[12]

Milestone learned his editing in the days of the silent screen, when the visual aspects of storytelling were even more important than they were with sound. As a young man learning his craft, he must have studied the outstanding examples around him, not just the work of the second-line directors he assisted but of the great directors, both American and European. Milestone acknowledges the influence of D.W. Griffith, "the father of American film," and the example of Griffith's dynamic editing in *Birth of a Nation* (1915) seems evident in the battle scenes of *All Quiet on the Western Front*.[13] From the early period of American film history Milestone has also admired James Cruze, Rex Ingram, and Marshal Neilan.[14] Although he left Russia long before the great days of the Soviet cinema, he must have been fascinated by the experiments of Eisenstein and his contemporaries. He points out that Eisenstein often referred to montage as "an American invention."[15] Also he is careful to differentiate between an Eisensteinian montage, which he compares to a mosaic, and the hackneyed Hollywood transition pieces contrasting newspaper headlines and rushing trains.[16] However, Milestone judges the most important influence on his filmic style to be German Expressionism, in particular the early films of F.W. Murnau.[17] Milestone knew both Eisenstein and Murnau in Hollywood, and their influence on his work is apparent in films as dissimilar as *Rain* and *Of Mice and Men*.

Milestone's most important films were made in the sound era, and his most interesting stylistic efforts combined the Expressionism he learned from the silent screen, especially from European emigrants like Erich von Stroheim, Ernst Lubitsch, and Karl Freund, with the developing Realism of the sound period. Obviously, technological development of sound film was necessary to portray Realism on the screen. Primitive photographic apparatus, monochromatic film, and poor lighting could produce only a flickering simulacrum of real life on the early screen. Most importantly of all, sound was necessary for film to recreate experience realistically; indeed, it is impossible to conceive of the silent film as ever being essentially Realistic. In a sense, sound added a whole new dimension to the medium, a dimension which transformed the stylized, often flat depiction of the silent screen into a more fully rounded representation of reality. Milestone was one of the first American directors to realize the artistic possibilites of sound, to use the sound track to complement his visuals rather than merely explain them. Like Ernst Lubitsch, Josef von Sternberg, and Rouben Mamoulian, he worked to free the early sound film from the limitations imposed by sound equipment and a stagebound mentality. His war classic, *All Quiet on the Western Front*, remains perhaps the most important example of the early sound film freed from the static strategy of other directors.

In the historical development of American film during the 1930s these general tendencies toward Realism created by sound were reinforced by the social problems of the Depression, as well as by the business trends of the film industry. The alienation of the unemployed and the dispossessed created a liberal response in all the arts. Literature, theater, painting, and music all sought to focus on the common (often the "mass") man and his situation. The critical canons in all these forms emphasized a Realistic response to the problems of the poor and the downtrodden, often depicted within clearly identified American settings. Milestone was a Holly-wood liberal who espoused pacificism in *All Quiet on the Western Front*, socialism in *Hallelujah! I'm a Bum*, and antifascism in *The General Died at Dawn*. His adaptation of Steinbeck's *Of Mice and Men* mirrored the regional Realism of art and literature and documentary film in the 1930's and 1940's. Thus Milestone's career paralleled the convergence of all those factors—technical, social, and artistic—which produced the great period of American cine-matic Realism, roughly between the early 1930s and World War II.

Finally, Milestone's style proves most interesting in its eclectic combination of Expressionistic and Realistic devices. Against the realistically developed *mis-en-scène* he will impose the frame of a door or window, as in the filming of the Ivers mansion in *The Strange Love of Martha Ivers;* within a long, smooth boom shot, he will edit tight close-ups, as in the marching sequences of *All Quiet on the Western Front;* against the invisible editing of exposition he will contrast a montage action sequence, as in the fight in *Of Mice and Men;* across a bright, well-lighted scene he will cast Expression-istic shadows, as in the early sequences of *Rain*. Most often these expressive devices underline psychological meaning. For example, the framing device of a window or a door functions within a realistic setting to symbolize some longing of his character for either entry or escape. The close-up on an important character cut into a long, smooth, following shot emphasizes individual feelings within a group action. The alteration of cutting speed indicates the excite-ment or panic of his characters. His changing balance of light and

shadow reveals his characters' hopes and fears. These blendings of
Realism and Expressionism often represent the larger artistic balances of Realism and Romance in the literary works he adapted for
the screen.

Often Milestone's matter and style interlock in shifting combina-
tions of Realism and Expressionism, Realism and Romance to find
artistic unity in their complex tensions. The present study will
elucidate these crucial tensions as it analyzes, in greater and less
detail, Milestone's thirty-eight feature films. Of course, it will take
into account many factors—literary sources, casting and production
values, financial problems, technological developments—but the
basic emphasis will be on the achievement of Milestone's very best
films as revealed in his artistic fusion of complex subject matter and
a style which balances filmic Expressionism and Realism.

The Director's Early Life

The director, Lewis Milestone, was born in Odessa, the Russian
Black Sea port, on September 30, 1895.[18] Until 1919 his name was
Milstein, like his younger cousin, the celebrated concert violinist
Nathan. The family, a widespread clan of prominent Russian Jews,
for the most part was comprised of successful business people and
community leaders. Milestone's father, a well-off manufacturer,
moved his growing family from Odessa to Kishinev, the capitol of
Bessarabia, in 1900 when Lewis was five. In this medium-sized
provincial city, the boy grew up in the tight-knit Jewish community,
attending Jewish schools where he studied several languages.[19]
Although his parents were liberal in their religious, social and
political attitudes, they still were conservative enough to discourage
the boy's first love for the theater. In an autobiographical fragment,
Milestone tells of his family's anger when he was observed playing
a bit role in a Russian play.[20] After the completion of his local
education, the young man was packed off to engineering college at
Mitweide, Germany, to study a subject more practical than dramatic
arts.[21]

Not surprisingly, young Milestone was quickly bored by his
studies, spending most of his time at the local theater. By the end of
his first term he was flunking his courses and longing for a chance to
do something more exciting.[22] His opportunity came when his father
sent him money to travel home for the mid-year holidays. Instead of
coming home to Kishinev, the enterprising young man set off for
the promised land of so many of his compatriots at that moment,
the United States of America. With two equally adventurous

and At 'Em. During this period he also served as gag man for comedian Harold Lloyd, assistant editor for matinee idol Sessue Hayakawa, and editor for the Fox Film Corporation.[35]

1923 proved an important year in Milestone's developing career. He moved to Warner Brothers with Seiter, serving as assistant director on *Little Church Around the Corner*. According to Milestone, Seiter was more interested in the golf course than in the studio, and the director allowed his assistant to appropriate many directorial tasks. Milestone was soon planning scenes, placing cameras, and directing players. He did his editing at nights and on Sundays so that he had time to learn the director's craft during the weekday shooting schedule.[36] He still worked as an editor, notably on the film adaptation of Sinclair Lewis's *Main Street*, directed by Harry Beaumont, as well as on *Where the North Begins*, the film debut of Rin-Tin-Tin at Warners, directed by Chester Franklin. This Alaska adventure established Milestone's reputation as a film doctor when he managed to hack a story out of the disaster filmed by Franklin.[37] After this success, Warners often lent the young editor out on assignment to other studios at several times his salary, an arrangement which naturally irritated Milestone.

At Warners Milestone continued to aid director Seiter in 1924, as assistant director on *Daddies* and as screenwriter on *Listen Lester*. He also scripted *The Yankee Consul* for director James W. Horne. All of these features were moderately well received, and Milestone was acquiring a reputation as a bright young man on the Hollywood scene. In 1925, the year he got his first chance at direction, Milestone followed Seiter to Universal to assist on several features including *Helen's Babies*, *The Mad Whirl*, and *The Teaser*, the last starring Seiter's wife, Laura La Plante. Milestone also scripted another comedy vehicle for Seiter and La Plante, *Dangerous Innocence*. Meanwhile, back at Warners, Milestone wrote the screenplay for *Bobbed Hair*, a satirical farce originally created by twenty authors ranging from Louis Bromfield to Alexander Woollcott. Between them, writer Milestone and director Alan Crosland managed to find enough plot in the book to showcase Marie Prevost, a Sennett graduate with talent for romantic comedy.

The Silent Movie Director

From the moment he had arrived in Hollywood, Milestone had wanted to be a film director because he believed it to be the easiest job in the world.[38] In view of his extremely thorough and very hard work on most of his films, his early conception must have proved inaccurate. Rather, movie direction was a prestigious and lucrative position which combined Milestone's abiding interests in the theater and in photography. After years of apprenticeship Milestone won his first chance at direction late in 1925.

According to Milestone, he had been pestering Jack Warner for some time about directing a feature, but the executive never managed to find him a property. Finally Milestone offered Warner a story idea he had created if he could direct it himself. Warner took the bait and gave him the director's job, with the assistance of another up-and-coming young man, Darryl F. Zanuck, as screenwriter.[39] Milestone's idea eventually became *Seven Sinners*, a mildly sophisticated comedy starring Marie Prevost as one of seven crooks who impersonate various folk in order to rob an unguarded mansion. The robbers arrive in ones and twos wearing varied disguises and trying to con the others out of a fortune in gems. After seven reels of complications and hijinks, Marie Prevost and Clive Brook see the error of their ways, outwit the other robbers, and turn the whole *ménage* over to the police. Following a short prison sentence, the happy couple are glimpsed in the final scene beginning a new career as burglar-alarm salespersons. The picture proved a moderate success with the critics and the public, and Milestone's career as a director was launched.

Within a few months Milestone, Zanuck, and Marie Prevost had cranked out another semisophisticated comedy, *The Caveman*, which was released in 1926. Adopted from a story by Gelett Burgess, the movie told of the reluctant romance between a coalheaver and a society beauty. The socialite, bored with her wealthy set, discovers the proletarian and passes him off to her friends as an eccentric professor. He soon becomes a social lion, and they fall in love, within the context of this new identity. The still-pretentious lady rejects him when he is unmasked, and he goes back to his former occupation. At the conclusion, however, he sweeps her away in his coalwagon, presumably to live happily ever after. The cast included the underrated Matt Moore as the coalheaver, as well as John Patrick, Hedda Hopper, Phyllis Haver, and Myrna Loy in her screen debut as a maid. Once again the movie was somewhat successful, with generally positive reviews and a favorable gross.

Because of a contract dispute *The Caveman* turned out to be Milestone's last film for Warners until *Edge of Darkness* in 1943. By 1926 the studio was paying Milestone $400 a week, a sizable sum for that era; on the other hand, they continued to loan him out as a film doctor at the rate of $1,000 a week and more. Milestone, understandably miffed, demanded the difference, and when it was not forthcoming he broke his contract with the studio. Warners promptly sued him and won, forcing the obstinate young director to go through bankruptcy in order to avoid the terms of the settlement.[40] Although he had to modify temporarily his newly acquired taste for good living, Milestone was soon working for Paramount. He had forcefully demonstrated his independence, and he had established his reputation as a maverick within the Hollywood system.

At Paramount Milestone became associated with silent star Thomas Meighan, who was looking for a director to do an adaptation of *The New Klondike* (1926), a story about the Florida real-estate boom of the late 1920s, originally written by Ring Lardner. Milestone decided to go on location to soak up local color, so he loaded Meighan and a crew of forty on a train and headed for Florida. The location shooting put the picture a notch above his earlier efforts in production values, in spite of a rather predictable performance by Meighan. The star impersonated a sincere baseball player, unfairly dropped by his team during spring training in Florida, who makes his fortune in real estate and wins his girl, in spite of some villainous tricks by his unscrupulous team manager and a crooked real-estate agent. The reviews were only lukewarm, but the film did well enough for Paramount to number Milestone among its rising talents. The director portrayed himself as such in *Fascinating Youth* (1926), a showcase film for the year's graduates of Paramount's "School for Stars," and Milestone also was reputed to be one of Hollywood's *bon vivants*. Later in the year he began another comedy for Paramount, *Fine Manners* (1926), with Gloria Swanson, but he quarreled with his star and left the film, which was later completed by Richard Rossen.[41]

Again Milestone's talents were recognized when he signed a four-year contract with Howard Hughes's Caddo Company. His first effort for Hughes, *Two Arabian Knights*, was released by United Artists in 1927. The film, Milestone's first depiction of war, was a rough-and-ready comedy obviously reminiscent of *What Price Glory?*, the Maxwell Anderson–Laurence Stallings stage hit of 1924, brought to the screen by Raoul Walsh in 1926. Not only did the director publicly admire the famous play, but one of his screenwriters, James O'Donahue, had written the screenplay of Walsh's screen adaptation. Milestone's principals included Louis Wolheim, the star of the stage production of *What Price Glory?*, in his film debut, along with William Boyd and Mary Astor as the other elements of the central triangle; Boris Karloff also had a bit part as a porter. Wolheim and Boyd played a feuding pair of doughboys, a sergeant and a private, captured by the Germans on the Western Front. Later they escape from a POW camp in Germany disguised as Arabs and wind up on a steamer to Palestine; on board, they discover and fight over a beautiful Arabian princess. Landing at Joffa they have to face the girl's irate father and fiancé, and in the process they are made Arabian knights in order to fight a duel with them. After a series of extraordinary adventures they finally leave the Holy Land for the States, still fighting over the girl. The film received a solid production, with sets by William Cameron Menzies and photography by Tony Gaudio. The movie not only proved a box-office smash, but it won Milestone the Oscar for Best Comedy Direction in the first Academy Awards presentation of 1927.

United Artists also released Milestone's next picture, *The Garden of Eden* (1928), starring the popular silent screen heroine Corrine Griffith. Adapted by Hans Kraly from a German comedy of the same title, the story was of the sort the screenwriter wrote for Ernst Lubitsch, while Milestone's visual production obviously recalls the work of Lubitsch. A variation on the Cinderella story, the slight plot has Miss Griffith first put upon as a chorus girl who wants to be an opera star and then rescued by a fairy godmother in the person of a wardrobe mistress (a baroness down on her luck) and by a rich Prince Charming at the Hotel Eden in Monte Carlo. The impressive production included lavish sets designed by William Cameron Menzies and some excellent camera work by John Arnold. With *Two Arabian Knights* and *The Garden of Eden*, Milestone had become an important director of comedy, both rough and sophisticated.

His next film, also produced by Hughes, demonstrated the director's lifelong resistance to stereotyping as he left the comedy genre with *The Racket* (1928), a tough gangland melodrama perhaps influenced by Josef von Sternberg's *Underworld* (1927). Milestone's entry in the gangland boom of the late silent period stars Thomas Meighan and Louis Wolheim as the antagonists, an honest police captain and venal bootlegger, with Marie Prevost as the chorus girl who tries to get the mobster's attention by flirting with his younger brother. The captain arrests the bootlegger, the

Milestone's famous "circles of entrapment" distinguish his silent films: (top) the soldiers surrounded by enemies in *Two Arabian Knights* (1927); (bottom) Marie Prevost surrounded by another kind of enemy in *The Racket* (1928). (Credit: Museum of Modern Art/Film Stills Archive)

kingpin of the Chicago underworld, but he is forced to release him by crooked politicians. Later the mobster kills a cop, and the Captain guns him down in a rousing finish. The screenplay by Chicago newspaperman Bartlett Cormack, from his own stage piece, proved taut and realistic, while Milestone's direction of Tony Gaudio's photography was technically deft. Some critics ranked the movie as the best of the plethora of silent gangster films released in the late 1920s and it was nominated for Best Picture in the 1928 Academy Awards.[42]

Milestone's last silent film was also a serious effort, one that did not succeed as well as *The Racket. Betrayal* (1929), written by Hans Kraly, portrays the tragic consequences of a love triangle. The stars are Emil Jannings, Gary Cooper, and Esther Ralston as, respectively, the mayor of a Swiss village, a bohemian artist, and a local beauty. The artist impregnates the girl and wanders off, leaving her to marry the unsuspecting mayor. The couple is blessed by two fine sons, and things seem settled until the artist returns. He tries to persuade the faithful wife to run away with him but only succeeds in killing her and fatally injuring himself in a toboggan accident. In a deathbed letter he reveals that he is the father of one of Ralston's sons; however, he names the mayor's son in an attempt to protect his own child. The mayor contemplates killing his boy, but is later reconciled to him by another letter of revelation. Although endowed with a good script as well as fine players, the picture falters because of poor production values and indifferent direction. Some of the Alpine sequences were shot on location at Lake Tahoe, but most of the studio shot exteriors and snowstorms are obviously faked. In particular, Jannings's attempt to dramatize the mayor's murderous impulses toward the boy proves quite ineffective. The film did employ synchronized music and sound effects, but it seemed corny and outdated to an audience avid for sound.

By 1929 sound had been established as the wave of the future in filmmaking, and Milestone was naturally interested in trying his hand at the new medium. He turned down a musical starring the Two Black Crows, a successful vaudeville team, and then accepted the assignment of *New York Nights,* an overwrought melodrama, which combined the genres of gangster and "show biz" movies. Released by United Artists, the movie was produced by Joseph Schenck as the first sound vehicle for his wife, Norma Talmadge, a popular star of the silent screen. Also featured were Gilbert Roland as Talmadge's husband and John Wray as her gangster boyfriend.

Roland is a songwriter who needs the gangster's help in plugging his latest effort. Talmadge tries to sweet-talk the gangster and, through a jealous mix-up, runs off with him, only to be reconciled with the songwriter when they all wind up in police court. The plot is from a justly forgotten play, *Tin Pan Alley* by Hugh S. Strange, and it represents Hollywood's desperate efforts to bring Broadway to the screen in the early years of sound.

In several ways, the film is best considered with Milestone's silent efforts, as it seems an obviously unimportant transitional piece. Like many early sound films it is shot from a few camera settings, and it is full of static scenes in which the cast is all too obviously speaking into hidden microphones. Milestone was so displeased with the final cut that he asked to have his name removed from the credits.[43] For some reason it was not. However, the film is not worth considering as Milestone's first sound work. Rather, his next effort, his master-piece, *All Quiet on the Western Front*, deserves that consideration.

2

The Early Sound Era

All Quiet on the Western Front

FILM HISTORIANS generally recognize *All Quiet on the Western Front* as a breakthrough film in terms of its use of sound. From *The Jazz Singer* (1927) to Milestone's masterpiece in 1930, motion pictures were rendered strangely static by the introduction of sound, a situation resulting from both the commercial and technical problems inherent in the early development of sound techniques. Originally sound was a gimmick introduced to increase the sales of movie tickets; audiences were happy to listen to anything, and for the most part they listened to established entertainments with sound properties—nightclub acts, vaudeville routines, and Broadway plays. The inherent stasis in these works was increased by early recording equipment, which was both delicate and cumbersome, impeding the movement which lends film its visual excitement. Milestone, along with other directors, like Rouben Mamoulian, Ernst Lubitsch, and Josef von Sternberg, could see possibilities in sound films not realized in the early transcriptions of theatrical works. In 1929 Paramount had offered Milestone the direction of a talking picture starring the well-known vaudeville team the Two Black Crows.[1] Milestone declined, concluding that the sound engineer would be the real director, which indeed was the case with his *New York Nights,* made the same year for United Artists. He studied the sound process carefully before making *All Quiet on the Western Front,* discovering that a film could be shot in traditional visual terms if postsynchronization were used for the sound track. To his company Milestone decreed: "... 'we shoot the way we've always shot.'" At the end of his career he would reminisce: "and that ... was the big sound revolution; it was that simple, all the tracking shots, for example, were done with a silent camera."[2] With

this simple and logical development Milestone was able to combine
the Realism of sound in both dialogue and effects with the Expressionistic visual techniques he had learned as a silent editor and
director.

All Quiet on the Western Front (1930) is generally regarded as
Lewis Milestone's masterpiece, his most important work in terms of
both subject and style. The majority of the contemporary reviews
were ecstatic, and the Motion Picture Academy recognized his
achievement with Oscars for Best Film and Best Direction. Since
1930 most critics have been generous with their praise, though there
also have been recent exceptions. This study will reiterate the
historical importance and artistic success of Milestone's creation,
while advancing certain reservations about the film by means of a
comparison with Erich Maria Remarque's classic novel, from which
the film was adapted.

Remarque's book had been published in 1929, receiving lavish
praise which generated sensational sales not only in Germany but in
the rest of the world. When the book sold well in America, Universal
Studios acquired the screen rights and began a search for a director
capable of doing justice to this important property. Someone at
Universal had been sufficiently impressed with *Two Arabian
Knights,* Milestone's earlier effort in the war-comedy genre, to offer
him a chance at the direction of *All Quiet on the Western Front.*
The young director was excited by the project, his first important
sound film as well as his first adaptation of a novel, and he settled -
for a relatively low salary in order to obtain the contract. Milestone
was also attracted to the project by the grim realism and antiwar
themes of Remarque's novel. At the end of his career, Milestone
could look back and say, "I've probably had my greatest successes
with war films because I've always tried to expose war for what it is
and not glorify it."[3]

In his adaptation the director had his first chance to translate a
powerful literary statement into cinematic language. For the most
part he succeeded admirably, producing the most realistic and
moving of American war films, perhaps the best war film ever made.
Undoubtedly the primary source of the film's power is to be found
in the novel's bitter but compassionate vision. *All Quiet on the
Western Front* remains an important, widely read book because,
like the film, it makes a definitive statement about modern warfare.
Remarque, a Western Front veteran wounded several times, wrote
the novel in the transition between the despair of the Weimar
Republic and the madness of the Third Reich. Remarque's message

was an agonized plea that the horrors of the Western Front's trenches never be repeated. The novel's thematic impact was subtly reinforced by its matter-of-fact style. The simple, straightforward style of Paul Baumer's case contrasts beautifully with the monumental terror of his experience. Remarque's novel was actually only one of a number of similar works which formed a movement in German literature between the wars sometimes called New-Realism. These New-Realistic writers turned away from the Expressionism of the 1920s in their attempt to objectify the horror of the war and the chaos of the peace.

Sound provided the primary impetus toward Realism in the films of the 1930s, though other social and artistic factors reinforced its impact as the dominant mode of the period. In *All Quiet on the Western Front* the technology of sound allowed Milestone to reproduce the terse, tough dialogue of Remarque's novel, assuring the film some degree of the novel's harsh Realism. Yet other influences pulled Milestone's version away from Realism, weakening the artistic balance between matter and style which informs the book. Milestone had done his apprenticeship in the era of silent Expressionism, directing seven silent features and editing many others. While he could celebrate the way sound had freed the directors from ". . . trying to tell the story through pieces of business and pantomime,"[4] his appreciation of German Expressionism and Russian montage pulled him toward Expressionistic overstatement in his translation of *All Quiet on the Western Front*. In short, Milestone's artistic training, in combination with the influences of the studio production system, tended, at least slightly, toward the romanticizing of literary properties so common in Hollywood adaptation.

Milestone's collaborators on the film may have exerted even more romanticizing influence. For example, the preliminary dramatic treatment of Remarque's novel was done by playwright Maxwell Anderson. Milestone admired *What Price Glory?*, Anderson's 1924 Broadway smash, written with Laurence Stallings, which traced the colorful adventures of Capt. Flagg and Sgt. Quirt on the Western Front. Milestone's *Two Arabian Knights* (1928) was suggested by *What Price Glory?* and by Raoul Walsh's film version of the play, made in 1926. Moreover, Milestone's choice for the role of Katcinsky, Louis Wolheim, played one of the two feuding doughboys in both the stage version of *What Price Glory?* and in Milestone's *Two Arabian Knights*. Thus the director's primary screenwriter and leading actor were both inclined toward dramatizing a rough-and-tumble camaraderie among the men in the trenches. Remarque treats *Kameradschaft* as a major theme in his novel, but his treatment avoids all the colorful heroics of Flagg and Quirt or Phelps and McGaffney. Wolheim's performance as "Kat" inclines somewhat toward those multiple recreations of a gruff and growling "Sarge" with a heart of gold familiar from dozens of Hollywood war movies.

The film's treatment of the central character, Paul Baumer, also edges toward sentimentality. In the novel Paul is portrayed as sensitive, naive, and innocent, yet Lew Ayres's characterization develops Paul beyond innocence to a sort of sophomoric saintliness. Some film critics even suggest that he becomes a sacrificial figure, another modern guise of a crucified Christ. Again director, writer, and player seem to cooperate in the transformation. The Christ images are developed in the graphic depictions of crosses and wounds, inventions of Milestone's directorial eye. Yet the characterization foreshadows also Anderson's heroic historical plays, particularly *Joan of Lorraine* (1946), the basis of the 1948 film *Joan of Arc* with Ingrid Bergman. Finally, the twenty-year-old Lew Ayres seems not quite capable of Paul Baumer's complex blending of innocence and bitterness. Although Ayres's conscientious-objector status during World War II underlined the sincerity of his personal convictions, his artistic development never grew beyond Paul Baumer grown into an adolescent Dr. Kildare.

The supporting company, both players and technicians, confirm similar developments; aside from Raymond Griffith's brilliant cameo as the French soldier Baumer fatally wounds and must watch die, the rest of the cast ranges from competence to schmaltz. Paul's classmates, the ironically named "Iron Men," prove rather callow youth, while the rougher peasant types are represented by Slim Summerville as Tjaden, a characterization close to the comic relief he provided in many Westerns. The novel's petty tyrants, Kantorek the schoolmaster and Himmelstoss the postman become a sergeant, are transformed by Arnold Lucy and John Wray into villains of the silent screen. Some officers on horseback reviewing the new recruits even look like clones of Erich von Stroheim, while Beryl Mercer as Paul's mother and Marion Clayton as his sister seem to have wandered in from a D. W. Griffith set.

More subtle influences were exerted by cinematographers Arthur Edeson and Karl Freund. Both men were noted for their silent films, Edeson's in Hollywood, Freund's in Germany. The screen credits of both men point toward an extension of Expressionistic style into the sound era, and their influence on Milestone's graphic conception of the adaptation was considerable. For example, it was Freund who suggested the famous concluding sequence of the film. In the novel Paul's death is merely reported in a tersely ironic epilogue; in the film his death is dramatized as he is picked off by a sniper while reaching for a butterfly. The invention is beautifully and thematically correct, but the sequence is handled in terms of Expressionstic cross-cut close-ups, brilliant in their own way but stylistically antithetical to the novel's concluding ironies. Of course the terse irony of the novel's conclusion almost of necessity escaped the filmic adapter. The novel is told from Paul's viewpoint, and the conclusion is a framing coda added by an omniscient voice. "He fell in October 1918, on a day that was so quiet and still on the whole front, that the army report confined itself to the single sentence: All quiet on the Western Front. He had fallen forward and lay on the earth as though sleeping. Turning him over one saw that he could not have suffered long; his face had an expression of calm, as though almost glad the end had come" (p. 256).[5] Only at the novel's conclusion does the reader discover the full irony of its title: the only quiet on the Western Front is the stillness of death. Milestone, of course, was forced to depict Paul's death in imagistic terms.[6] He comments: "Each of our portentous endings seemed worse than its predecessor, and I kept throwing them away."[7] Finally Freund suggested the butterfly idea, but Milestone, against his own advice, ends with a further visual and audial crescendo. After Paul's death the image of the "Iron Youth" marching to their first engagement is superimposed over a massive battlefield graveyard, a forest of white crosses. In the background the orchestral strains swell from the simple harmonica accompaniment of the death scene. In both theme and style this last shot symbolizes the whole process of filmic transcription: the antiwar feeling is overstated by the Expressionistic device of superimposition, a gesture which would become a cliché conclusion for war films.[8]

Not all the changes from the novel work to the film's detriment. As in many filmic adaptations, the screenplay tightens the plot, avoids some repetition, and excises some digressions. In general, the screenplay gains a good deal for what it sacrifices. The objectivity of the camera eye balances the loss of intimacy in transforming Paul's story from first to third person. The thematic embellishments of an Expressionistic style for the most part match the ironic underlining created by Paul's understatement. Finally the chronological and geographical simplification of the plot compensates the loss of complexity with the increase in order, logic, and thematic emphasis.

After the credits the film opens on the homefront at the beginning of the war: the novel begins *in medias res*, about midway in Paul's war experience, and his earlier life is recalled in reminiscence. In some ways, the order of the screenplay better emphasizes the basic mode of the novel, a sort of anti-*Bildungsroman* (development novel). Since Paul Baumer is the writer of the work, it might also be considered a sort of anti-*Kunstlerroman* (artist's novel). Remarque seems to be consciously reversing the usual patterns of the genre by having his hero schooled in death rather than life. An excellent definition of the *Bildungsroman* appears in Suzanne Howe's *Wilhelm Meister and His English Kinsmen:* "The adolescent hero of the typical apprentice [novel] sets out on his way through the world, meets with reverses generally due to his own temperament, falls in with various guides and counsellors, makes many false starts in choosing his friends, his wife, and his life work, and finally adjusts himself in some way to the demands of his time and environment by finding a sphere of action in which he may work effectively."[9] Paul's false starts result from the bad counsel of his early father figures, particularly his own ineffectual father and the schoolroom tyrant Kantorek. The Western Front is an environment which allows no real maturation; the "Iron Youth" are quickly old before their time. Finally death remains the only adjustment to this world at war; as Paul's comrade Albert puts it, "The war has ruined us for everything" (81).

The film's opening sequence underlines this sense of the war as a destructive educational experience. The scene is Dolbenberg, Paul's hometown, where the townsfolk prattle about the glory of the war as a local regiment parades through the streets, their rifle barrels sprouting bouquets of flowers. Milestone deftly frames his shots through a series of doors, windows, and arches creating a visual sense of the civilian view of the war, a viewpoint heard in the dialogue. The butcher and the postman agree that it will be over in a few months. Milestone's camera tracks all this action deftly, finally pulling back from the martial band to reveal Paul Baumer's classroom. Here the director handles sound imaginatively, as the passing band drowns out the professor's lecture; he is held in a medium-long shot, working his mouth but communicating nothing, and, when he is at last heard, his patriotic ranting has already been characterized by the military march. Milestone cuts back and forth between the schoolmaster and his rapt audience, "The Iron Men of Germany," and as he raves on about the "Fatherland" the camera pulls tighter and tighter in close-ups revealing the fanaticism in the old man's vision. By contrast, the close-ups of the starry-eyed youths reveal their innocence and naiveté. One by one they assent to Kantorek's call for immediate enlistment; then the camera pulls back to view the whole room, now alive with cheering, singing students, and the seemingly endless parade still passing by outside the windows.

Most of the first sequence was developed from a brief reminiscence in Chapter 1 of the novel; the film's second sequence, the training camp, follows other bits of reminiscence from the novel's second and third chapters. In the first shot, a heavy gate opens to reveal the huge paradeground from the perspective of the recruits who are entering another stage of their development. An aerial shot also establishes both the immensity of the camp and the relative unimportance of this group of recruits. However, a series of close-ups on the marching column identifies Paul and his comrades in a pattern of presentation which will be repeated to the conclusion of the film. Again the group is framed in a barracks door as they receive their first orders; inside they are framed by bunkbeds as they change from civilian clothes to uniform. Slim, healthy bodies become visual analogues to their exuberant shouts and boasts. Suddenly Himmelstoss, the Postman turned Sergeant, appears to shape up his recruits. Although actor John Wray overdoes the role, Milestone neatly tracks the martinet as he strides between the parallel lines of schoolboys. Ominously he tells them to forget everything they ever learned, and that he will make soldiers of them even if it kills them in the process.

On the drillfield the boys are seen with their weapons, their individual identities lost in a universal pattern of uniforms, packs, and spiked Prussian helmets. Himmelstoss is panned upward from his shiny boots to his glittering helmet. He enjoys himself immensely as he forces the recruits to crawl through acres of mud, screaming at them to keep their faces in it. Up and down, left and right, the group marches and flops, with camera close-ups on muddy faces and boots; the recruits are beginning to sense some of the ugliness of war. When Himmelstoss calls on them to sing a patriotic song as they march, the response is much different from the classoom. At last, two von Stroheim–like officers announce from their lofty perch on horseback that this group of "Iron Youth" are ready for the front.

The sequence of the arrival at the front is not found in the novel, though a few of the details are taken from the arrival of later shipments of cannon-fodder. This sequence demonstrates the strength of chronological and geographical order, though it also exhibits some weaknesses in terms of clichés about the first experience of green troops. Remarque began his novel with a well-integrated group of veterans and comrades; Milestone has the schoolboys and the peasants come together with understandable awkwardness. Again the sequence opens with a shot through a frame, here the window of a railroad station in a front-line town. Through the window the recruits receive their first view of the results of war, ruined buildings and Red Cross cars full of wounded, and of the causes as shells began to fall into the scene. Milestone suggests the general confusion by moving masses of men in various directions across the screen. Huge gun carriages rattle down the middle of the road, moving in the opposite direction to the marching recruits. The director also manipulates the movement between shots as he intersperses close-ups of individual faces and boots within the sea of soldiers. Once again a doorway serves as a framing device as the group enters a bombed-out house, the billet of the Second Company.

Here Paul and his comrades meet the other soldiers in the company, Westhus, Detering, and Tjaden. After some slightly corny humor about the poor food, Tjaden mentions "Kat" Katcinsky (Louis Wolheim), who is out foraging for food. Kat is introduced by the familiar movie device of a discussion which creates a sense of anticipation then fulfilled by cutting to the character, seen here in close-up as he crawls through the railroad yards. This introduction represents the treatment of Kat in the film, as a character slightly larger than life, the inevitable "savvy Sarge" of many war movies. Kat easily obtains an entire pig, which he carries back to the billet wrapped in an officer's coat. Inside, he allows the recruits to share in his plunder at the cost of their brandy and tobacco rations.

Kat is characterized as the "Papa" of the group, by Tjaden as well as the recruits. When they move up to their first assignment, stringing barbed wire across a section of the front lines, Papa Kat leads the children. In the text this action in Chapter 4 is familiar routine to the veteran Second Company. In the film it is a frightening initiation to war for the young recruits. As they march toward the lines Milestone's camera tracks along with them, occasionally pausing to recognize an individual as they furtively look back to the safety now left behind. Their pace slows until they are far behind Kat and the other veterans, and the father figure is forced to admonish them like children. Kat tries to prepare them for the shock of shellfire, warning them to bury themselves in the lap of Mother Earth, but his words are inadequate to the experience itself. In a notable preservation of realistic detail Behm and several others foul their pants in a paroxysm of fear. Behm's fear proves prophetic; the most hesitant to enlist, the last to be signed up, he is the first to die. Blinded by a shell splinter, he staggers screaming out of the trench and is cut down by an enemy machine gun. Two of the others risk their lives to reach him, but he is already dead when they pull him back into the trench. Here is the harsh reality of war, which contrasts with the romantic words of patriotic songs and speeches. Throughout the scene Milestone works with uncompromising realism. The sights and sounds of barrage are fearfully real, the terror and agonizing fear of the troops clearly depicted.

This scene proves only a prelude to the first major battle, which follows before the "Iron Youth" can recover from the shock of Behm's death. First, they are quartered in a front-line dugout under heavy shellfire for three days, with only the trench rats for company. The dugout scenes are generally handled in a theatrical manner; the dugout interior forms a stage and the group of soldiers play the scene before a stationary camera.[10] As the intensity of the shelling increases, the camera begins to pick out the individuals who are beginning to crack. Franz Kemmerich becomes the most notable example, screaming in horror into the camera lens brought in for a tight close-up. When part of the ceiling collapses under a direct hit Kemmerich runs wailing into the trenches, where he is badly wounded by shell fragments. A tracking shot which follows Kemmerich along the trench also establishes the setting for the major battles of the film. As soon as the others have returned to the dugout after helping Kemmerich, a whistle shrills the warning of an enemy charge.

The Second Company pours out of the dugout entry along the trench taking their positions on the firing lines. The ensuing fight is the most interesting sequence in filmic terms, one where Milestone frees his camera from the necessity of sound to rise high above the battlefield in extended high-angle traveling shots. Essentially the sequence follows Chapter 6 of the novel in considerable detail, but with a much greater Expressionism in style. In the novel Paul's viewpoint does not rise omnisciently above the action; he cannot see the whole battle and is concerned with the little ring of fighting around him. Milestone's direction captures the wrenching horror of the fight, but from a slightly different viewpoint, one suggested, perhaps, by D. W. Griffith's *The Birth of a Nation* (1915).

As in Griffith's battles, the audience follows the ebb and flow of the action, charge and retreat and countercharge: great masses of men move in massive groupings intercut with significant individual details. The enemy charges across "no-man's land" from left to right; then they veer directly into the camera. The charging mass is intercut with the intent faces of the waiting riflemen and machine-gun crews. As they open fire the crosscutting develops into a montage recalling the early Eisenstein. The arc of the machine guns' field of fire is duplicated by the arc of the camera's horizontal pan, and the hammerlike strokes of the machine guns' bolt-action mechanisms are carefully matched to the tumbling bodies struck down by the bullets. Milestone says of this effect: "One of the ideas that paid off big for us was to have man after man go down with the equal rapidity of a machine gun bullet leaving the barrel."[11] Suddenly the enemy is leaping into the trenches, as extremes of angle and distance quickly alternate, approximating the rapid and radical dislocations of battle. The camera tracks along the trench, revealing hundreds of individual combats. The company retreats but artillery fire and hand grenades force the enemy backward, and the whole grim choreography of death is played in the opposite direction—right to left. Now the comrades are mowed down like wheat in a field by enemy machine guns; then they leap like savage animals into the melee in the enemy trenches. Slowly they too are forced back by heavier firepower, and at last they return to their original position; their trophies are a blood-soaked loaf of bread and a bottle of wine with a broken neck, grim sacramentals of war's awful sacrifices.

The next scene marks the beginning of another major sequence, one of rest and quiet after the action and noise of the battle. The novel is also structured by a series of such contrasts; the film organizes the pattern by building to the crescendo of the first battle, retiring to the comparative peace of the rear, and then repeating the pattern twice again. This scene, an orgy of eating at a field kitchen, actually forms Chapter 1 of the novel; in the film it comes at almost the midway point. Within the scenes a major change involves the transposition of several antiwar speeches to a single conversation following the meal. Parts of Chapters 3, 9, and 12 are brought together here to make a major antiwar statement after the recruits have experienced the full horror of battle. The logic of this presentation seems sound, but a comparison with the novel demonstrates that this emphasizing of the antiwar themes is perhaps too insistent, almost as if the audience is being presented with the "moral" of the story.

Another scene in this sequence, the death of Franz Kemmerich in the dressing station, the major event of the novel's second chapter, is marked by pathos, but Milestone barely skirts sentimentality. Instead of a mobile hospital, the film's dressing station is a bombed-out church complete with Gothic crosses to advance the crucifixion theme. The parallels with Kemmerich, who has lost his leg, are made obvious emotionally, while the ironic note of the scramble to get the dying man's boots is underplayed. In general, Paul's bedside manner seems more young Dr. Kildare than Remarque's tough comrade. Finally, as Kemmerich dies, Paul prays over him with great emotion. The same words are found in the novel, but they are

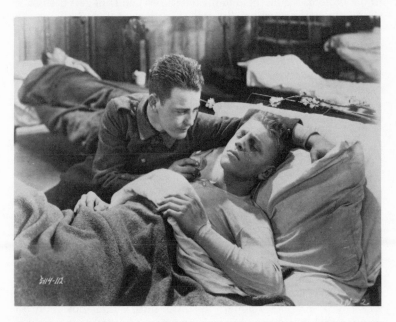

Paul Baumer (Lew Ayres) at the bedside of his dying comrade Franz Kemmerich (Ben Alexander).

internalized; Paul thinks: "the whole world ought to pass by this bed and say 'That is Franz Kemmerich, nineteen and a half years old, he doesn't want to die. Let him not die' " (32). Said aloud, with eyes upraised, Milestone approaches bathos in his depiction of both Franz and Paul.

Fortunately the next sequence redeems the filmic vision of the story by picking up Franz Kemmerich's boots as a visual motif. Paul's boots fill the frame as he emerges from the dressing station, and as the camera tilts upward Franz's boots are in his hands. He runs wildly back to the field kitchen, while other soldiers joke that he must have stolen the boots. After Paul tells the story of Kemmerich's death, the fine boots go to Müller, and the camera follows them in the march back to the front. Then they are the focus of a charge across "no-man's land," until a sudden explosion drops Müller's body into the frame. Next Peter inherits the boots, and again the camera eye picks them out of a marching column. The boots mount the parapet of a front-line trench and then Peter slides to the bottom, a bullethole in his temple. When Paul gets the boots, the pattern changes briefly. Another dugout scene allows the younger men to worry that the war has ruined their chances for life even if they escape the dangers of the front. As in the antiwar conversation earlier, several parts of the novel are brought together here, and the "lost youth" or anti-*Bildungsroman* theme seems somewhat overstated. As this boot montage also marks the passage of time, the young recruits are developing as veterans, soldiers with a past but no future.

The next two scenes are among the most powerful in the novel; occurring in Chapters 4 and 9, respectively. Their juxtaposition in the film chances emotional excess, but Milestone's deft direction realizes both nicely. In the first scene a heavy bombardment catches the company passing by the graveyard of the church earlier used as a dressing station. The effects of the earlier battles ae recaptured, again by the careful handling of extras and explosives, as well as by artful camera work and complex cutting. The troops caught in the confusion of the shelling move in every direction seeking cover, and close-ups of frightened faces are carefully intercut. Again the cross becomes an important motif as the troops hide behind the grave markers. When Paul is wounded for the first time, nicked in the wrist by a shrapnel splinter, he dives into a shell hole only to discover that it is in actuality an open grave. Milestone again frames the face of his young protagonist, this time in an angle formed by a piece of a coffin. This visual motif will persist to the conclusion, as this close-up is very similar to the one which directly proceeds Paul's death as he looks out of a square observation hole in the parapet of the trench.

Paul recoils in horror from the symbolism of death inherent in his shelter, so he races from the graveyard, only to encounter an attack by enemy infantry. Once more he takes cover in a shell crater, as the enemy troops leap over him in their advance and retreat. The extreme upward angle realizes Paul's personal terror that they will leap into the hole with him. He draws his knife in preparation for hand-to-hand fighting, and when one French *poilu* lands near him while dodging German fire Paul stabs him several times. As the French retreat the area around the crater becomes a no-man's land. Thus Paul is trapped in another grave, this time with a man in the ghastly process of becoming a corpse. Night turns the scene into a near Gothic horror, and at first Paul tries to stay as far away from the dying man as possible. His groans and sobs at last force Paul to approach him, to try to ease his death as much as he can. As in the novel he catches water from a puddle and wets the other's lips, but the wounded man is beyond help. Raymond Griffith's portrayal of dying and death creates a brilliant tour de force within the general framework of the film. His wide-open, death-shocked eyes remain one of the film's most powerful images, as well as a powerful statement against war. Milestone's intercutting of close-ups with a medium shot of the two soldiers huddled together draws the full emotional power from the scene. Particularly fine is Lew Ayres's choreography around the dead body of his new comrade; he whimpers at the dead man's feet, searches his clothes for identification, rages at him, pleads with him, and finally begs forgiveness. Some of Ayres's lines, including another prayer, seem more senti-mental than the novel's, where the same words are presented as interior monologue. However, the scene works very effectively, and the linking of these two "grave" images from different sections of the book proves another instance of the screenplay's tightening in terms of the logic of repetition. When Paul finally gets back to the company, Kat serves as father-confessor and absolves him from his feelings of guilt. Kat points to a sniper on the parapet above them who is gloating about a kill. Both conclude that "After all, war is war."

After Paul has killed for the first time he badly needs to escape the horrors of the war. Luckily the company is given a short rest in a rear area where Paul can forget his new knowledge by drinking beer in the easy camaraderie of the canteen. Only one detail disturbs their fun; on the wall of the canteen a theatrical poster teases the troops with the image of a pretty young girl. Her petite image flanks a mirror which reflects the grizzled veterans (the year is now 1917). Soon Paul and the others are gathered in front of it, considering the possibilities for romance in the area. Their feelings of lust soon propel them out to bathe and barber, and then to cajole the French girls in the village. Paul and his friends find three mademoiselles hungry enough to trade their bodies for bread and sausage. A minor subplot involves removing one friend, Tjaden, from the competition, a humorous rendering of the "all's fair in love and war" theme. As in the novel, the love scene develops real feelings as the young German men and the young French women express a sense of each other which goes beyond the tawdriness of their reality. For this moment, they are comrades thrown together by war, forced to try to understand each other as people, as Paul was forced to know the dead comrade of the shell crater. Though some of the book's ironies are cut, for the most part the film avoids the possibilities for sentiment lurking in romantic involvement, and the scene proves successful as another part of Paul's education as a man.

The company's return to the front soon separates Paul from his brunette *bonne camarade*. Almost immediately a serious wound interrupts Paul's experiences as veteran at the front. Unfortunately the film moves Paul's wound from his leg (the boot motif) to his side (the Christ motif). Also, Paul, not Peter, is the soldier who escapes the hospital "dying room," a resurrection after his crucifixion. Finally, Paul comforts his friend Albert Kropp, who has lost a leg, much as he did Kemmerich in the earlier scenes. Thus the hospital scene verges on the sentimental portrayal of the wounded veteran presented in many Hollywood movies.

As indicated above, Paul's return home on convalescent leave also suffers from excessive sentimentality, as the homecoming exhibits all the emotion of a Griffith reunion. The drab picture of the empty streets stands in stark contrast to the film's opening shots; the only soldiers here are wounded veterans, one without a leg, ignored by the harried civilian population. Paul's reunion with his family is the film's low point, though the introduction of the butterfly motif in Paul's collection will become important for the conclusion. One scene in this sequence, his return to the classroom, proves another fine interpolation by the screenwriters. In the novel's seventh chapter Paul talked with uncomprehending civilians, including his old professor, Kantorek, now a draftee himself. In the film, Paul finds the professor harranguing another group of potential "Iron Men," a class even younger and more innocent that Paul's. The scene perfectly replays the first classroom episode, but in this instance Paul makes the speech, one of the most moving in the film. He tells the boys, who want to hear of heroism, that the soldier's only concern is staying alive. "It is not beautiful and sweet to die for the country . . . it is better not to die." Here his audience jumps up to jeer at the "coward" and drive him from the classroom. Paul soon leaves to return to the front, unable to stomach the hypocrisy of the homefront. As if in confirmation of his feelings, he discovers the Second Company now manned by boys of sixteen and seventeen. Only a few of the old veterans are left, Tjaden and Kat most notably. As at Paul's first arrival, Kat is out foraging for food When they meet and sit to talk, Paul feels he is really home. He hears the sad stories of Westhus and Detering and the others, now dead or seriously wounded, but word of the Armistice is in the air. The sky is full of enemy aircraft, symbolic of the Allied material strength forcing Germany toward surrender. One of the planes drops a bomb near the two comrades, and Kat is wounded. He has been hit before, so he tells Paul not to worry and to carry him off to the aid station. As they cross the open field, another bomb explodes and a splinter of shrapnel kills Kat without Paul's knowledge; as they walk Paul reminisces aloud about their first meeting and the first combat. Paul, contrary to Kat's instruction when Behm was killed during the first action, has carried a corpse to the aid station under enemy fire.

With his true father figure dead, Paul loses his grip on life. In spite of the impending Armistice he feels as if he has no future in war or in peacetime. On a quiet afternoon in October of 1918, a day which would be reported "all quiet" in the official dispatches, Paul sits lost in his thoughts, as a soldier's harmonica plays softly in the background. His face is framed by a square lookout hole in the parapet of the trench. From the square he sees a butterfly alight on a rusty tin can The camera travels from Paul's smiling face to the butterfly, following Paul's line of vision. The butterfly is a bright spot of natural beauty in the wasteland of the trenches; it also represents Paul's lost youth and innocence, the days of his butterfly-collecting at school. Slowly he rises above the sandbags to reach for it. Milestone cuts to a French sniper poised behind a log. The sniper sights down on Paul, aiming left to right; Paul slowly extends his arm, reaching right to left. Three times Milestone crosscuts, each time drawing closer to his two subjects; then the crack of the rifle and the whine of the bullet stops the harmonica music. In the final frame Paul's hand, shown in close-up, relaxes in the peace of death.

As mentioned earlier, Milestone's conclusion, suggested by cameraman Karl Freund, beautifully captures the feeling of the novel's understated conclusion. In some ways this development even surpasses Remarque's as it draws together a number of notable image patterns which represent the tensions existing between war and human nature. Yet even this beautiful piece of film alters the matter and the style of the novel to some extent. When the concluding image, the superimposition of the young recruits marching to their first action over a hugh forest of gravemarkers, fills the screen, a banal movie orchestra supplies the audial counterpoint.[12]

This double conclusion represents the filmic adaptation of the novel at its best and its worst. At its best Milestone's film proves an imaginative cinematic translation which balances the Realism of sound against the Expressionism of image from the silent film. At its worst, the movie romanticizes the novel through a sentimentality also inherited from the silent screen. Both Remarque's and Milestone's *All Quiet on the Western Front* possess undisputed historical and artistic importance, created for the most part by meaningful tensions between subject and style. In the final analysis, however, these tensions are better maintained in Remarque's literary work. Milestone's film remains a classic, but a classic appreciated with certain reservations, reservations generated by Milestone's artistic temperament and the studio system.

A recent made-for-television film adaptation of *All Quiet On The Western Front* demonstrates that a simplified filmic Realism does not render full justice to the novel. Norman Rosemont's multimillion dollar production in 1979 proves remarkably faithful to the novel in plot, tone, and theme. Delbert Mann's direction is deft, if not inspired, and the international cast, headed by Richard Thomas as Paul and Ernest Borgnine as Kat, is capable, if not much more so than Milestone's. Even the battle scenes, filmed in Eastern Europe, are as well mounted. Yet the whole effect seems flat in comparison with both the original novel and the classic film version. A comparison of the two films shows how Milestone's stylistic daring captures more of the book's raw power than the more pious, stolid approach of Rosemont and Mann. This comparison proves both how much Milestone changed Remarque and how much he recreated Remarque's unique vision. *All Quiet On The Western Front* remains Lewis Milestone's most important film.

The Front Page (1931)

Following the success of *All Quiet on the Western Front,* Howard Hughes offered Milestone the direction of a film version of the Ben Hecht–Charles MacArthur Broadway hit of 1928, *The Front Page.* Milestone had already done successful work for Hughes's Caddo Company, notably *The Racket* (1928) and *Two Arabian Knights* (1927), the World War I comedy which earned him the chance to direct Remarque's anti-war novel. As usual, Hughes tried to exercise control over the production of *The Front Page,* and he rejected Milestone's first choices for the role of the rowdy reporter Hildy Johnson—James Cagney and Clark Gable. According to Milestone, Hughes considered Cagney "a little runt," while Gable's ears reminded him "of a taxicab with both doors open." So the part finally fell to Pat O'Brien, who had done it in the Chicago stage production of the play. *The Front Page* marked the actor's film debut, establishing him as a screen star. O'Brien does a creditable job as Hildy, but it seems the film would have been livelier with either of Milestone's choices, as the young Irishman O'Brien proves too much the matinee idol for the role of a rough-and-tumble newshound. Of course, Milestone did have the pleasure of telling Hughes, "I told you so," when Cagney and Gable became major stars. However, Hughes later had the same dubious pleasure after Milestone advised the producer to sell Jean Harlow's contract for a paltry sum because the director felt that though she was very pretty, she simply could not act.[13]

Casting became the major production difficulty in the Milestone filming of *The Front Page.* Not only was Pat O'Brien too clean-cut and sincere as Hildy Johnson, but his antagonist, the ruthless editor Walter Burns, was toned down considerably by the dapper Adolph Menjou, who had played only sophisticated ladies' men on the screen before *The Front Page.* A comparison with the later film versions, Howard Hawks's *His Girl Friday* (1940) and Billy Wilder's *The Front Page* (1974), clearly demonstrates the weakness of casting in the 1931 production. Hawks makes Hildy a tough-talking news-paperwoman, beautifully portrayed by Rosalind Russell, with Cary Grant as her antagonist, while the 1974 remake uses Jack Lemmon and Walter Matthau, two great comedy actors, as reporter and editor. The minor roles are perhaps stronger in Milestone's original, but the central weaknesses in casting the pivotal pair make the later versions more enjoyable movies.

Milestones's *The Front Page* remains the finest film, the best artistic success, of the three. At the height of his creative powers, the director brings to the production such style and panache that a clearly second-line literary vehicle is transformed into a first-rate film. The weaknesses of all versions of *The Front Page* can be traced to the Hecht-MacArthur play, an improbable blending of Realism, melodrama, and comedy. In an epilogue to the first edition of the play, the authors, both former Chicago newspapermen and later-day members of that city's literary renaissance, admit their mixing of genres and modes. They started to write an intellectual analysis of the newspaper world, but the result was "a romantic and doting tale." "The same uncontrollable sentimentality operated in our treatment of Chicago . . . as a result *The Front Page*, despite its oaths and realisms is a Valentine . . . a Ballad." [14] This curious sentimentalizing of reality has its moments; after all such sentimentality has been one of the staples of the American popular press as well as the popular stage. The authors follow neither the Realistic nor the Romantic thrust of their materials to artistically logical conclusions; instead they settle for the unmotivated resolutions of melodrama. Today *The Front Page* can be clearly seen not as part of the great traditions shaping modern drama, but as an extension of the sentimentalism which characterized the American popular drama of the nineteenth and early twentieth centuries. Hecht and MacArthur are more comparable to Belasco or Fitch than O'Neill or Elmer Rice, their collaborative effort more reminiscent of *Ten Nights in a Barroom* than *Desire Under the Elms*.

Still, the multiple stage and screen revivals attest to the play's power as entertainment in its own right. Milestone's eclectic film style proves itself capable of finding the best of this literary vehicle. "I saw it as a comedy-melodrama, or a melodrama with comedy overtones," he told an interviewer. [15] Thus Milestone wisely decided to stress the play's lighter elements and to ignore the strains of Social Realism. Most important, he emphasizes the romanticized personal relationship between the tough reporter and the ruthless editor, recalling the love-hate relationship of his protagonists in *Two Arabian Knights* (1927), as it works itself out in near farcical knockabout comedy. On the other hand, he plays Earl Williams's execution and especially Williams's romantic relationship with Mollie Malloy as pure melodrama. Serious, realistic, and even poignant bits from the play are dropped from the film; for example, Mrs. Schlosser searching for her drunken reporter-husband, Woodenshoes's "psychological" theories on the causes of crime, and much of the realistic detail, including the pathetic anarchism of Earl Williams, the satire on the Red Scare, and the topical references to Chicago. Milestone does create considerable realism in *mise-en-scène* effects probably attributable to this earlier work in *The Racket* (1928), but the film's dominant style is Expressionistic. Milestone uses several framing devices, a quick crosscutting between scenes, a moving camera intercut with close-ups, the juxtaposition of angles and distances, and a number of trick shots. Overall, the deft combination of Realistic *mise-en-scène* with an Expressionistic camera style draws the best out of the realistic, melodramatic, and comedic elements of the original *The Front Page*.

The film opens with a trick set-up of the titles as part of the front page of a metropolitan tabloid. As the pages of the paper turn the names of the production personnel are cleverly worked into the print, and finally the faces of the players are presented in news photographs. The story itself begins with a title reminiscent of a silent film: "Our story takes place in a mythical kingdom." Although this title's real purpose is probably as a disclaimer to placate the politicians in Chicago, it also serves to emphasize the romantic elements in the work itself. Milestone's *The Front Page*, even less than Hecht's and MacArthur's, will be no Realistic exposé of urban corruption or the nefarious methods of big-city newspapermen; rather, it is another cinematic celebration of the rough-and-tumble friendship of two strong men.

Milestone mentions in an interview that he naturally tried to open the play up by moving outside the single stage setting of the press room in the Criminal Courts Building.[16] The play opens inside this room, but Milestone moves outside it to the courtyard of the County Jail where the gallows are being prepared for the hanging of Earl Williams, an addled anarchist accused of killing a Black policeman in a scuffle following a demonstration. The contrasting close-up of a sandbag used as a stand-in for Williams and longshots of the gallows itself complement the "gallows humor" of the executioners. This short sequence is dark and tense, almost like something out of Fritz Lang's crime dramas, and it creates a mood of heavy melodrama occasionally reiterated later in the film, particularly in Mollie Malloy's suicidal leap and in occasional cuts to the gallows used to punctuate pauses in the action. A series of extremely angled shots connect the courtyard and the press room as the cops and reporters exchange harsh banter about the execution scheduled for the following morning.

Inside the press room the reporters are engaged in a penny-ante poker game accompanied by irreverent wisecracks. The *mise-en-scène* proves grimly realistic, with careful detailing, including girlie pictures on the wall, establishing the mood of tough, seedy masculinity. Even within the confines of the room Milestone creates a sense of movement and excitement by pacing the dialogue extremely rapidly and by cutting quickly from individual to individual and from individual to group shots. His deft handling of the camera also includes a number of moving camera shots, pans around the circular table, for instance, which extends the sense of constant action. The treatment of sequences in the press room recall the dugout scenes in *All Quiet on the Western Front* while anticipating the bunkhouse scenes in *Of Mice and Men*.

The reporters include Edward Everett Horton in a great performance as the hypochondriac pseudopoet Benzinger, Walter Catlett as the pop-eyed smart aleck Murphy, and Frank McHugh as the cynical newshound McCue. In contrast to the central grouping of "gentlemen of the press," the other minor parts are rather cornily presented. Mary Brian is too sweet as Hildy's intended, Peggy Grant; George Stone's portrayal of Earl Williams is overstated; and Maurice Black as Diamond Louie is a stereotyped Italian thug. Interestingly enough, Milestone himself plays a bit part as a reporter in one crowd scene.

As they talk, reporters note that one of their number, Hildy Johnson, is missing, and they speculate on the rumor that Hildy is quitting the *Herald-Examiner* to get married. Of course they don't believe this, but still they can't understand why Walter Burns keeps calling and asking for Hildy. Again opening up the action, Milestone cuts to Walter Burns pacing like a tiger in his lair, the city room of the *Herald-Examiner*. With a wonderful pair of extremely long tracking shots Milestone follows the editor through the city room past whirling presses to the loading dock, where he finds a gang of truckers in a crap game. Here he snarls an order to find Hildy Johnson. These tracking shots, which were becoming something of a Milestone trademark, perfectly place Walter Burns within the context of his world, the newspaper, a world where he is in full command.

The search for Hildy also leaves the confines of the stage in a quick montage of speakeasies, chorus lines, and houses of ill repute. The rather clear implication of Hildy owing two dollars at the parlor house may seem daring for the period; but the Hayes Office wasn't yet established in 1931, though worse than this would bring it into being. Finally Walter himself locates Hildy, with Peggy, purchasing a marriage license at City Hall. They plan to marry and leave that evening for New York, where Hildy has been promised an advertising job by Peggy's uncle. Burns gets his star reporter's attention by pulling a false fire alarm and then hustles him off to Pollock Mike's speakeasy for several shots of rye. All of this interpolated action works nicely to establish the central characters, introducing them much earlier and much more fully than the stage version. Finally, Hildy sneaks out of the ginmill through the men's-room window; his action is captured in a long shot which catches the escaping reporter framed by a window and the pursuing editor in the men's-room door. As in *All Quiet on the Western Front* and earlier films, the director uses naturalistic framing devices, particular doors and windows, to establish contexts for the presentation of character.

When Milestone cuts back to the press room of the Criminal Courts Building for Hildy's arrival, he follows the dialogue of the play closely, but as earlier he speeds the action through rapid-fire exchanges, quick cutting, and constant camera movement. When Hildy comically waltzes with the cleaning lady, the camera follows them in a lilting dance itself; and when the other reporters surround Benzinger to sing a jeering refrain in response to his free plugs for the restaurant which provided Williams's last meal, the camera dances up and down with their movement. Milestone claims to be the only director to master the technique, and he still refuses to explain how he created this particular shot.[17] (It would appear he used some sort of flexible camera sling, and the effect anticipates the hand-held shots of recent years.) All of this bravura camera work would prove more significant if it expressed more important themes. The dancing camera might well express the dislocations of some mad dance, some witches' sabbath, but the extremity of the device in connection with Benzinger's venial journalistic sin merely calls attention to itself as a device.

The arrival of Mollie Malloy turns the mood from madcap comedy to melodrama once more. The traditional whore with the heart of gold, Mollie has befriended Williams and insists that he is innocent of the policeman's death. Her entrance is dramatically framed in the windows and doors of the press room as she berates the newsmen for hounding poor Williams to the gallows. Effectively played by Mae Clark (most famous for her next picture, *The Public Enemy*, with James Cagney), Mollie begins to work on the sentimental souls beneath the tough hides of the reporters. Later the venal sheriff (Clarence Wilson) enters, bearing tickets to the hanging as if they were passes to the Policeman's Ball. Hildy returns to defend Mollie and denounce the sheriff, thus demonstrating his basically sound moral sense. The sheriff positively gloats over the fact that after one more interview with a noted "alienist," (or psychoanalyst in our sense) Williams will be declared sane and thus ready for execution. It seems that the sheriff and his brother-in-law, the mayor, feel that Williams's execution will secure the "colored vote" in the upcoming municipal elections and guarantee them another term at the public trough.

The sheriff's plans are blasted by Williams's escape. In an improbable piece of psychodrama, the alienist gives Williams the sheriff's gun to reenact the crime; Williams shoots the professor, chases off the sheriff, and escapes. In addition to dramatizing this action, only mentioned in the play, Milestone gives the audience the excitement of speeding cars and chattering machine guns. Hildy, who was just ready to leave and meet his girl at the station, follows his reportorial instincts and begins to cover the story for Walter Burns. Peggy and her mother arrive at the press room, trying to get Hildy on to the train for New York. He holds his post, however, and sends them on to the station, promising to meet them before the train leaves. Their departure is followed by the arrival of the mayor, played in pompous windbag fashion by James Gordon, who predicts the speedy demise of Williams. When the Mayor takes the sheriff aside to learn the story of the escape, they are interrupted by a messenger (Slim Summerville) from the governor bearing a pardon for Williams. They persuade him to pretend he could not deliver the pardon with the promise of a lucrative sinecure as Keeper of the City Seal. Meanwhile, Williams crashes through the window of the press room while Hildy is left alone trying to call Walter Burns.

Again the melodrama increases as Mollie returns and joins forces with Hildy in order to protect the condemned man. They hide him in Benzinger's roll-top desk, the most prominent piece of furniture in the press room. When the others return, Mollie stands up to their threats and finally leaps from the window into the courtyard in order to distract them from their search. This melodramatic sequence is beautifully stylized as two long tracking shots follow Mollie advancing against and retreating from her enemies; then a high-angle shot isolates her broken body in the courtyard several stories below the press room window. Mollie is only hurt by her fall, and she is taken off to the prison infirmary to recover from her injuries. Walter arrives and, when told of this new development, he formulates a plan to smuggle Williams out of the building and credit the *Herald-Examiner* with his capture. Peggy's mother reappears, threatening to reveal the story, and Walter has her packed off to Pollock Mike's by one of his strongarm men, Diamond Louie. Next Peggy is driven off by Walter's insults, and then Benzinger is kept from opening his desk by the promise of a better job on the *Herald-Examiner*. Later the sheriff, the mayor, and the other reporters return to question Hildy and Walter about Williams's whereabouts. In quick succession, Peggy's mother is brought back by the police after a car accident freed her from Walter's henchman; Williams's hiding place is comically revealed when Walter pounds his fist on the desk to emphasize righteously his innocence, and in the nick of time the governor's messenger reappears, after a change of heart, to reveal the attempt to bribe him.

After much confusion, Walter, Hildy, and Peggy are left alone in the press room. Clearly Hildy must make his choice between the other two and the ways of life they represent. Peggy plies him with promises, Walter with reminiscences, while Hildy wavers between them. Finally Walter gives in, urging Hildy to make the train, marry Peggy, and start a new life. He even finds a wedding present, a watch given to him by the "Big Chief himself" and inscribed "To the Best Newspaperman I Know." After the lovebirds leave, Walter picks up the telephone and instructs his assistant to call the police in the first town where the train stops; he wants Hildy Johnson arrested for stealing his watch! As with the credits the film's final word is interestingly presented; on a large mock-up of the words "The End" beneath a large question mark, Walter and Hildy perch, seemingly together again after Walter's final trick.

The Front Page ends on a note of stylization which not only replicates its opening but underlines the mode of romantic comedy. The central relationship, between Hildy Johnson and Walter Burns, is also reiterated, asserting the American filmic ideal of strong male friendship. This masculine romance, replayed so often in the films of Hawks, Walsh, Ford, and other classic Hollywood directors, is also important in Milestone's world. In the war movies, most notably

All Quiet on the Western Front, it offers the only solace to lonely soldiers, while in *Of Mice and Men* it similarly supports the exploited ranch hands. In those films the strong relationships of strong men are realistically treated; in *The Front Page* the relationship is sentimentalized in knockabout comedy. The tensions between star reporter and wily editor are comically resolved, just as the tensions created by the impending execution of Earl Williams are melodramatically resolved by a last-minute pardon. The Chicago scenes give the play and the film an air of reality, but in the final analysis the sentimental world of romantic comedy prevails. These difficulties are inherent in Hecht and MacArthur's literary vehicle; others were created by the casting of the principals imposed by Howard Hughes, but Milestone's deft stylistic juxtaposition of realistic and expressionistic elements makes the best of the production, creating the most cinematically interesting, if not the most entertaining, version of *The Front Page*. Milestone's accomplishment was recognized when *The Front Page* received an Academy Award nomination for best film, and the film must have proved entertaining enough to its audience as it grossed over half a million dollars.[18] The success of *The Front Page* also created a spate of newspaper films, so that the type became almost a genre during the 1930s.

Rain (1932)

The nomination of *The Front Page* for the Motion Picture Academy's Best Picture Award not only affirmed the success of Milestone's second important sound film but confirmed the directorial talent already recognized by the Academy in *Two Arabian Knights* and *All Quiet on the Western Front*. Although *The Front Page* lost the Oscar to Wesley Ruggles's *Cimarron*, perhaps the worst movie ever to win Best Picture, Milestone's reputation was enhanced when he topped a list of the "Ten Best Directors" compiled by *Film Daily* from a poll of 300 movie critics. David O. Selznick made a "handshake deal" with Milestone to form a small independent production group under the creative control of filmmakers themselves. Others Selznick intended to form units with included King Vidor and Ernst Lubitsch. However, the Hollywood money men were not ready to relinquish any of their power over production, even to this array of talent, and Selznick failed to solicit any support for his group.[19] Milestone also negotiated with RKO for the production of several films a year, but this deal also failed to materialize. Early in 1932 Milestone accepted the job as production head for United Artists. His own first production was *Rain* (1932), a screen adaptation of the stage version of Somerset Maugham's famous story, starring Joan Crawford and Walter Huston.

Rain is a curiously neglected work in the Milestone canon. Neither the reviewers nor the public thought much of it in 1932: and, for the most part, later scholars and critics have judged it no better than an interesting failure. Even Milestone himself takes this general position on the work: "Joan Crawford wasn't up to it, and the picture couldn't get off the ground—although there are quite a few things in it I like."[20] At first the project did not interest him at all, as he thought that the play was dated and that no actress could approach the Sadie Thompson created by Jeanne Eagels in the Broadway version of 1922. Finally Milestone accepted the challenge of adaptation and, in spite of his own disclaimers and the verdicts of almost everyone else, he did a very creditable job of filming Maugham's famous tale. With more control in casting he might well have created a movie classic; as it exists, Milestone's *Rain* must be judged one of his most interesting films, a complex cinematic rendering of a literary classic and a film which deserves much more attention and praise than it has received.

Certainly Milestone's *Rain* is the most interesting recreation of Maugham's story. His film's place in the long history of the tale as told in print, on stage, and on the screen not only provides comparative perspectives but establishes clear critical contexts for viewing Milestone's accomplishment. W. Somerset Maugham, a writer of an autobiographical and journalistic bent, began with the reality of a story given to him during a Pacific Ocean trip in 1916. The prototypes of his principal characters sailed with him to Pago-Pago, where they were all stranded for some days waiting for another ship. Maugham's role as observer falls to Dr. Macphail in the story, and Macphail gives the reader Maugham's observations of the others. The dramatic climax was invented, but it had been anticipated in the careful delineations of the other characters. The Reverend Davidson, a megalomaniac South Seas missionary, and his equally narrow-minded wife are shocked by the behavior of Sadie Thompson, a young woman of dubious background and motivations. Davidson becomes obsessed by the idea of saving the fallen sister; and Sadie succumbs to his fanatical fervor only to triumph bitterly when she seduces him. In a fit of guilt and despair Davidson cuts his throat, leaving Dr. Macphail to puzzle out the meaning of

the events. Under the title "Miss Thompson" (which was the real
name of the tart who served as the model for the title character), the
story appeared in H. L. Mencken's *Smart Set* and later was
published in Maugham's collection *The Trembling of a Leaf* in
1921. This volume of stories set in various corners of the Pacific
received mixed reviews, but the tale of Sadie Thompson was almost
universally applauded.

A young playwright named John Colton was struck by the
dramatic possibilities in the story and discussed them with
Maugham, who also wrote for the theater. Because of other commitments, Maugham could not undertake a dramatization and gave his
permission for Colton to do one if he wished. Colton, with the
collaboration of another young writer, Clemence Randolph, quickly
created a script, found enthusiastic backing, and mounted a production. Under the title *Rain* (a title also given to the story in
subsequent reprintings) the play opened in 1922 for a run of almost
three years, with the self-doomed Jeanne Eagels in the central role.
The play has been revived often, perhaps most notably in 1935 with
Tallulah Bankhead as Sadie Thompson. Although the stage version
generally preserves the power of Maugham's story, it does weaken it
somewhat by confining the action to Trader Horn's outpost, by
simplifying character (Davidson becomes more mad and vicious,
Sadie more innocent and put upon), and by adding a plot strand
involving Sgt. O'Hara, a tough marine who falls for Sadie and who
walks off arm in arm with her at the final curtain. Movie versions
began in 1928 when the silent *Sadie Thompson* appeared with
Gloria Swanson and Lionel Barrymore in the central roles; they
were directed by Raoul Walsh, who also played the part of the
erstwhile Sgt. O'Hara. A stage musical version of the play starring
June Havoc in 1944 evidently influenced *Miss Sadie Thompson*
(1953), directed by Curtis Bernhardt and featuring Rita Hayworth
as another singing version of Sadie.[21] The two sound movies have
been shown frequently on television, perhaps creating a new and
more receptive audience for Milestone's neat stylization.

Given the problems of his literary sources and of the production's
casting, Milestone does artistic justice to his conception of *Rain*. The
story proves difficult to dramatize because its extreme tensions and
their shocking resolutions are more aptly presented through an
observer character who can render them obliquely, thus defusing
their inherent melodrama. Maugham's story ends with the short
paragraph: "Dr. Macphail gasped. He understood." Macphail's

understanding can reverberate over the story, but dramatic and filmic versions must objectively present material which the Doctor knows only imaginatively. Beyond this inherent problem, the dramatists weakened the story by giving the characters less probable motivations and providing a rather false "happy" ending. Additionally, they also create a good deal of stage business and "snappy" dialogue which had aged badly even by 1932.

Milestone also faced real difficulties in casting. In particular, his producers wanted the box-office attraction of a top female lead in the role of Sadie Thompson. Joan Crawford was among the most popular leading ladies in 1932, but she had demonstrated dramatic ability only in *Grand Hotel* among her dozen or so major appearances. Her performance in *Rain,* like the film, has been generally panned and almost every comment on the film insists she was miscast. The critics have probably viewed the tale as a vehicle for Mae West. Viewed today, Crawford's interpretation generates considerable power. After all, Maugham's Sadie is a sister under the skin to the attractive but deadly "queen bees" portrayed by Miss Crawford in myriad later films.[22] Sadie's venality always seems a veneer on Crawford, but the essential dynamics of the character, peculiar sexual tensions rooted in sadomasochism, exist at the core of the characterization. In her autobiographical work, *A Portrait of Joan,* Miss Crawford wrote that she was haunted by the Sadie Thompsons of the past and that her insecurities made her far too emotional in the role. Yet her emotions are essentially Sadie's, so that it seems hard to discover a screen actress who would have done better with the role.

Walter Huston's characterization of the maniacal missionary Davidson has also received scant approval. Like Crawford, he does become excessive in places, but the emotional extremity of a fanatic Puritan blazes forth quite convincingly. The principals are wrong only in the nuances, not the essentials of interpretation; rather, it is the supporting cast who sink the production. Only Guy Kibbee as Trader Horn and Walter Catlett (Murphy of *The Front Page*) as Bates are at all adequate, and both are broad characterizations created by the dramatists for comic relief. The rest of the cast are uniformly unconvincing, indeed almost amateurish. William Gargen proves too boyish and innocent as Sgt. O'Hara, a man who should know his way around after twelve years in the Marines. Beulah Bondi makes a nagging caricature of the repressed Mrs. Davidson. Matt Moore and Kendall Lee (the future Mrs. Milestone) are

particularly undistinguished as Dr. and Mrs. Macphail, casting
which creates real problems as Macphail's role is important in terms
of viewing the other characters. The over-and under-acting of the
subsidiary cast seriously impinge on the central players and perhaps
helped create the unfair press the performances of Crawford and
Huston received.

Milestone did have solid support from his production unit, as,
aside from casting, the production values are excellent. Maxwell
Anderson, the gifted playwright and screenwriter who scripted *All
Quiet on the Western Front*, does a fine job of reshaping the play for
the screen, often reintegrating elements from Maugham's original
story. Locations on Catalina Island and an evocative studio set
designed by Richard Day are beautifully captured by Oliver Marsh,
the cinematographer, and Duncan Mansfield, the editor. As in *All
Quiet on the Western Front* and *The Front Page*, sound is used quite
effectively, particularly the sound motif of Sadie's honky-tonk
gramophone records.

Finally, it is Milestone's feel for *mise-en-scène* and for evocative
detail and cutting that makes the film artistically interesting. The
director seizes on symbolic detail and shapes it as creatively as in *All
Quiet on the Western Front*. Almost no one has mentioned the
intriguing landscape and background shots in the film, or the scenes
of the Samoan natives at work and play. These elements are
important for contrast in the story, but, of course, are lost in the
stage version. Milestone rescues them and presents them in almost
Eisensteinian montage. Remember that Milestone had defined
montage as the careful extension of detail toward meaning. Here
the details of setting are extended toward the meaning of the action
within the contexts of nature. Both Reverend Davidson and Sadie
Thompson embody unnatural attitudes toward life in nature, particularly in terms of sexual expression. Davidson is sexually repressed,
seemingly continent; Sadie is sexually promiscuous, as well as
mercenary. A middle ground is inhabited by the Macphails, the
Horns, the natives, and the sailors. Thus the rain of the title
becomes a force of natural vitality and growth; perhaps excessive in
the South Seas, like the sexual customs of the natives, but this is the
real world. For the central characters the rain becomes oppressive,
confining, fundamentally disturbing, and against this natural backdrop Davidson and Sadie enact unnatural dramas in place of normal
human relationships.

Milestone had many filmic sources for this evocative use of detail

from the troubles of the times. However, the public chose not to be diverted by *Hallelujah, I'm a Bum*, though it received some good reviews. The problem of this entertainment fantasy was that it brushed reality just enough to confuse its audience. Americans in the winter of 1933 were not in the mood to be advised that the life of a hobo was the road to true happiness, especially by a star earning $25,000 a week. Indeed, as the title indicates, *Hallelujah, I'm a Bum* is a Hollywood fantasy on the theme of voluntary poverty, but the script by S. N. Behrman from a story by Ben Hecht evokes just enough Realism to blur the mode of the film. This confusion is increased by the strange device of "rhythmic dialogue," created by musical dialoguers Rodgers and Hart, by some difficulties of casting, and even by Milestone's eclectic style. Finally, *Hallelujah, I'm a Bum* is interesting only as a rather bizarre failure.

Al Jolson's film career had stalled after the great success of his early talkies for Warner Brothers like *The Jazz Singer* (1927) and *The Singing Fool* (1928). In 1933 Jolson was still considered a leading entertainer, though off the screen for three years, and Joseph Schenck signed him to a fabulous contract for United Artists. Jolson was to make three or four pictures at $25,000 a week, with a total guarantee of $2 million. *Hallelujah, I'm a Bum* was to have been the first of these films; it turned out to be the last as well. The movie was given a lavish, million-dollar-plus budget with first-rate casting and production values, yet it still flopped. Its failure was through no fault of Jolson, who gave the best performance of his film career. Unlike his earlier talkies, the movie presents a re-strained, mature interpretation of his role as Bumper, the hobo mayor of Central Park; yet after *Hallelujah, I'm a Bum*, Jolson's film career never flourished, in spite of several other comeback attempts.[26]

Milestone came to the film as a second choice for director. According to his own reminiscences, Schenck hired a friend of Milestone's, Harry d'Abbadie d'Arrast, who had directed Adolphe Menjou in a number of successful films, to direct the piece in the manner of a French boulevard play. After the first day's rehearsal d'Arrast insisted that he couldn't work with Jolson and demanded a change in stars. Instead, the director was fired, and Milestone took over.[27] He then hired Richard Rodgers and Laurenz Hart to liven the script through the device of rhythmic dialogue, which they had just employed successfully in Rouben Mamoulian's *Love Me To-night* (1932). (Milestone specifically denies the influence of Mamoulian or Lubitsch on *Hallelujah, I'm a Bum.*)[28] This rhythmic and rhymed dialogue, delivered in somewhat sing-song fashion, resembles *recitative* in opera, adding another fantasy note to the work. Rodgers and Hart also contributed two notable tunes, the lively title number and the lovely "You Are Too Beautiful," which became something of a standard over the years. In *Musical Stages,* his autobiography, Rodgers admits he liked the film, but he succinctly identifies its major problem: ". . . we were defeated by the theme, which didn't strike many people as something to laugh about."[29]

Other replacement problems accrued as the production developed. Roland Young, who was Jolson's foil, the playboy mayor based on New York's Jimmy Walker, became ill and almost half the footage had to be reshot with his replacement, Frank Morgan.[30] This veteran does well as the blowhard politician (recalling the Chicago mayor of *The Front Page*), but the plot also requires him to be the love interest for a much younger Madge Evans, a development which fast becomes a histrionic embarrassment. Also embarrassing are the roles of silent comics Harry Langdon, Chester Conklin, and Edgar Connor. Langdon does a few good comic turns, but his part is basically preposterous. He is forced to rhyme lines like these to the assembled hoboes:

> I accuse you all of wasting your time,
> While I slave away for the City.
> You're parasites all! You're Brothers in Crime!
> When the revolution comes you won't sit pretty!

Chester Conklin, of Keystone days, plays Sunday, a horsecab driver who has secured his place through the benevolence of Bumper and the mayor. Edgar Connor is nothing beyond a stereotype as Bumper's tiny black sidekick, Acorn. (For example, when asked to clean a goose for cooking he pulls out a straight razor as his implement.) By contrast Tyler Brooke, Bert Roach, and Dorothea Wolbert do well with some minor comic roles.

Milestone's contribution to this strange gathering of talents is essentially stylistic. Assisted by cinematographer Lucien Androit and art director Richard Day, Milestone turned the Riviera Country Club of Pacific Palisades into Central Park. Musical director Alfred Newman assembled a full-sized orchestra on the fairways and created for the film the free and easy feel of later outdoor musicals.

The city settings have a sort of Art-Deco look which contrasts nicely with the natural freedom of the park. Most importantly Milestone uses a lively Expressionistic cinema style which matches the twists of Hecht's and Behrman's plot and the turns of Rodgers and Hart's rhythmic dialogue. As usual, Milestone's camera is constantly moving, and perhaps more than in any other of his films, he uses contrasting shots to create striking montage effects. For the most part, this style is well matched to such substance as exists in this very insubstantial piece, but Milestone's stylistic tricks remain only devices for telling a frothy story. Style never reveals real meaning, because Milestone's literary vehicle essentially provides none.

The tramp exists as a comic foil for an overorganized society in both serious and popular art throughout the twentieth century. The most famous example is, of course, Charles Chaplin's screen persona, the Little Tramp. Chaplin's tramp is at once less and more than this audience; he is both a poor and miserable outsider (indeed a scapegoat to be driven out) and a free spirit associated with the

Bumper (Al Jolson) and Egghead have a bit of trouble with the Central Park police in *Hallelujah, I'm a Bum.*

vital forces of nature, a hero who throws off the bonds of an
unnatural social order. Perhaps the most complex evocation of these
themes is found in Chaplin's *Modern Times* (1936), a film created
in response to the same world which spawned *Hallelujah, I'm a
Bum*. The inherent weakness of the tramp as symbol exists in the
inclination toward sentimentality; the scapegoat becomes the innocent victim, the free spirit does not have to pay the price of his
freedom. In some of his less thoughtful works even Chaplin sinks
into sentiment; lesser artists were often drowned in it.

The 1930s seem a strange period for sentimentalizing tramps, but
the sound comedies and musicals of the decade often did just that.
Hallelujah, I'm a Bum recalls not just Chaplin and Rene Clair but
numerous films by Frank Capra, Preston Sturges, Gregory La Cava,
and others. In these myriad 1930s fantasies, the bum is no derelict
but a Thoreauvian type (often with a fortune in the bank) or a good
man temporarily down on his luck. His life-style by contrast
demonstrates the weaknesses of a restrictive society, in particular
the pomposity of an easily satirized high society. In these fantasy
visions, some compromise is generally reached; the tramp figure
retains his sense of freedom while assuming greater societal responsibility (often symbolized by marriage to a vital heroine). *Hallelujah,
I'm a Bum* presents a clever variation on this pattern by having
Bumper fall in love with the heroine while she is an amnesia victim
and then having her fall out of love with him when she regains her
memory of the Mayor, her first love. However, the movie misses
both happy fantasy or meaningful reality by making Bumper and
his pals sympathetic, sentimental sterotypes, while implying just
enough reality to preclude belief in the ennobling effects of sleeping
on park benches.

Not that *Halllelujah, I'm a Bum* isn't an interesting film—certain
moments are fine, and generally the first half of the film remains
very watchable, especially for a film buff. Anyone interested in
Hollywood history, particularly in the careers of Jolson, Langdon, or
Milestone, will still discover much of interest here. As in *The Front
Page*, the setting of the titles establishes the mood of comic fantasy.
The production data is presented against a series of cartoon images
depicting the free and easy life of the traditional, bindle-carrying
hobo. Against these images the lively title tune introduces the
movie's other musical motifs obviously representing the freedom of
life on the open road. Recalling the nature imagery of *Rain*,
Milestone opens with a shot of wild geese in flight, an image of

natural freedom. Cut against this shot, Frank Morgan as the mayor sights his shotgun on the V-shaped formation. In quick cuts, he drops one from the flight, but it is recovered by Bumper and his pal Acorn. They in turn are apprehended by the mayor's entourage, but he effects their release as they are all old pals. Bumper is the hobo mayor of Central Park, and every day he meets the mayor for lunch at the Casino-in-the-Park. Of course, Bumper eats at the trash bins, while the mayor lunches in luxury, but the two men have the greatest respect for each other as symbols of life-styles opposite to their own.

Now it seems that both mayors are far from their constituencies, somewhere in the Sunny South. Bumper always heads South to avoid wintering in the park, while the mayor is sojourning in the Southland on the rebound from a broken romance. In order to escape the restrictions of his official party, the mayor decides to dine with Bumper, who cooks the goose that Acorn razor-cleans. During their dinner the mayor prevails on Bumper to reform and do something useful, but the hobo king praises the glories of the free life to the accompanying "yassuhs" of Acorn. When they part, they all promise to meet for lunch at the casino in the spring.

The next sequence shows them traveling back to the city. Bumper and Acorn walk, hitch a ride on a wagon, and then walk some more, while the mayor travels in the comfort of a private Pullman car. Yet the tramps are indeed happier, as the mayor still suffers from heartaches. In a neat bit of flashback, the mayor contemplates his beloved's picture and suddenly the picture comes alive to tell the story of their spat. Evidently their quarrel involved money, indicating that Bumper's earlier remarks on the subject might have been more accurate than the mayor would allow. The mayor is evidently keeping the lovely (and much younger) June Marcher in a fancy apartment. Opening the door (with his own key) he discovers June giving an old flame some money, and he leaves in a huff. Now he is returning at her request with one last hope of reconciliation.

Bumper's arrival is depicted first, a welcome relief from the corny melodramatics of the love plot. In fact, Bumper's return to his old tramping grounds becomes the best sequence in the film, one with great promise not fulfilled by succeeding events. Moments after he gives his special whistle, the nearly empty park is filled by streams of hoboes converging from every side. Now Milestone's visual style reverts to montage, moving his camera in long following shots of the central pair intercut with quick shots of the converging followers. Finally they all come together in a central arbor where the camera circles around Bumper as his followers crowd about him to hear his words. His message is another rendition of the gospel of voluntary poverty, as he reclines on the large, comfortable limb of a tree.

Milestone introduces Langdon by suddenly cutting away to frame the path once more. Into the frame march the mechanically stepping legs of Egghead, the whitewing of the park. Egghead is so called because he is a sort of halfbaked economic theorist of Leftist-persuasion. If the mayor represents the follies of Capitalism, then Egghead embodies the greater errors of Communism. Bumper, of course, is the Thoreauvian American who strikes the balance between extremes by eschewing both Communist theory and Capitalist practice. Egghead, though another old friend, undertakes to lecture Bumper about his duty to the workers, but Bumper comically puts him off, guiding him through the park in a long tracking shot. While Bumper and Egghead walk and talk, Acorn and the others slyly steal all the trash from the pushcart and scatter it on the path behind them. When Egghead reaches the end of the path, he turns to doubletake at the littered pathway. Undaunted, he draws his trash stick and proceeds to clean the park again.

Egghead, who parallels the mayor in symbolic function, also represents the problems of the film's thematic confusion. The whitewing is obviously intended as a comic Communist, the silly Leftist who often appears in 1930s entertainments. Yet Langdon's lines include such stinging epithets as "Hoover's Cossacks" for the park's mounted policemen. In later years, commentators including Milestone himself pointed to bits like this as indications of liberal daring. However, the context of Egghead's lines makes such reasoning seem an afterthought, for they seem to have been intended to satirize radicalism. Instead, however, they raise the spector of socioeconomic conflict in a way not calculated to entertain a Depression audience in search of musical-comedy diversion. Langdon's physical appearance also works against any comic intent of his role. Egghead is clearly based on the persona created by Langdon for the silent screen. Although the same air of madcap infantility still exists in the character's white makeup and black mascara, now he seems very worn and tired, at once a baby and an old man. The association with the real Langdon behind Egghead, another silent star ruined by sound, only reinforces the sense of American innocence and success lost in the Depression. In *Hallelujah, I'm a Bum*

Langdon seems somehow closer to the characters of Beckett or Brecht than of Sennett.

After leaving Egghead, Bumper and Acorn set out for their luncheon date with the mayor at the casino. On their way they encounter another silent comic, Chester Conklin, as Sunday, the horsecab driver. Sunday is sneaking a nap at the head of the cab line when Bumper and Acorn jump in, ordering him "to the Casino!" Sunday doesn't realize who he is transporting until he arrives and turns to receive his fare; then all three of the old friends enjoy a good laugh, with even Sunday's old nag joining in. A diagonal wipe, one of the many visual tricks Milestone unveils in his film, cuts to the mayor on his way to lunch with June. He must stop on the way for the laying of a school cornerstone, which makes one of the better comic bits of the film. In the role of the pompous politician, Morgan is a delight, and Milestone shoots the scene in series of deft angles which underline the jokes of the assembled schoolchildren and construction workers. In the midst of this satire of unresponsive urban politics, the kids sing "My Country 'Tis of Thee" while Milestone cuts between the freckled faces, creating a bit of Americana worthy of John Ford. Then as the noon whistle blows, everyone immediately departs: kids, teachers, workers, and the mayor's official party.

At the casino, Morgan has to revert to his romantic role, with unfortunate results. Whenever the film shifts to the romantic plot it comes to a standstill because of bad scripting and hammy acting. This sequence does some nice crosscutting between the lovers in the restaurant and the tramps at the trashbins, but the few good bits of visual humor are lost in the labored convolutions of the plot line. The lovers make up, and in a game of greenback poker (using the serial numbers of bills to construct imaginary poker hands) the mayor slips June a $1,000 bill. She leaves her purse behind, and it is wrapped up with the table linen and later winds up in Egghead's trash barrel. Bumper finds the purse and resolves to return it, but in the interim the mayor has learned of the loss and accuses June of sending the money to her former lover. In her anger at this false accusation, June leaves her apartment before Bumper can arrive with the purse, and the lovers are separated once more. Their separation is exaggerated when June leaps into Central Park Lake in an apparent suicide attempt. Bumper, now returning through the park, rescues her, but the shock of her action has caused amnesia.

Bumper falls for the girl (he calls her Angel), and with the aid of
Sunday secures her a place to stay.

Interspersed in these plotty developments are two fine sequences
with the bums in the park. After Bumper found the purse, Egghead
demands half since it was found in his barrel; then the other tramps
claim their share also. Bumper tries to escape them all, but they trail
him through the park in a number which recalls his return to the
park earlier in the picture. Again the scene is well orchestrated and
choreographed, and it ends with Bumper confronting a sea of faces.
Again the presentation is in montage fashion, and this angry crowd
seems straight out of a Russian revolutionary scene. Of course, there
will be no revolution on the Hollywood screen, as Bumper convinces
his comrades that they are better off without money: after all, they
have the grass and the trees. An interesting sidelight here is
Bumper's insistence that Egghead be consistent and give up his
claim to the money; the movie revolutionary always sells out when
faced with the temptations of greed.

Although Bumper could not return the purse to June, the mayor
arrives to receive it, and its return makes him so happy that he gives
Bumper the $1,000 bill to divide among his friends. With a few
dollars each, the hoboes pursue their favorite pleasures: some are
seen cooking chickens over open fires; others play cards; others,
including Egghead, drink up a little fun. On his nocturnal stroll
through his domain, Bumper sings the title song, seemingly content
with his lot in life and blissfully unaware of the scene's contradiction
of his earlier speeches. The tramps are happier with a little lucre,
but perhaps this scene is intended to demonstrate real communism
as all share alike, with only the Communist Egghead drinking more
than his fair share.

Directly after this scene, Bumper rescues June/Angel, and the
movie sinks into sticky sentimentality. Head over heels in love,
Bumper turns his back on his principles and gets a job to support his
beloved. (None of the men ever seems to consider the possibility
that June/Angel might support herself!) After setting her up in
Sunday's spare room (much to the suspicion of Mrs. Sunday)
Bumper goes to the mayor for a job. Soon both he and Acorn are
laboring in a bank (the capitalistic system), Bumper as an executive
and Acorn, true to type, as the washroom attendant. Meanwhile the
mayor, who thinks June has gone off with her former lover, slips
into the bums' role, drinking heavily and wandering in the park.
Bumper now enters the park only after work, and at the end of the

work week his former followers grab him and hold him for trial as a traitor to his own cause. This proves to be the last good scene in the film, as the wit in the speeches of accusation and defense is again matched by Milestone's deft camera movement. Bumper is finally acquitted on the grounds of insanity; love has driven him mad!

The love plot also drives the audience to distraction as Bumper simpers like a teenager on his first date. During his visits to Angel's room he does get to sing a few songs, including the standard "You Are Too Beautiful," yet this part of the film falls almost completely flat. Needless to say Milestone's style flattens out also, almost as if he lost interest in the proceedings entirely, and it seems to take forever for the easily anticipated plot developments to grind to a resolution. Bumper visits his old pal the mayor, sees him mooning over June/Angel's picture, and brings him to her. This reunion shocks her out of amnesia and into love with the mayor; now out of love with Bumper, she forgets the hobo entirely. Bumper reverts back to his tramp role, and one final shot takes him back to the park and a reunion with Acorn and Egghead.

Unfortunately, this pat resolution doesn't really resolve the problems raised by the characters' actions. Instead it merely ends a rather muddled story on a note of complacency. *Hallelujah, I'm a Bum* is not so much a bad film as it is a strange one. In spite of a fine performance by Jolson, some good tunes by Rodgers and Hart, and a lively directing job by by Milestone, the film fails both as entertainment and art. The incredibly corny romance plot is not balanced by enough scenes in the park to make it good entertainment, while the ambiguous handling of the social problems undermines the film as art. In particular, the film's ambiguity about economic issues undoubtedly upset a Depression audience, just as it shattered any artistic unity Milestone might have created. *Halleluah, I'm a Bum* was a flop in 1933, and today it can only be evaluated as an interesting failure. It can also be considered as the last film in the cycle of Milestone's early sound efforts; unfortunately it points forward to failures of the mid-1930s rather than back to Milestone's first successful sound films. (It continues to have a strange history. It is now being distributed under the title *Heart of New York*, despite the fact that this title leads to confusion with another Warner Brothers (1932) film directed by Mervyn LeRoy.)

3

The Later Sound Period

The Mid-1930s

AFTER COMPLETING *Hallelujah, I'm a Bum* Milestone began
work late in 1933 on a much more serious project, a film about
recent Russian history tentatively titled *Red Square*. Laurence
Stallings (coauthor with Maxwell Anderson of *What Price Glory?*)
developed a screenplay from Ilya Ehrenburg's *The Life and Death
of Nikolai Kourbov* (1923), while Milestone returned to Russia for
the first time since 1912 in order to plan locations and solicit Soviet
support for the project.[1] Evidently he could secure neither Soviet
cooperation nor American financial backing, and the project was
shelved permanently. In 1934 Milestone also negotiated unsuccessfully with the British producer Alexander Korda about a film version
of H. G. Wells's *The Shape of Things to Come* (1933).[2] The project
would have been interesting as Milestone's only science-fiction
effort, though it was probably better directed by William Cameron
Menzies, frequently a set designer for Milestone, as *Things to Come*
in 1936.

In 1934 Milestone left United Artists for Columbia, lured by a
contract which promised 50 percent of the profits, where he directed
The Captain Hates the Sea for Harry Cohn.[3] The film is inevitably
called "*Grand Hotel* at sea," but the comparison proves rather
unfair. Edmund Goulding's 1932 screen adaptation of Vicki Baum's
bestselling novel featured talents like Greta Garbo and Joan Crawford as well as Lionel and John Barrymore in a complex anthology
of melodramatic personal tales showcased within the setting of the
grand hotel. Two years later in early 1934, United Artists, released
Transatlantic Merry-Go-Round, directed by Benjamin Stoloff, a
seeming reprise of *Transatlantic* (1931); Stoloff featured the popular
radio comedian Jack Benny and a number of other Hollywood

Contrasting moments in Of Mice and Men: *George (Burgess*
Meredith) and Lennie (Lon Chaney, Jr.) in fear of pursuers
(top), and joyful over a new puppy (bottom).

regulars, in a spoof of *Grand Hotel*. Milestone's effort also utilizes
the anthology concept, as a disparate group of characters are mixed
together by the confined setting of the ocean liner at sea. However,
Wallace Smith's scenario (from his own story) lacks both the
effective drama of *Grand Hotel* and the successful satire of *Transatlantic Merry-Go-Round*. Rather *The Captain Hates the Sea* proves
a very uneven, disconnected, rambling piece, featuring such diverse
talents as John Gilbert, Victor McLaglen, Alison Skipworth, and the
Three Stooges.

Gilbert, a silent star shipwrecked by sound, was coaxed from
retirement by Milestone to play an alcoholic writer drying out on a
cruise. The part definitely proved type casting for the hard-drinking
Gilbert, and, as with the character he played, Gilbert's drinking got
successively worse as the liner sailed on. Isolated on a rented
steamer off the southern California coast, often unable to work
because of the star's massive hangovers, the rest of the cast joined
the party with smuggled booze. Production grew slower when
Milestone discovered other cast members as drunk as Gilbert. Cohn
reportedly shot off a cable to Milestone at sea, "Hurry up. The cost
is staggering." The witty director fired a message back, "So is the
cast!"[4]

Gilbert, as the alcoholic writer, observes the other characters and
serves as an integrating device for telling their stories. Walter
Connolly portrays an irritable captain who hates not only the sea,
but the ship, the crew, and the passengers. Victor McLaglen is a
private detective, disguised in order to trail Wynne Gibson, who is,
in turn, posing as a librarian. Alison Skipworth plays a large, loud
widow with marriage on her mind, while Leon Flynn is the madcap
steward. The ship's orchestra turns out to be the Three Stooges.
Some of the antics are amusing, but they are strangely negated by
the melodramatic bits. In all the film has a sort of improvised air, as
if Milestone were making it up as he went along. Perhaps, given the
working conditions on shipboard, this was exactly what he did. The
overall effect was, in the words of the *New York Times* review,
"generally meaningless."[5]

The problems of this production hardly endeared Milestone to
Harry Cohn or Columbia, and in all probability he returned their ill
feelings. In any case, Milestone moved to Paramount in 1935,
signing a lucrative contract to work under new production head
Ernst Lubitsch. Cecil B. DeMille, Rouben Mamoulian, and Josef
von Sternberg were also at Paramount in the mid-1930s, but for the

most part they all were producing second-rate work under the pressures of studio politics.[6] Milestone proved no exception to this pattern: his first two efforts for Paramount were musical programmers that might have been shot by almost anyone in the studio, films he himself dismisses as "insignificant."[7]

Milestone's first effort for Paramount, *Paris in the Spring* (1935), seems intended to follow a pattern established by Lubitsch, a romantic farce set to music and directed with zest and sophistication. Although Milestone demonstrated something of the "Lubitsch Touch" in *The Garden of Eden*, his efforts at sophistication prove inept here. Although Hans Dreier and Ernst Fegte provided a reasonable facsimile of Paris, which Ted Tetzloff transferred capably to film, the scripting and casting presented problems which Milestone could not master.[8] The story turns on the worn device of rejected lovers joining forces to make their ex-lovers jealous. In this case, the rejects, played by Italian singer Tullio Carminatti and a very youthful Ida Lupino, meet atop the Eiffel Tower, where they have come to end it all. Instead they resolve to pretend romance and capture the attention of Mary Ellis and James Blakeley, who in turn form an alliance in reaction to the new pair. Carminatti had co-starred with Grace Moore in Columbia's successful, operetta-like *One Night of Love*, and Paramount was using Mary Ellis, a versatile singer and actress, in the same type of role.

A comic mix-up follows when the newly formed pairs spend the night together after a sham wedding in the country, though the original pairings are restored in time for the happy ending. Carminatti and Ellis sing a few good songs, including the title number, but otherwise the proceedings are pretty dull. Even when Milestone tries to liven things up with some fancy camera work on a bizarre set, such as a revolving stage supported by human statues, the effect is only to emphasize the essential flatness of the tale.

Anything Goes, Cole Porter's Broadway musical of 1934, was brought to the screen by Milestone in 1936. Although the story seems just as silly as *Paris in the Spring*, the literary property proves stronger in terms of tunes like the title number, "I Get a Kick Out of You," and "You're the Top." Ethel Merman and Bing Crosby perform these hits quite capably, and Charles Ruggles provides some nice comedy relief. The love plot, which again features Ida Lupino, slows the piece down with the improbabilities. Recalling *The Captain Hates the Sea*, the setting is an ocean liner, splendidly created by set designers Drier and Fegte, and like the early film a number of complicated plot strands are pulled together for a happy ending. In all, *Anything Goes* still seems a pleasant musical entertainment, but one that might have been created by any studio workhorse. It seems that Milestone has little feel for the musical genre, though he was always careful with the use of music in his other films. His two efforts for Paramount were his only work in the genre, and like most of his genre pieces they are competent but little more.

Fortunately, the director's personal life proved more successful than his artistic efforts; in 1935 he married Kendall Lee Glaezner, the actress who played Mrs. MacPhail in *Rain* under the name Kendall Lee. Milestone had courted her since they met, and the couple lived very happily until Mrs. Milestone's death in 1978. The couple had no children. Over the years the Milestones were among the most gracious of Hollywood hosts, giving parties which attracted the cream of the film community.

The General Died at Dawn (1936)

After this string of three insignificant studio pieces—*The Captain Hates the Sea, Paris in the Spring,* and *Anything Goes*—Milestone regained his stride as a superior cinematic craftsman with his next effort, *The General Died at Dawn* (1936). This fine film has been neglected by most historians of the period, though some critics found it very good indeed. For example, in *Hollywood in the Thirties,* John Baxter calls the movie, "one of the Thirties' undoubted masterpieces."[9] Such high praise seems somewhat lavish, but the film holds up very well both as entertainment and art. Milestone obtained the story from an unpublished novel by Charles G. Booth, a work not much better than a pulp serial, but in the welter of high adventures he discerned an important sociopolitical theme—the tension between democracy and authoritarianism. He then persuaded Leftist playwright Clifford Odets to build a screenplay around this central tension, and he obtained the services of a fine cast and crew. His own technical and stylistic expertise then shaped the whole into a solidly successful film.

However, the film, fine as it is, cannot be ranked with Milestone's superior efforts—*All Quiet on the Western Front* and *Of Mice and Men.* As in *The Front Page* and *Rain,* the crucial points of contrast between great and good are scripting and casting. Odets was the darling of the literary Left during the depression decade, but his later works display a penchant for preaching and melodramatics which he mastered only in his early plays *Waiting for Lefty* (1935) and *Awake and Sing* (1935). The playwright was able to elicit the central theme of democracy versus repression from the pulpy background of *The General Died at Dawn*, but only by forcing high blown dialogue worthy of a New Deal speechwriter into the mouths of the "Terry and the Pirates" characters he inherited from the original source. The *Time* reviewer observed that "plaintive radicals" quipped after the opening night, "Odets, where is thy sting?"[10] The comic-strip adventures of the original plot force the capable but limited cast into high-action melodrama. As entertainment the movie often becomes strained and overdone, while as art it advances its themes more as platitudes than hard-won wisdom. Thus the film's success is real, though limited, the case with most of Milestone's efforts.[11]

The General Died at Dawn resembles nothing else in the Milestone canon. As always he was highly eclectic in sources and influences, ready to tackle any project which took his fancy. The exotic setting of the Far East often attracted purveyors of popular culture and during the 1930s the exciting drama of civil wars and international conspiracies made China the perfect place for high adventure. Milestone's Chinese film is both thematically and visually reminiscent of earlier Hollywood efforts, as different as Josef von Sternberg's *Shanghai Express* (1932) and Frank Capra's *The Bitter Tea of General Yen* (1933). Since both directors were old friends of his, Milestone might well have been influenced by their choices of materials and their styles of handling them. Technically, Milestone was assisted by an excellent supporting crew. The Chinese sets by Hans Dreier and Ernest Fegte never betray the Hollywood backlot, though the faces of the extras are often not very oriental. Werner Janssen's music, a special symphonic score composed for the film, also works quite well. Most importantly, the camerawork of Victor Milner and the editing of Eda Warren helped Milestone create one of the smoothest presentations of his career, a film which is always economical yet exciting in its style. As befits the subject this style proves essentially Expressionistic, with as many inventive bits as any of Milestone's films. Stylistically, *The General Died at Dawn* remains a bravura effort of split screens and match dissolves, almost a compendium of things a camera could do to tell a story.

In *The General Died at Dawn* casting parallels scripting in both strengths and limitations. From the central trio of Gary Cooper, Madeleine Carroll, and Akim Tamiroff down to bit appearances by Milestone, Odets, and rising novelist John O'Hara, the cast is uniformly fine. At the center of the story is another O'Hara, the character portrayed by Gary Cooper, who seems almost an inevitable choice for the portrayal of a sincere, sensitive American, tough enough to tackle a Chinese warlord. Throughout his career Cooper mastered such roles for dozens of Hollywood directors; his prototypical part came in the same year, 1936, when he played Longfellow Deeds in Frank Capra's *Mr. Deeds Goes to Town*. From *The Virginian* (1929) to *High Noon* (1952) he presented a laconic Western hero, perhaps second only to John Wayne in his characterization of that archetypal American. Yet it is often in his offbeat roles that he is best seen—as the legionnaire in *Morocco* (1930), as Lt. Frederick Henry in the original *A Farewell to Arms* (1932), or as a British officer in *The Lives of a Bengal Lancer* (1935). In *The General Died at Dawn* he combines his fundamental American rectitude and innocence with just enough cynicism and eccentricity to become believable. His characterization of O'Hara is not quite three dimensional, but it proves more than adequate for the melodramatic adventures provided for him by Odets and Milestone.

O'Hara may be the protagonist of the story, but his antagonist, General Yang, gives the movie its title. In essence the film tells of the warlord's defeat and death, symbolically the dawn of a new life for the downtrodden peasants of his province. Yet Yang cannot be a one-dimensional villain or he will not support his dramatic or thematic position in the film. The general is brutal, cruel, almost sadistic, but he has courage, cunning and a kind of sinister grace. Yang represents not just the evils but the temptations of totalitarianism; as played by veteran Akim Tamiroff, he exudes an inscrutable charisma which fascinates his enemies as well as his followers. Replete with cast rubber oriental eyelids devised by Milestone, Tamiroff's Yang seems a demonic half-caste, a frightening combination of oriental fanaticism and Western technical expertise. In all, he represents a worthy antagonist for the American democrat in the person of O'Hara.

However, the real surprise of the cast turns out to be Madeleine Carroll as Judy Perrie, O'Hara's love interest, who also proves a foil in another sense than Yang. Judy's father is an old China hand, a weak and venal American type, who has sold out to the general. So Judy is still an American, though she has been raised in China. She at first lacks the fortitude to declare her love for O'Hara and her support for the peoples' cause. In the course of the film she moves from the negative influence of her father to the more positive influence of O'Hara, finding her real self in the process. Unlike the usual adventures of the exotic movie, Judy is not strong, hard, and amoral; rather she is lost, weak, and world-weary, though with the strength to save herself if aided by the right man. It is a complex, demanding part, and Madeleine Carroll gives perhaps the best performance of her career in realizing at least some of its nuances. She obviously sinks into sentimentality and melodrama on occasion, but altogether her performance provides just the right balance for Cooper as O'Hara.

The minor roles are uniformly well handled also. Carter Hall is suitably craven as Judy's father, though his venality is somewhat excused by his tubercular condition. Dudley Digges conjures up an inscrutability to match General Yang in the role of his democratic foe, Mr. Wu. A greedy Britisher out to serve the general, aptly named Mr. Leach, is nicely handled by J. M. Kerrigan. William Frawley proves both amusing and believable as Brighton, a hard-drinking American dealer in smuggled guns, though a contemporary viewer finds it difficult to see Frawley as anyone except Fred Mertz of the "I Love Lucy" television series. All of Yang's insidious Chinese henchmen are well cast and well played by oriental actors familiar in face if not name from Charlie Chan mysteries and World War II action movies.

With his usual penchant for unusual presentation in the titles, Milestone opens with a tracking shot of Shanghai harbor which depicts a fleet of junks, a forest of masts and sails. Drawing in on one sail, Milestone uses it to project the main title. Later he pans among the junks to find other sails for other titles. The opening anticipates that used in Milestone's next film, *Of Mice and Men*, where, after preliminary action, the titles are projected on a boxcar door. This opening also anticipates the conclusion of the film, which takes place on Wang's junk anchored in Shanghai harbor. In general, the stylized sails set the visual ambiance of the film, a partially realistic, partially expressionistic evocation of the Orient in all of its exotic and exciting appeal.

Moving away from this center of civilization, the opening sequence presents the barbaric ravagement of the warlord's upriver province. Again anticipating *Of Mice and Men*, Milestone opens with the sky, a somber backdrop for carrion birds. A contrasting shot shows the scorched earth of a village street littered with corpses, the result of Yang's revenge. Then a long, left-right pan presents the general's legions, the cause of the destruction, marching through a wheat field, oblivious to the life around them. Next he cuts to a convoy of motorized troops led by a luxury car of American make. These close-ups reveal the driver, Yang's Oxford-educated assistant, his German aide-de-camp, and the warlord himself. The car passes directly over the camera, and another file of marching men ominously fills the frame. Again the sky and the birds of prey are shown, and finally, again, the deserted street. Careful pacing is complemented by the musical background, which perfectly matches the mood of the connecting shots.

This montage sequence, which runs less than a minute, economically and expressively establishes both the menace of Yang's terror and its cruel, mechanical nature. The general's military juggernaut seems a merciless force, almost like the forces of natural disaster, an earthquake or flood. Yet the mechanized efficiency of this force most terrifies; like the war machines in *All Quiet on the Western Front*, Yang's convoy represents the fearful evolution of modern destructive technology. This mechanical force in the hands of an authoritarian dictator threatens the existence of all civilization, a situation evolving around the world in the mid-1930s.

By contrast the next sequence opens with a crowded street scene in the provincial capital: a column of refugees from Yang's terror moves past impassive spectators. Tracking from right to left against the flow of the refugees the camera picks up the trenchcoated figure of Gary Cooper as O'Hara. He pauses to lift a child who has fallen from a refugee cart; clearly, he is sensitive and kind enough to help the Chinese people. As he stops to watch the refugees he hears another American talking about what a good business the general makes for the enlightened Westerner. In a neat bit of characterization, the American asks the man for a light, and when none is forthcoming knocks him flat. As he leaves he explains the moral of the action to the amazed businessman: just as he had no light to proffer, neither did the peasants have the tax money to please the greedy warlord.

The following scenes quickly and efficiently set up the plot. O'Hara, accompanied by his pet marmoset, Sam, receives his orders at the local hotel. He is to take a money belt loaded with gold back to Shanghai and purchase guns from Brighton for the rebel forces forming against General Yang. The rebel contact advises caution because Yang's agents are everywhere, even in Shanghai. As O'Hara pauses at the door, a typical Milestone use of a framing device, the rebel leader warns him, "From the moment you close that door the fate of the people of this province is in your hands." O'Hara with typical American bravado asserts that he will get through.

Milestone uses a bravura touch to introduce the next scene; he match dissolves from the white porcelain doorknob to a billiard ball, a ball which is then played by Peter Perrie. Around the billiard table he whispers with Oxford, Yang's chief assistant, who was last seen in the general's fancy car. The scene itself is expressively and brilliantly handled. The single light over the billiard table leaves the rest of the room in darkness, and the shadows serve to conceal identities and motives. The audience strains to hear the whispered conversation, punctuated by Perrie's tubercular cough. The shifting allegiances here are well caught by the changing angles and distances of Milestone's camera, as well as by the muffled sound track. It appears they know of O'Hara's mission and that Perrie has been engaged to stop him. His daughter, Judy, sitting to the side in the shadows, is included in the plot when she rises to take her turn at the table. Oxford comments ambiguously on her beautiful form, and remarks that a beautiful woman can lure a man to do many foolish things. Hearing this, Judy storms out, pausing only long enough to view herself in a mirror, as if trying to discover her own identity. Perrie imploringly follows her, while Yang's lieutenant is left thoughtfully racking up the billiard balls.

The next scene takes place in the Perrie's hotel room, next to O'Hara's. The window looks out onto the teeming streets, and the contrast between the masses outside and the pair incestuously locked within is emphasized by Milestone's deft camera work. To reach the room, they quickly pass through a series of dark streets and doorways as if threading a maze. At first Judy refuses to take part in Perrie's schemes, but her father prevails on her sympathies by parading his illness and his weakness. He desperately wants to return to America for his last months, back to an innocent vision of the Hudson River Valley. Judy cannot resist this appeal to her basic loyalties, and she agrees to participate if O'Hara will not be killed.

Again moving economically, Milestone cuts to the departing train (distressingly American in prototype to the discerning eye) and a number of neat tracking shots through the station crowd. Judy has evidently lured O'Hara aboard, but as she sits alone in her compartment her uneasiness is evident in constant chain-smoking and nervous gestures. Finally O'Hara appears, again framed by the compartment door; the entrance recalls the introduction of Joan

Crawford in *Rain*, a triptych of shots, first the exotic pet marmoset, then the long legs (anticipating his entrance in *Saratoga Trunk*, 1945), then Coop's handsome face reflected in the door-length mirror. Judy has just studied herself in the same mirror, and the mirror motif raises the theme of concealed identities. O'Hara is playing a role and so is Judy, but she knows his while he has yet to fathom hers. Beyond disguises, the questions of basic identities and motivations are also raised by this neat bit of imagistic characterization. Then O'Hara moves impulsively, kicking down the folding table between them and taking her in his arms. She pulls away and tries to warn him obliquely of her purpose, but she finally allows him to hold her and talk of his mission. O'Hara's speeches here project not only his romantic biography, but his philosophy of life. He has a background of oppression himself, and he asks, "What better work for an American than fighting for democracy?" After this impassioned credo Judy kisses him for the first time, and their romance is sealed.

At this point, Milestone crosscuts to Yang's forces waiting to ambush the train; the general sits impassively in his staff car knowing that his agents have done their work. Back on the train, O'Hara takes Judy to the dining car, where Perrie is also having his dinner. All the principals are in place for the action. Looking once more at her watch, Judy begins to tell O'Hara of the plot against him but it is too late. The train screeches to a halt, Yang's soldiers swarm aboard, and soon the warload is holding court in the dining car. The choreography here is well handled with the principals moving up and down the long aisle of the car, engaging each other in accusation and insult. True to Odets's Leftist bent, O'Hara characterizes Yang as "a strikebreaker" among other things. The warlord also demonstrates his cruel power by ordering one of his guards to commit suicide over a minor offense and then relenting only at the last minute. This development anticipates the conclusion by preparing the audience for the bizarre motivations which effect the lovers' escape. General Yang directly confronts O'Hara with a bayonet, in a nice piece of angle shooting, and quickly discovers the gold in the money belt beneath the American's clothes. Next he gives the money to Perrie, who is to proceed to Shanghai and purchase the guns from the American smuggler Brighton. O'Hara is kept behind as a hostage, and once again Judy is torn between father and lover. As the guards escort him through the dining car,

General Yang (Akim Tamiroff) holds court on a train in *The General Died at Dawn* and threatens O'Hara (Gary Cooper) with a bayonet.

O'Hara stops near Judy. When she rises, he slaps her across the face. As Perrie flinches, Yang smiles inscrutably in the background.

Thus far, about one-third of the way into the film, Milestone has managed to balance the serious theme and the pulp-magazine story material in an evocative thriller. Unfortunately, as is often the case in Milestone films, the final two-thirds quickly race downhill into melodrama. In this case, it would seem that the adventure plot overwhelmed both Odets and the director, so that the one forgot his ringing speeches about democracy and the other neglected his expressive style. Whenever either Odets or Milestone tries to reconstruct the earlier mood, their efforts seem strained and out of place. For example, at one point Milestone uses a five-way split screen in order to follow the fortunes of all his characters. Starting with Wu and Chan in the center of the screen he introduces the others sequentially in each corner in visual complement to Wu's speculations about them. Yet the device, for all its cleverness, calls

attention only to itself and to the muddle of plots at this point in the
work. Vertical wipes used to move from one short scene to another
also demonstrate that simply too much is going on in the cops-and-
robbers business of the concluding two-thirds of the film.

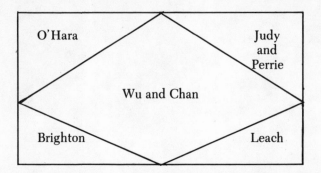

After Yang and O'Hara leave, the train continues on to Shanghai,
where Judy and Perrie proceed to the Mansion House, which is
managed by Mr. Wu, the Shanghai leader of the rebellion against
Yang. Wu identifies Judy by the marmoset she has adopted after it
was separated from O'Hara, and he grills her about the American's
fate. She reveals his capture by the warlord's men, but conceals her
father's part in the scheme and the information that Perrie now is in
possession of the gold. In the meantime, Perrie has decided to
doublecross the general, and he converts the gold to cash and buys
passage to America. Another complication ensues when a British
"angle man," as he calls himself, one Mr. Leach, becomes suspicious
of Perrie and trails him to the hotel in hopes of cashing in on some
nefarious dealings. Meanwhile, back at Yang's junk, O'Hara mouths
a few more impassioned lines and then escapes. He makes it to
Shanghai, though wounded, and reveals Perrie's part in the plot
to Wu.

Wu shrewdly confronts O'Hara with Judy, opening the door
which connects his office with the bar and billiard room of the hotel.
This mutual revelation is carefully shot both ways through the frame
of the door, which separates the lovers physically. O'Hara accompanies Judy to her room, where she tries to explain herself. The
scene is dramatically overdone, indicating the film's irreversible
slide into melodrama. The plot continues to thicken also as Perrie
overhears the lover's conversation and pulls a gun on O'Hara,

forcing him to shoot Judy's father in self-defense. Almost immediately Leach gets the drop on O'Hara, but Wu in turn extricates the American from this danger. Now, incredibly enough, General Yang and his cohorts, sinisterly attired in trenchcoats and carrying Lugers, arrive to capture everyone else. As a contemporary critic remarked, the only people missing from the hotel room were the Marx Brothers, recalling the famous stateroom scene from *A Night at the Opera* (1935).[12]

The warlord hauls them all off to his junk in the harbor, where he threatens them with unspeakable tortures unless they come up with the money. Actually, none of them knows its location as Perrie had hidden it in the lining of Judy's suitcase but was dispatched before telling her. The foggy, fearful night aboard the junk is expressively presented, though by now the film is sinking fast into a sea of melodrama. Judy offers to take Yang's wrath by pretending to know the location of the money and trading the information for the release of O'Hara and Wu. This scene, as the lovers withdraw into a convenient niche of the cabin to be alone, becomes extremely sentimental. Cooper and Carroll are presented in soft, backlit close-ups constructed around lines like, "We could have made wonderful music together."

Then improbability follows sentimentality in the creation of melodrama. Yang's gang had also seized Chan and Brighton, the gunrunner, from the hotel. Poor Chan is tortured to death as an example of what might happen to the others, but Brighton, in a drunken stupor, snoozes through it all. Meanwhile Leach is shot by the firing squad, and Judy is dragged off to be shot. Finally awakening, Brighton demands another drink and starts rummaging about in the suitcases trying to find a bottle. Instead he discovers the money and decides to fight his way out with it. In the resulting confusion, he fatally stabs General Yang. The dying warlord gives orders that his personal guard execute all the prisoners and then commit suicide. O'Hara quickly sizes up the psychology of the situation and talks Yang into leaving them behind as witnesses to the glory of the suicidal act. The mass suicide is very powerfully presented, with two rows of soldiers facing each other, Lugers at arms' length, firing in obedience to Yang's orders. The mechanical precision of their bizarre military drill recalls the terror of the opening sequence and underlines the irony of their fate. They have lived by military terror, and they die in the same manner. As the general finally expires, the dawn lights the faces of the survivors. In a long pullback shot Milestone captures the whole junk in the frame as O'Hara and Judy run along the deck into each other's arms.

This shot also anticipates a memorable pullback in *Of Mice and Men* as George and Slim separate in search of Lennie. Of course, there the figures move apart rather than together, so that camera movement matches character movement; it is the meaning of the movement which separates the two shots artistically. In *Of Mice and Men*, the shot works expressively yet still organically within a generally Realistic framework to underscore a powerful emotion. In *The General Died at Dawn*, the visually pleasing shot calls attention to itself as another device decorating a strained, melodramatic plot. Thus the differences in scripting and casting create the final differences between the two films in terms of style. *Of Mice and Men* is a great movie, as the next section will demonstrate; *The General Died at Dawn* is in many ways a good movie, both serious in intention and entertaining in execution, though it falters under the weight of its melodrama. However, it deserves to be better known and better appreciated that it is, for as right-minded Hollywood melodrama it ranks only a notch below the classic of the type, Michael Curtiz's *Casablanca* (1943).

Of Mice and Men

The General Died at Dawn was released late in 1936, while Milestone's next film, *Of Mice and Men*, did not appear until very late in 1939. This three-year hiatus in the director's development seems puzzling, especially as he should have been at the height of his career. A number of problems were involved: unsuccessful projects, broken contracts, and lawsuits. Yet behind these demonstrable details of Hollywood business life the film critic senses a fundamental conflict. Milestone wanted to make serious movies, though he had not directed one since *Rain* in 1932; *The General Died at Dawn* was only a moderately successful attempt to do something serious with a studio property. In his attempt to find meaningful projects Milestone ran afoul of the studio system, so much so that he was essentially pushed outside it for several years at an important point in his development. Happily he was able to return with one of his finest films, *Of Mice and Men*.

After completing *The General Died at Dawn*, Milestone contemplated several serious projects. The first was a film version of Vincent Sheean's autobiography, *Personal History* (1935), which was filled with colorful incidents from the author's career as an international correspondent in North Africa, China, and Palestine. Walter Wanger was to have produced the film, but for whatever reason it never went into production.[13] Later, Alfred Hitchcock directed it for Wanger as *Foreign Correspondent* (1940), a thriller typical of the British director. Like the unrealized *Red Square* in 1933, this uncompleted work might well have proved quite interesting for Milestone in terms of subject matter and film technique. In 1937 Milestone and Clifford Odets prepared a screenplay based on Sidney Kingsley's Broadway hit, *Dead End* (1935), for Sam Goldwyn. However, the production was given to William Wyler, who used a different screenplay for his 1937 film version. Again Milestone's film might have proved more interesting than Wyler's, as the Odets screenplay stays much closer to Kingsley's original play.

Late in 1937 Milestone signed a contract with Hal Roach to film an adaptation of Eric Hatch's novel *Road Show* (1934), the story of a traveling carnival. According to the original contract Milestone was to have received $5,000 a week for a minimum of sixteen weeks of work, but after ten weeks of shooting Roach removed the director, claiming that he was making a serious drama from a comedy vehicle.[14] Early in 1938 Milestone sued Roach for $90,000 in salary arrears, interest, and damages. The director won the initial decision, but Roach dragged out the appeal over the rest of the year. Finally the producer settled out of court, offering Milestone part of the production costs for a projected screen version of John Steinbeck's *Of Mice and Men* in lieu of the disputed salary.

Before filming the Steinbeck novel, however, Milestone pushed out another programmer, *The Night of Nights*, for Paramount in early 1939. This project evolved when Pat O'Brien (the Hildy Johnson of Milestone's *The Front Page*), was idled along with a full production crew by a last-minute change in script assignments.[15] Milestone and Donald Ogden Stewart threw together a scenario and filmed the result in three months. Milestone's contribution to the plot included the reminiscence of a fist fight between Walter Catlett and Louis Calhern, both Milestone friends, which resulted in their lifetime expulsion from an actors' club. The brawlers became the star (O'Brien) and the producer (Roland Young) of a hit play, friendly rivals recalling the reporter-editor relationship of *The Front Page*. This introductory material is rather well done, and promise is created when the actor ruins his career with drink and abandons his wife and daughter. Then, moving forward eighteen years, the resolution involves a reconciliation with the daughter (Olympe

Bradna), who has become a star in a revival of the play the father first triumphed in eighteen years earlier. O'Brien dies a contented man in her dressing room on opening night. As is often the case with Paramount's second-line offerings, Hans Dreier's sets are the best feature of the film.

Milestone's *Of Mice and Men* was almost completely a personal project, a labor of love. The director had read John Steinbeck's novel (1937) and seen the play (1938), immediately concluding that the story would make an excellent film.[16] In New York during his period of inaction, Milestone called the play's producers and suggested a partnership for producing it as a film. Surprisingly they assented; it turned out later that they were miffed because Harry Cohn of Columbia had taken an option on the property but later turned it down because he feared the censors. Milestone worked up a screenplay with Eugene Solow and later took it to Steinbeck for approval. Though the author made a few minor changes, he essentially approved of the script. Next Milestone had to sweat out a session with the studio censors and the Hayes Office, but again the changes were minor.[17] With Roach's money, Milestone was in business.

As was usual when he had control, Milestone cast very carefully. Out of budget constraint and artistic preference, Milestone preferred to work with comparative unknowns. Burgess Meredith, who had appeared on Broadway in several plays by Maxwell Anderson, was probably the best known member of the cast. His version of George Milton adds a touch of stylized lyricism to the production. Lon Chaney, Jr., played Lenny in a Los Angeles production of the play, and the film offered this ill-used actor a chance to escape monster roles. B-Western star Bob Steele was typecast as Curly, while Betty Field had her first important role as his wife, Mae. The rest of the cast—Charles Bickford as Slim, Roman Bohnen as Candy, and Leigh Whipper as Crooks—are uniformly excellent.

Milestone also conferred carefully on visual motifs with art director Nicolai Remisoff and with Steinbeck himself, who took the director to the real ranch which had been the scene of the real action inspiring the novel. Veteran cameraman Norbert Brodine competently filmed the piece, while Bert Jordan provided expert editing. The director was also much concerned with sound motifs, and he persuaded well-known composer Aaron Copland to do the musical score, which has since become a concert favorite.

In spite of this array of talent and a Best Picture nomination for the banner year of 1939 (when Victor Fleming's *Gone with the Wind* swept the Oscars), the movie failed at the box office. In desperation United Artists even tried to sell it as a "sexploitation" picture, using posters which featured Betty Field in seductive poses and catchlines like "Unwanted, she fought for the one thing which is every woman's birthright."[18] However, the artistic success of the film guaranteed its eventual reputation as a Hollywood classic, and as a staple in film programs. As Steinbeck himself wrote to his agents, ". . . it is a beautiful job. Here Milestone has done a curious lyrical thing. It hangs together. . . ."[19]

A comparison of serious American fiction with film versions reveals that John Steinbeck has proved the most cinematically adaptable of our major novelists. At least two great films have been adapted from Steinbeck's fiction—Lewis Milestone's *Of Mice and Men* (1939) and John Ford's *The Grapes of Wrath* (1940)—while two other films—Milestone's *The Red Pony* (1949) and Elia Kazan's *East of Eden* (1955)—are at least very good.[20] Steinbeck's novels possess qualities which make them inherently adaptable for the screen; his individualized characters, strong narrative lines, and colorful settings are all as valuable in the film as they are in fiction. Yet more subtle consideratons of style, mode, and medium yield greater insights into the filmic adaptability of Steinbeck's fiction, particularly when attention is focused on the chronological pattern of these adaptations. The two great films were made from Steinbeck's most realistic novels at the high point of American cinematic realism in the years just prior to World War II; thus the convergence of literary and cinematic mode and style occasioned the successful screen adaptations of Steinbeck's fiction to the film medium.

In a general sense the matter, the manner, and the method employed in *Of Mice and Men* are realistic. Steinbeck's short novel and the stage version he wrote from it present a topic that was common in the 1930s—the lives and deaths of little people disoriented and dispossessed by the conditions of the modern world. The book's accurate and dispassionate portrait of agricultural life in California during the Depression prefigures Steinbeck's next novel, *The Grapes of Wrath*. Like that novel *Of Mice and Men* shows people reduced to animal status by social pressures.

Of Mice and Men's characters, especially Lennie, seem almost animal-like in their simplicity, but Steinbeck is careful to portray lives shaped by social as well as natural forces. Lennie cannot control his natural impulses and dies like a hunted animal, while

Slim, who controls his passions as expertly as his mule team, lives on as the aristocrat of merit, providing what leadership and order are found in the ranch world. George exists somewhere between these poles, poetically dreaming of order and harmony on "a little place," while still desiring the easy pleasures of pool hall, barroom, and brothel. Thus behavior is motivated by the whole spectrum of human involvements with society, and social morality is as much a theme in *Of Mice and Men* as it is in *The Grapes of Wrath*.

Steinbeck's stylistic techniques are realistic also; the point of view is third person. It is an objective, carefully distanced viewpoint, as dispassionate as the camera lens:

Evening of a hot day started the little wind to moving among the leaves. The shade climbed up the hills toward the top. On the sand banks the rabbits sat as quietly as little gray, sculptured stones. And then from the direction of the state highway came the sound of footsteps on crisp sycamore leaves. The rabbits hurried noiselessly for cover. A stilted heron labored up into the air and pounded down river. For a moment the place was lifeless, and then two men emerged from the path and came into the opening by the green pool. (p. 2)[21]

Steinbeck seems almost to be anticipating a film version of the book in his descriptive, documentary prose. The same vision is maintained throughout the short novel. Each chapter is introduced by a detailed report of the setting and then dialogue is simply recorded with no authorial directions. This methodology increases both the complexity and the ambiguity of the work because of the lack of editorial judgment. Steinbeck does not comment on his characters through symbol or symbolic action. Although Lennie is depicted through images of rabbits, mice, and birds, he is not an animal; he is to some undetermined extent a responsible human being, and he must live in society as such or be destroyed. The antiomniscience of viewpoint and imagery increases the complexity and ambiguity of characterization, placing *Of Mice and Men* solidly in the tradition of literary realism.

Milestone's film version parallels Steinbeck's *Of Mice and Men* in its antiomniscient viewpoint. His camera angles from prologue to epilogue are always at eye level, thus involving the viewer much as he would be involved by watching the action unfold in real life. The director's framing, especially in the outdoor scenes, opens wide vistas of natural and social contexts for the immediate action. His composition, though careful, is also detailed and complicated; the bunkhouse and barn interiors exemplify this method in the contextual details of social and animal life—pin-ups, bunks, harness. Even within the bunkhouse or the stables at night the light of kerosene lamps is bright and clear enough to illuminate the nuances of relationships, as in the shooting of Candy's dog. His editing utilizes long takes from George and Lenny's first conversation, while tracking shots connect the players' complex action.

In perhaps the first use of this now common device, Milestone opens with a prologue before the credits, one which establishes the serious intentions of the film. The audience sees the drama of real life, rather than the details of Hollywood production. More importantly, the prologue sets mood and tone while establishing themes and motifs which will be continued throughout the film. Steinbeck preserves a greater dramatic unity by opening and closing his narrative at the narrow pool, but Milestone achieves greater dramatic force by translating George's remarks about the trouble at Weed into an exciting chase sequence. The prologue also works toward realism as it extends the action of the narrative from the small world of the ranch to a larger world of Weed and the Salinas Valley country, and finally, by the implications of the hoboes on the train, to all of Depression-stricken America.

The opening shot establishes the nature-man-society balance which will become thematically important throughout; as the music rises dramatically, swirling stormy clouds darken the sky.[22] After studying the sky, the camera looks down from eye level to examine a rabbit and a flock of quail. The inhabitants of this natural world feed peacefully until human legs intrude into the frame; as the camera pulls up to eye level, the audience sees George and Lennie running wildly. Several quick cuts of the pursuing posse and their quarry capture the excitement of the chase, while in the background the thunder rolls and Copland's music swells. Trapped like rabbits, the pair begin to panic until George leads them into an irrigation ditch; this immersion is accompanied by a cloudburst which evidently discourages the hunters, who have leaped across the ditch without discovering their prey. The emotional mood of the film (fear, frustration, hate), characterization (George as the leader, Lennie the follower), style (eye-level shots, careful framing in outdoor scenes), and theme (the relationship of human and animal worlds) are all established.

The next scene consists of one long, panning shot which shows George and Lennie still running, now at night, to catch a moving freight train. When they climb into an open boxcar, George closes the door, and against this background the credits are presented. After the credits the train fades into the distance, and the next sequence is in the interior of a bus; the other passengers are scanned as the camera settles down for an extended take of George and Lennie in the front seat talking about their new jobs at the ranch. Again this sequence is added by Milestone, made up from a few retrospective remarks by George, and again it works to open up the context of the action. The bus is full of other ranch hands like George and Lennie, and the bus driver remembers taking them to Weed. George becomes angry and defensive at the bus driver's remarks and creates a confrontation, after which the driver puts the pair off to walk the rest of the way to the ranch. After several miles of hot pavement, George hurls a clod of earth at a signboard depicting a businessman enjoying the comfort of an air-conditioned train, a life-style in easy contrast to his various modes of transportation. The shot of George and Lenny trudging down the dusty highway past the billboard seems suggested by one of Dorothea Lange's documentary photographs for the Farm Security Administration. In general, the visual ambience of. Milestone's film, like John Ford's adaptation of *The Grapes of Wrath*, seems strongly influenced by the documentary film and photography of the 1930s.[23]

The next sequence presents Chapter 1 of the novel or Act 1, Scene 1, of the play. George and Lennie stop to rest beside a narrow pool of the Salinas River, and George decides to spend the night there enjoying their last freedom before their new job. Milestone's version stays very close to the dialogue of the play, and his filmic style develops a similar sense of intimate realism. After filming the pair approaching from a slight distance, the camera moves in like another person joining their conversation. Many of the cuts are held for long periods as both men are balanced in the frame; about the only cutting in the scene is from one speaker to another. In fact, editing becomes nearly invisible; it does not, for example, focus on Lennie's dead bird (a mouse in the novel) as a symbol, but only as a part of a developing pattern of nature images within the context of the entire Lennie-George relationship. Milestone does add one piece of dialogue to the scene; the last thing George says before they sleep is that "A man sure feels free when he ain't got a job . . . and when he ain't hungry."

Their arrival at the ranch the next day proves the wisdom of these words. The boss is angry because they have missed a half-day's work, and he makes it plain that working on this ranch will be no picnic. In handling the interview with the boss before the arrival at the bunkhouse Milestone reverses Steinbeck's order of events, though each event is substantially reproduced. This method seems to work better, providing a greater contrast of life in nature and life in society. These greater complexities of social life are mirrored in the increasing use of deep focus and in the greater detail of *mise-en-scène* composition. The scene opens as Candy, the aging bunkhouse swamper, leads George and Lennie across the ranch yard toward the boss's office; they are seen through the open window of the office and in the context of the cluttered desk and files. As they enter, the camera examines all the details of the interior, which is perfectly arranged to present the complicated hierarchy of the ranch as a business society. During the interview Milestone holds very extended shots on the carefully composed grouping of the four figures, with dramatic emphasis provided by shifting of the figures in front of the camera (the boss rises from his chair, Candy shuffles, Lennie cowers, George puffs himself up defensively) instead of by camera movement or cutting.

Steinbeck used a sort of verbal *mise-en-scène* in the depiction of the bunkhouse. Milestone picks up this cue and translates this picture perfectly to film. He has his camera at eye level, inside the door, ready to follow the trio through the room and to locate them against all of the details Steinbeck mentions, while adding a few, such as girlie pictures tacked to the walls. George's argument with Candy about the possibility of bed bugs is neatly framed by two stacks of bunks and again done in an extended shot. In both novel and play Steinbeck brings the other characters into the bunkhouse, including the boss for the interview. Milestone has the other characters presented outside, in the office, or against the natural backgrounds of ranch activity. Crooks, the black cripple who serves as stablebuck, limps by; Curly, the boss's son, rides up on a movie cowboy's white horse; Mae, Curly's wife, is playing in the barn with her fleecy puppy; Slim, the muleskinner, is first seen behind his twelve-mule team. Milestone also builds more tension by inventing a fist fight between Curly and Whit, a young ranch hand, then moving to direct confrontations of Curly with Slim, George, and Lenny. Although this movement seems a little plotty in comparison with the novel, it works nicely here to widen the contexts of animal and natural images.

Milestone very carefully orchestrates these scenes in terms of composition. Mountains, barley fields, and farm machinery are balanced to emphasize the movement of characters. Curly advances through the moving belts of the threshing machines; Mae peeks out from between the wagons at Slim; George has Lenny lift a wagon on his back in a demonstration of his superhuman strength. In the movements between each of these confrontations Milestone draws back for distanced shots which locate the characters in the full context of the ranch and the natural world. Even here he holds the shots and lets the action play in front of the camera; farm wagons criss-cross in right-left, left-right lines of movement—a sort of ballet which gives a lively feeling to the bucolic life. Against this backdrop we see Lennie's brute strength, Mae's lust, and Curly's brutality; only Slim, the muleskinner, and, to some extent, his new friend George, know how to harness nature in an orderly way.

Milestone uses dinner time as a transitional device to several scenes which bridge the gap between afternoon and evening in the novel and the play. Instead of having George and Slim talk in the bunkhouse, Milestone films their conversation while riding in, washing up, and eating dinner. These scenes allow Milestone to do some nice *mise-en-scène* composition with visual elements like the sinewy bodies of the ranch hands in the outdoor washhouse and the heaping piles of plain food on the tables of the cookshack. He also interpolates a contrasting dinner scene at the ranchhouse with considerable by-play between Curly and Mae.

The long sequence which forms Chapter 3 of the novel and Act II, Scene 2 of the play, the shooting of Candy's dog, demonstrates basic human solidarity. Carlson, a seasoned ranch hand who seems second in command to Slim, has been after Candy to get rid of his old sheepdog because it smells up the bunkhouse. All the men commiserate with Candy, as almost all of them have dogs of their own, but finally they all agree that Candy would do better to shoot the old dog and take a pup from the litter Slim's bitch has just dropped. When Candy cannot bring himself to do it, Carlson volunteers to shoot the dog with his pistol. Milestone handles the potentially melodramatic scene with a fine restraint, using the devices of cinematic realism to limit the sentiment inherent in the subject (though the musical background is somewhat overdone). The scene unfolds within the *mise-en-scène* earlier established in the bunkhouse, playing itself out in extended shots of the whole group debating the fate of Candy's dog. Many of these shots are angled through the bunks or other bits of furniture, giving a fuller context to the drama pictured. Only when Candy hears Carlson's shot does the camera close up on him isolated in his bunk. The scene requires this extended treatment because it prefigures Lennie's death at the conclusion of the film.

Lennie is not present in the bunkhouse; rather he is out in the barn playing with the pup Slim has given him. Milestone cross-cuts back to the ranchhouse to show Mae alone, pacing and brooding; when she flips on the radio, the raucous swing music contrasts with Aaron Copland's quiet background score in the bunkhouse scene. The radio irritates Mae's father-in-law, so she decides to visit her puppy in the barn. Slim and Crooks have also headed to the barn to look after the mules, and she takes the opportunity to talk to Slim about why he absolutely rejects her (another scene invented by Milestone); but Curly, who is always checking on her movements, uses their proximity and the gift of the puppy to cause another confrontation.

The resulting fracas leaves George and Lennie together in the bunkhouse, where they can discuss their plans. They are not alone, though, for Candy is still quietly curled up in his bunk. When George begins another description of their little place, the camera holds on him and Lennie for a full five minutes; slowly, in the far background shadows, Candy changes his position as he hears their plans for the little place. Then he gets up and crosses the room, filling the opening between George and Lennie. Hesitantly, he asks to be included in their plans; now alone without his old dog, he must have some companionship. As he tells George that otherwise he faces only the county home, the camera moves to a close-up of his broken face and then, through quick cutting back and forth, unfolds their debate. Candy has $340 to contribute toward the purchase of the ranch. George climbs into his upper bunk to think the proposition over; the camera now looks over his shoulder down at the expectant Lennie and the hopeful Candy. Suddenly George jumps down. They will do it. They almost dance between the stacks of bunks, while the camera holds all three yelling out their contributions and desires. Overall, the whole sequence is a splendid example of how cinematic style can evoke the full power of dramatic performances.

The next sequence, Lennie's fight with Curly, begins with extended shots of the group returning to the bunkhouse; Slim verbally puts down Curly, and then Carlson does the same. In his frustration Curly turns on Lennie, and Milestone uses his quickest cutting and most dramatic montage effects to achieve the sense of physical urgency the scene requires. The cuts jump from one combatant to the other, and to the circle of ranch hands urging Lennie to defend himself. Finally the badgered giant catches one of Curly's fists in his big paw and slowly crushes it. The camera holds a long close-up on the fist, and Copland's music also rises to a crescendo. Fortunately, Slim is able to browbeat Curly into covering up the fight, saving Lennie's job.

Milestone interpolates the next scene—Saturday night in the town barroom. Not only does it give him the opportunity for another realistic *mise-en-scène* composition, but it again extends the contexts of the central narrative. George is tempted by booze and floozies, but he limits himself to one beer, and leaves to mail a money order as a down payment on the little farm. Almost the whole sequence is shot from directly beside the booth where George, Whit, and Carlson sit with three good-time girls. This set-up also allows Milestone to reemphasize one motif, the tawdry dreams of Hollywood; the girls introduce themselves as Marlene Dietrich, Jean Harlow, and Greta Garbo; "Garbo" even camps, "I vant to be alone."

The real Greta Garbo's publicity-oriented aloofness exists in direct contrast with the realistic loneliness of Steinbeck's characters. One of the most lonely, Crooks, the black stablebuck, is featured in the next sequence, when Lennie, finally tiring of his pup, visits his room in the barn. At first Crooks refuses to let him in, because he is refused admittance to the segregated bunkhouse. But Lennie's innocence encourages Crook's trust, and this human contact opens him up to Candy also. Soon Crooks is also in on the "little place" plan; when George returns from town all three are drinking, smoking, and singing. Crooks's room, actually the harness room of the barn, gives Milestone another carefully detailed setting that carries symbolic overtones. As Crooks himself says, he has his own room, but also his own dung heap. The whole sequence is shot much in the same style as the bunkhouse scenes, and when Mae intrudes once more, Milestone has the opportunity to do some nice choreography with his figures before the camera.

Unfortunately, the boss finds Mae with the men and tells Curly when he returns from town; Curly, unable to start a fight, throws her out the next morning. Milestone adds this scene between Mae and Curly, and it works very well in terms of motivating Mae's subsequent behavior toward Lennie. When she goes to the barn to retrieve her pet, she finds Lennie mourning over his puppy, the pup having gone the way of his mice and birds. Mae wants any sort of human response, and she begins to flirt with Lennie. Steinbeck sets the scene in the barn with its naturalistic implications; Milestone cinematically realizes them by photographing against this realistic backdrop and by viewing his characters through the perspectives of rails and pens and hay bales. As Lennie and Mae talk, the camera does more close-up work than it has throughout the film. Each character is locked in his own dream—Lennie's of the little place, Mae's of Hollywood.

The unintended murder is handled deftly and with considerable decorum. Originally Milestone had thought of having Mae killed by someone else in order to preserve audience sympathy for Lennie; Steinbeck, rightly, protested that such a move would dissipate the tragic inevitability of the conclusion.[24] Quick cutting captures the physical tension of the scene, and the camera holds a long close-up on Mae's shoes suspended a few inches above the ground by Lennie's iron grasp on her throat. Her left shoe dangles, then drops off, and a few seconds later Lennie lets her crumple to the barn floor.

Until the discovery of her death, life goes on much as usual. After Lennie runs, Slim's bitch comes back to her pups; Candy comes in and picks one out to be his; George and Crooks play at horseshoes. Candy and George discover the crime as the dog comes to them carrying Mae's shoe in its mouth. George decides, with Slim's approval, that he must kill Lennie himself so that the lynch mob organized by Curly won't get a chance at him. This final sequence is reminiscent of the prologue and the first scene at the narrow pool in both action and treatment. George and Slim race to the pool and quickly find Lennie. Slim walks off as Milestone crosscuts to the posse led by the sheriff and to the mob led by Curly. The camera holds extended takes of George and Lennie as George delivers his customary monologue; now as George describes the little place he has Lennie look across the narrow pool and imagine what it will be like. In a final act of human imagination Lennie does see the future that George so movingly presents. The camera holds on them together for several minutes and then follows George as he pulls back and takes the pistol from beneath his jacket. Like Carlson he is a careful shot; he fires once, and turns his head in horror at his act. Milestone has Lennie fall into the pool, once again immersing himself as he had in the prologue. The director also adds an epilogue in which Slim joins George, an act of supportive comradeship, and George, at Slim's urging, surrenders the gun to the sheriff, who has arrived with the posse.[25] Then after they have walked off, Copland's theme music rises and a final pullback shot holds on the same scene as the seasons change—leaves fall and a squirrel scampers on the fallen tree where Lennie sat. Recalling the rabbit and quail of the prologue, the natural movement poetically states that Lennie has returned to the nature which he loved, leaving George to the greater complexities of human nature in its social organization. The excellent cast, the creative technical staff, and the director's thoughtful combination of their efforts into an extension of the novel's realistic thrust all combine to make Milestone's version as powerful as Steinbeck's. Milestone created from *Of Mice and Men* a great film, one which demonstrates the convergence of realistic fictional and cinematic styles.

Milestone's Hollywood reputation took another upward turn after *Of Mice and Men,* and he signed a contract with RKO, where he was given his own production unit. In quick succession he ground out two light comedies with an aging Ronald Colman as the lead. As Milestone himself has remarked "This particular pair of comedies were of the kind you did if you hoped to stay in motion pictures, in the expectation that the next film might give you a chance to redeem yourself."[26] Both were scripted by John van Druten from light stage vehicles. *Lucky Partners* (1940) evolved from a Sacha Guitry play *Bonne Chance,* with Colman as a Greenwich Village pseudoartist who goes halves on a lottery ticket with Ginger Rogers as a brunette bookstore clerk. When they win $6,000 Colman whisks her off on a cross-country trip, to the chagrin of her insurance salesman fiancé (Jack Carson). After some bedroom knockabout, Colman carries Ms. Rogers off to Niagara Falls.

My Life with Caroline (1941) was based on Louis Verneuil's *Train to Venice,* though the action again is transposed to New York. Colman here plays a successful publisher troubled by a flighty wife, the Caroline of the title, portrayed by British actress Anna Lee. Several suitors, including Reginald Gardiner and Gilbert Roland, offer to help her find the "real" Caroline. Colman persists through it all, and wins Caroline back at the conclusion.

Either film might have been directed by any of a dozen studio regulars. Both have moments of wit and smooth cinematic integration of dialogue, but overall they are simply uninspired fare.

Once again Milestone's career seemed in the doldrums. However,

My Life with Caroline was released in August 1941. Within a few months America would be at war, and one of the home-front industries would become the production of war movies, a genre neglected in the 1930s. Milestone, his reputation for *All Quiet on the Western Front* still alive, would soon enter another career cycle, one which would prove much more important than his return to light comedy at RKO.

4

The War Years

Hollywood at War

LEWIS MILESTONE established his directorial reputation with the critical and popular success of *All Quiet on the Western Front,* Hollywood's most important antiwar film. Although the movie's pacifist attitude was inherent in Remarque's novel, Milestone undoubtedly shared the writer's ideological position. The director was always known as a liberal intellectual, and both the film and his comments on it indicate an artistic commitment to the powerful antiwar statement made by the book. When he directed the film in 1930, Milestone reflected the feelings of most Americans; the Great War had been fought to end all wars, and the world wanted no others. In spite of the popular and artistic success of *All Quiet on the Western Front* Milestone did not make another war film until 1942. This twelve-year span between works in the same genre probably can be explained by the isolationist attitudes of the 1930s. War films were not popular during the decade, and Milestone himself possibly felt that he had made his personal statement about war, and needed to make no other. Then World War II changed everything; Hollywood found it both patriotic and profitable to turn out topical war films, while Milestone's personal position on war was fundamentally altered by the terrors of totalitarianism.

Like many liberal intellectuals, Milestone viewed the rise of totalitarian Fascism with considerable alarm; born a Russian and a Jew, he would have had a natural insight into the dangers posed by the arming and the expansion of Nazi Germany. The director's opposition to totalitarianism was evident in *The General Died at Dawn,* made in 1936, an adventure film set against the background of war and scripted by Leftist playwright Clifford Odets. The title character, General Yang, is an obvious stand-in for all the totalitar-

ian militarists then flourishing. After Pearl Harbor, Milestone, like
most Americans, became convinced that armed resistance to Fascism was the only course of action right for free men. War was still
a horror, but it was a horror created by an evil system; the only way
to end it sucessfully was to conclude the war Hitler and his allies
had started. Therefore, Lewis Milestone placed his art at the service
of an ideal, the defeat of Fascist totalitarianism.

The predominance of this ideal and the general climate of opinion
in wartime Hollywood obviously limited the artistic complexity of
Milestone's later war films. It was one thing to present pacifist
statements in a vehicle which concerned a foreign army in a war a
decade or more past; it was quite another to portray realistically our
own cause in war still raging around the world. Like most Hollywood movies made during World War II, Milestone's efforts tend
more toward propaganda than art. Yet these films should not be
dismissed out of hand, as some critics have done. The transformation
of his attitudes toward war was a viable intellectual position, one
Milestone shared with many decent people during the 1930s and
1940s. The director still viewed war as horrible, and its participants
as human beings, both ally and enemy. Although none of Milestone's later war films achieved the artistic success of *All Quiet on
the Western Front*, they often present moments of insight and
power. In addition, they were always good, if melodramatic, entertainment, as well as fine propaganda for the Allied cause.

Milestone's first film about the Second World War concerned the
Eastern, not the Western, Front. *Our Russian Front* (1942) was a
compilation documentary edited from Russian newsreel footage of
the Nazi invasion of the Soviet Union which began in June 1941.
The project was proposed by Dutch documentary filmmaker Joris
Ivens, who began his career with poetic fantasies like *The Bridge*
(1928) and *Rain* (1929), but who soon moved toward more realistic
documentaries, most often of Leftist sympathies, such as the Russian
made *Komsomol* (1932) and the great documentary of the Civil War
in Spain, made in connection with Ernest Hemingway, *Spanish
Earth* (1937). Ivens came to the United States in 1940 to work with
Pare Lorentz at the Government Film Service. Naturally, he sym-
pathized with the defenders of Russia, and he managed to obtain a
scant 15,000 feet of Soviet news film. As the recent television series
"The Forgotten War" indicates, the Soviet cameramen extended
the Russian tradition of cinematic art to the subject matter of war.
Their work is much more impressive than that of the other Allies,
and from it Milestone and Ivens edited a striking film. Although

taken from actual newsreel footage, the film depicts such dramatic events as villagers putting their own homes to the torch. The commentary written by Elliot Paul and spoken by Walter Huston to the accompaniment of Dmitri Tiomkin's music somberly noted that ". . . there are no noncombatants in this war." The film stresses overall contribution of the Russian people in the war against Fascism, anticipating the subject matter and themes Milestone would dramatize in *The North Star* a year later. Finally, *Our Russian Front* is not a great documentary; in its urgent didacticism it crowds too much material into its forty-five minutes. At the same time, it remains important both as a document of the Russian Front and as an indication of Milestone's changing attitudes toward war.

Edge of Darkness (1943)

These changes in attitude become even more evident in his next full-scale production, *Edge of Darkness*. Late in 1942 Milestone was hired by Warners on a one-picture contract to direct the film based on William Wood's popular novel of the same title, published in the same year. Future director Robert Rossen served as the screenwriter in the first of three successful collaborations with Milestone. Although Wood's novel and Rossen's screenplay both shaped the vision of the film, there is little doubt that it represents Milestone's new vision of war. In the director's own words: "The picture has done away with disillusionment. We know the enemy we are fighting and we are facing the stern realities of the present war. The moral of *Edge of Darkness* is 'United we stand, divided we fall.' That is the great lesson of our time and the keystone for victory for the democratic cause."[1] Given this thematic oversimplification, it is not surprising that even a sympathetic contemporary critic judged the film "only a surface conception of the complicated tragedy of Norway."[2] Like *The North Star*, the film which followed it, *Edge of Darkness* presents a melodramatic, Hollywood version of an occupied nation during the Second World War. It is strong melodrama to be sure, with at least two brilliant sequences, but like the other films Milestone made during World War II *Edge of Darkness* displays severe limitations created by the propagandistic weight of its message.

Aside from difficulties of theme and story, *Edge of Darkness* also labors under other production problems. As Milestone himself observed, the cast is "an extremely mixed" group.[3] Errol Flynn and Ann Sheridan are the romantic leads, a local fisherman who becomes the leader of the resistance and the strong-willed daughter of the local doctor. Although Milestone insists that Flynn is an underrated actor, his performance, like Miss Sheridan's, rarely rises above looking stalwart and strong. Like most of the cast, the central pair make rather strange Norwegians; it seems they have just dropped in from *Dodge City* (1939), another adventure in which they costarred. Others in the cast display more inspired histrionics: they include such veterans of the stage as Roman Bohnen (Candy in *Of Mice and Men*) as a local storekeeper, Ruth Gordon as Ann Sheridan's mother, and Judith Anderson as the local hotelkeeper. Yet none of these interpretations, particularly Miss Anderson's, could be considered believable. More convincing are Walter Huston (Mr. Davidson in *Rain*) as the conservative doctor, Morris Carnovsky as the venerable schoolteacher, and Helmut Dantine as the psychotic Nazi commandant. The rest of the cast is eminently forgettable. Aside from the difficulties of characterization and casting, Milestone's players evidently had severe personal problems during the production. Flynn was indicted for rape, though later exonerated (a doubly ironic situation as his beloved is raped by the Nazis in the course of the movie). Ann Sheridan left her husband, George Brent, perhaps because of Flynn. Judith Anderson and Ruth Gordon were embroiled in legal controversy because of their commitment to a stage play. Thus the director was probably happy enough even to finish the picture.[4]

Beyond casting, other production problems hampered the film. Most of the exteriors were shot near Monterey, California, the closest approximation of Norway Milestone could find. Of course, Monterey has an ocean, docks, and a cannery, but otherwise bears little resemblance to the Norwegian coastline. Milestone employed painted backdrops to evoke Norway, but all they suggest is the ersatz quality of the whole effort. The opening sequences are so clearly shot with model planes and boats that any sense of reality is immediately destroyed. Nor is realism restored by the frequent sight of mountains painted on studio flats or the frequent rasp of New York accents from both Norwegians and Nazis. The only plus in the production is the musical score by Franz Waxman; though somewhat overdone in Hollywood lyric style, the motifs created by the Norwegian national anthem (for some reason sung in the original language) and the stirring hymn "A Mighty Fortress Is Our God" powerfully underscore the film's two fine sequences.

These two successful sequences aside, Milestone does only a competent job in terms of cinematic style. For the most part he films the story in an unobtrusive but undistinguished realist style.

Few extreme effects are attempted, yet the plain style seems more motivated by a failure of creativity than a commitment to realism. Although Milestone moves through his story crisply and clearly, few of his films exhibit so many Hollywood studio clichés. For example, byplay between Flynn and Sheridan is most often shown by intercutting a two-camera take of their exchanges, a dull practice Milestone generally avoids. However, like almost all of his films, *Edge of Darkness* occasionally exhibits the Milestone touch in the management of actors or the manipulation of camera.

The screenplay, for all its allusions to Ibsen, also falls into dramatic clichés. The method is retrospective; the film opens on October 28, 1942, with a German patrol plane spotting the Norwegian flag flying over the small fishing village of Trollness. A patrol boat lands a force of troops after the report and discovers a silent shambles in the streets of the village. Every foot of town is littered with the corpses of the dead, Norwegian and Nazi. The only sounds are made by the seabirds and a single gibbering civilian, later identified as the local Quisling. The patrol makes its way to the local military headquarters, a former hotel, where it discovers more bodies, including the commandant's; he has obviously committed suicide. From here the story flashes back to the events which led up to the carnage witnessed in the streets and the hotel. Sometime in the previous summer an SS man had arrived in Trollness to appraise the local situation. Naturally the commandant had to brief him, using a model of the village constructed in his office to demonstrate his points (unfortunately, the use of the model only underlines the fact that the whole set is a mockup). As he mentions each of the local leaders, the camera cuts to them, rather lamely identifying and characterizing the group.

The discussion of Flynn takes the camera to his fisherman's shack where he is discussing his plans to leave for England with Ann Sheridan. She urges him to stay and continue to serve his country by leading the resistance, though the audience can easily detect her personal motivations. Flynn's course of action is changed when a wounded partisan staggers through the door with the Nazis in hot pursuit. Flynn hides the man, eludes the Nazis, and secures Walter Huston's medical aid. Later he discovers that a neighboring village, supplied by British arms, has revolted against the Germans in a bloody shootout. Heartened by this news, Flynn elects to stay and await word from England. Surprisingly enough it comes from the visiting SS officer, who turns out to be a British agent in disguise.

The plot continues to thicken when on the next morning the

doctor announces that his son, a collaborationist in Oslo, is returning
to the village to help his Quisling brother-in-law run the local
cannery. Walter Huston as the doctor is the film's most complex
character, torn between the defiant patriotism of his daughter and
the accommodating attitudes of his son and brother-in-law. A visit
to his brother-in-law (nicely played by Charles Dingle) provides an
opportunity for Milestone to pan through the factory, showing the
workers sabotaging their machines under the noses of the Nazi
guards. At the factory the doctor has an opportunity to reject the
brother-in-law's Quisling overtures; later he gets word of a town
meeting to be held under the cover of a church service.

This church scene becomes one of the two excellent sequences in
the film. Flynn has brought everyone together to discuss the decision
to take the British arms; once the commitment is made, they will all
be in it together. The wounded veteran of the recent uprising tells
his story to the group so that they will know the dangers they face in
accepting the supplies. Many oppose the idea. The local pastor is a
sincere pacifist, and he counsels his flock to make the best of the
present situation. The venerable schoolteacher admits that he
doesn't know the answer to this knotty question. The doctor
prescribes caution, pointing out that no situation is simply black or
white. Milestone deftly cuts between close-ups of these individuals
and overall shots of the group; whenever the Nazi patrols pass near
the congregation bursts forth with "A Mighty Fortress Is Our God."
Finally strengthened by the hymn, the majority prevails, and they
all agree to accept their roles as rebels.

A number of subplots add to the central tension of the story.
Paralleling the central love interest between Flynn and Sheridan are
two less perfect romances, one between Judith Anderson and a
humane Nazi and another between the psychotic commandant and
a pathetic camp follower. Both loves are doomed to failure, but they
do humanize the enemy, making them something more than the
mechanical monsters of most propaganda films. (Both the film and
the novel on which it was based actually were criticized for being
too generous to the Nazis.) Johan's return also has complicated the
family situation at the doctor's house and leaves Huston more
confused than ever. Meanwhile, the long awaited arms arrive
(aboard an obvious model submarine), and Miss Sheridan feels
compelled to denounce her brother as a traitor. As she speaks the
camera pulls in quickly on her, catching her in a dramatically
effective close-up.

The Nazis, suspecting that rebellion is afoot, become more demanding in their confiscations, shown in a neat montage; finally they seize the fishing fleet itself. The commandant also orders that the school be made into a blockhouse, necessitating a conflict with the old schoolteacher. This philosophical septuagenarian infuriates the Nazi with his talk of truth and justice. In his barely controlled rage the commandant orders the old man's possessions burned in the town square. This powerfully symbolic scene forms the second fine sequence in the film. Looking down at the square Milestone has four columns of German infantry form a square within the square. Then a long pan follows a wagon loaded with books and furniture within both squares; as the Nazis soak the cart with gasoline, the doctor looks around at his townspeople. The camera cuts between him and his viewpoint, a near 360-degree circular pan, also interspersed with upward angles on the coarse, brutal faces of the soldiers. When the cart is set alight, the old teacher falls to the ground and the camera closes on his weeping face. Suddenly the crowd rushes forward from all sides, as Milestone uses four quick cuts to depict the closing square. However, Flynn and the other leaders finally restrain the people, as they are not yet ready to fight. Flynn rushes to the church tower and rings the bell to distract the crowd. Then the pastor bravely enters the inner square, lifts the old man in his arms, and walks out. When he begins to sing the Norwegian national anthem all the others join in, and soon the crowd moves away in four directions. The day has been saved, even as the town has symbolically triumphed over the garrison. Throughout this fine scene Milestone builds tension with expert cutting which is complemented by a dramatic use of sound. The scene recalls the very best of his work, and it still can evoke an emotional response from the viewer.

Unfortunately, the rest of the movie falls off from this high point. In the next scene, the old teacher points out the lesson of his experience: the individual cannot stand alone. Convinced at last, the doctor also joins the resistance group, just in time to hear that his daughter has been raped by one of the Nazi soldiers. As in *Of Mice and Men,* Milestone discretely shoots the rape scene at a downward angle. Sheridan walks through the empty church; then the camera follows her legs, which are tripped by a pair of jackboots; next he cuts outside the building to the mechanically marching boots of a Nazi patrol. Sheridan convinces Flynn not to seek personal revenge, but she does not reckon on her father, who waylays the rapist and kills him with a blow of his heavy cane. In reprisal, the commandant orders that the doctor and the other ringleaders all be shot in the town square.

Again the square of soldiers is formed; this time it surrounds the eight leaders digging their own graves before they are to be shot. Suddenly the national anthem rings out once more as the other villagers, armed with British weapons, advance from four sides. Now even the pastor plays his role in the rescue; standing in the church tower as if to bless the condemned prisoners, he suddenly whips out a tommy-gun and mows down the firing squad. The battle is on. In the town square, on the waterfront, at the hotel, Flynn, Sheridan, Huston, and the others lead the valiant villagers in a rout of the degenerate Nazis. Although there is some good combat work in this long sequence, as well as some good action cutting, overall the battle is strictly standard war-flick fare. As Bosley Crowther put in his *New York Times* review: ". . . so many have not fallen so graphically since the United States Cavalry and Mr. Flynn died very gallantly with their boots on back there at the Little Big Horn."[5] Everyone turns out as the heroes anticipated; even the pastor becomes a tiger. On the other side, the doctor's son finds his courage and warns his father's group of an ambush at the cost of his own life. Also, the commandant's whore denounces him as a coward and a brute; he shoots her and then himself as the hotel falls to the partisans. Finally, the women and children are sent off to England in the fishing fleet, and the men take to the hills to begin guerrilla warfare.

Now the story flashes forward to the present once more. The German officer finishes his report with the lie that the commandant died like a hero. He then orders the Norwegian flag lowered and the Nazi emblem raised. As one soldier raises the swastika flag, the retreating guerrillas pick him off, and the flag sags downward once again. Milestone superimposes the column of guerrilla fighters over a long view of the town; on the sound track the voice of President Roosevelt praises the courage of Norway. His final words are: "If anyone doubts the democratic will to win let him look to Norway."

Indeed Norway made an apt symbol of resistance to Fascism, and it was more often used in this fashion than any of the other occupied countries. A film with a stronger literary base, Irving Pichel's *The Moon Is Down* (1943), from John Steinbeck's play, proved stronger than *Edge of Darkness*. In turn, Milestone's entry was better than Hollywood's *Commandoes Strike at Dawn* (1943) or the British-made *The Avengers* (1942). Like his other war films from this period, *Edge of Darkness* proves a cut above than the average product in the genre. Marked by occasional touches of his best style, it finally is weighed down by its singleminded theme, its frequently weak scripting, its "mixed" casting, and its limited production values. Like *The North Star* and *The Purple Heart*, his next two films, Milestone's vision of occupied Norway proves to be effective melodrama, good entertainment, and fine propaganda, but not the stuff of which great films are made.

The North Star (1943)

With *The North Star*, Milestone moved back to territory more familiar than the occupied Norway of *Edge of Darkness*. His Russian film is titled after the name of a farming commune on the Bessarabian frontier with Poland, a fictional place not far in imagination from Kishinev, the capital of Bessarabia, where Milestone was raised, or from the real villages portrayed in the Soviet newsreel footage he edited into *Our Russian Front* a year earlier. Yet for all this connection with reality, the Eastern Front of *The North Star* finally becomes even less real than the ersatz Norway depicted in *Edge of Darkness*. Although the production credits of *The North Star* are impressive, the end product is not. A Sam Goldwyn production, with script by playwright Lillian Hellman, music by composer Aaron Copland, sets by William Cameron Menzies, and photography by James Wong Howe, *The North Star* promised great things it never delivered. Nor can the blame for the failure be attributed to casting; Walter Huston, Erich Von Stroheim, and Walter Brennan are excellent in secondary roles, while Anne Baxter, Dana Andrews, Jane Withers, and Farley Granger (in his first screen appearance) are better than adequate in the romantic leads. The problem lies in the artistic climate of wartime Hollywood. As in so many other films of the period, the excesses of patriotism and propaganda overpower what might have been a fine effort, producing a melodramatic fantasy notable only for its good intentions.

Not that the film is a complete failure, given its basic purpose. Critic Bosley Crowther would say of it in his *New York Times* review: ". . . this lyric and savage picture suggests in passionate terms the outrage committed on a peaceful people by the invading armies of Nazi Germany. And it offers a clamorous tribute to the courage and tenacity of those who have sacrificed their homes, themselves, and their families in resisting the Fascist hordes." In other words, *The North Star* is good Propaganda, though Crowther must admit that the peacetime opening is more operetta than documentary and that the wartime conclusion is more melodrama than reportage. Yet he excuses these lapses by noting that "*The North Star* has so much in it that is moving and triumphant that the sometime departures from reality may be generally overlooked."[6] Other reviewers in the national media were even more generous in their praise; clearly *The North Star* was responsive to the American mood in 1943.

Such was the case with most Hollywood products in the early 1940s, the period of its greatest financial, though not artistic, achievement. Hollywood naturally viewed the war in terms of entertainment and melodrama. The world's most devastating conflict, the most important event in modern history, was perceived within the limitations imposed by commercial filmmaking. The American feature film presented a fantasy world war which combined in varying doses the clichés of established genres—the Western, the horror film, the costume romance, and the "Woman's Picture." As one wag put it: "How could we have won the war without John Wayne?" This question proves provocative under thoughtful examination. Wayne and other cinematic war workers on the home front perhaps made as important a contribution to the victory effort as anyone. Certainly the image of national purpose which emerged from hundreds of war movies must have had an important psychological effect on wartime America.

Hollywood's glamorous imagery extended beyond the fighting Leathernecks and Rangers of the American forces; our allies were presented in the same simplistic terms. In fact, they were often less realistically portrayed because of Hollywood's unfamiliarity with other cultures. Central and eastern Europe, for example, existed only as the setting for prewar musicals and Gothics; thus the war on the Eastern Front became singing and dancing peasants versus monsters in uniform. Examples include *Hostages* (1943), *Chetniks* (1943), and *None Shall Escape* (1944), concerned, respectively, with Czechoslovakia, Yugoslavia, and Poland. Our major Eastern ally, the Soviet Union, also was often represented in reverential fashion; aside from *The North Star*, other examples exist in *Mission to Moscow* (1943) and *Days of Glory* (1944).[7] These films, and others like them, were to haunt their creators in the McCarthy era, when various witchhunters would try to sniff out any sympathy with Communism. In most cases, this romanticizing of the Eastern Front seems more commercially than politically motivated. The mass media, somewhat in response to government pressure, portrayed all of our allies as the good guys, the Soviets included.

More astute film critics like James Agee recognized the real danger in such Hollywood histrionics. Writing of *The North Star* Agee asserts that the movie consists of "... one long agony of meeching, sugaring propitiation, which as a matter of fact enlists, develops, and infallibly corrupts a good deal of taste, courage, and disinterestedness ... every resourcefulness appropriate to screen romance is used to make palatable what is by no stretch of the mind romantic."[8] In a similar vein Mary McCarthy concludes an omnibus review in which she savages several war flicks, including *The North Star*, with this observation: "Beside this, a documentary like the ones the Marines have done of the capture of Tarawa seems exotic and almost untrustworthy. It is a shock for us to realize that the dead Marine will not come to life in the next war movie."[9] In short, the Hollywood war films, Milestone's included, forgot the lessons taught by *All Quiet on the Western Front:* he forgot the reality of war.

Of course, some efforts are better than others. The most notable exception to the Hollywood tendencies are the excellent documentaries, Frank Capra's "Why We Fight" series, often made by Hollywood personnel in the service of the government. Exceptional dramatic films, for example Hitchcock's *Lifeboat*, from Steinbeck's screenplay, also stand out. And for all their failings, Milestone's war movies remain better than average, something between the patriotic praise of Bosley Crowther and the intellectual indictment by James Agee. *The North Star* proves perhaps the most interesting of these films in its strange blend of corny romantics and occasional moments of cinematic insight.

As usual, Milestone handles the titles very nicely. Against the backdrop of several bucolic scenes Aaron Copland's lilting music creates a sense of harmony in nature. In succession herds of cows, horses, and sheep are led across the scene by sturdy, happy collective farm workers. If all the peacetime background was as quietly and effectively done, the film would be a good deal stronger, possessed of some of the strength of Russian films, Eisenstein's *Bezhin Meadow*, for example. Milestone cuts to the old man Karp driving his wagon through the early morning streets of the village. Almost immediately the mood of reality is broken, as the set is an obvious Hollywood backlot version of a Russian commune. Karp is played

by Walter Brennan, and the role verges on the lovable old coot
Brennan often portrayed; here it takes a few minutes to recognize
the venerable character actor, and throughout the film Brennan
becomes Karp, in the process creating one of his finest screen
performances. The camera tracks him neatly in a shot that has the
Milestone signature on it; the picture shows some promise. This
promise fades as the action progresses; Karp waves good morning to
a flock of cute little school girls and then to a honking gaggle of
geese and then to a crusty old grandmother. The viewer is soon
expecting a song, perhaps by Bing Crosby or Danny Kaye.

Karp's morning ride serves to introduce all the major characters
as he moves among the houses of the commune. First he calls on his
old and good friend Kurin, the village doctor and a world-famous
pathologist. Walter Huston, the doctor in *Edge of Darkness*, again
plays this part in *The North Star*, and as always he does very
creditably with it. In fact, Dr. Kurin is one of two complex,
interesting characters in the work. Evidently he has settled in *The
North Star* village in order to stay close to his roots in the Russian
earth; in his dual role of doctor-scientist he combines the man of
intellect and action. He shares his home with his devoted cousin,
Anna (Barbara Everest), and his young grandchildren, Claudia (Jane
Withers) and Grusha (Eric Roberts).

Later Karp's travels take him past the homes of Boris (Carl Reid),
who is the father of two fine boys—Kolya (Dana Andrews) and
Damian (Farley Granger). Kolya is an air force bombardier, on leave
at the moment, and Damian is the leading student at the local high
school. At the opening of the film the two young men are planning
a walking trip to Kiev in the company of Claudia, Grusha, and
Marina, the teenaged daughter of the commune chief, Rodian
(Dean Jagger). Marina is played by the box-office lead, Anne Baxter,
fresh from a fine performance in Welles's *The Magnificent Amber-
sons* (1942). Although she is too old for the part, Baxter does well
with it, as do all the other young people. Granger is refreshing and
convincing as a young idealist, while Andrews is as forthright and
decent in his martyr's role here as he was as the innocent victim in
Wellman's *The Ox-Bow Incident* (1943). The problem with all of
these young enthusiasts is their single-dimensional, unchanging
sincerity. One as well expects them to get together a musical show
in the commune barn as to fight a war.

With his characters identified, Milestone moves toward deeper
characterization by showing them in their daily routines. He cuts

between the families eating breakfast and preparing for school or
work. The younger people are all buoyant at the prospect of the end
of school, Midsummers Day, and their excursion to Kiev. Some dark
forebodings are introduced by radio reports of German inhumanities
in Poland and by the school director's somber speech about the
students' future. In the school Milestone does a nice bit of montage
cutting as the children sing a Russian anthem which proclaims them
worthy of the future, words by Ira Gershwin and music by Aaron
Copland. The adults meanwhile are gathering the early harvest to
load in a waiting freight train. This task is quickly finished, and all
move on to the festive supper planned to celebrate the day. Here
the operetta analogy really takes hold with fifteen-minutes of
singing and dancing. This whole sequence seems rather silly as it
does little to advance the story, while it reduces the major characters
to fugitives from a musical comedy. However, the scene is beautifully handled by Milestone in terms of concentric circles, circles of
picnickers, dancers, and actors, all circled in turn by his camera.
Perhaps Milestone was reminiscing about his youth, perhaps imitat-
ing the Russian popular films of the sound period which were always
breaking into song and dance. In any case the sequence makes no
sense in terms of the plot, and it does much to create the overall
inanity that finally destroys the film.

The evening's dance and the next morning's walking tour establish the love relationships so important to Hollywood wartime
melodrama. Damian and Marina provide the central love interest;
they have been in love since early childhood, and they promise to
stay in love forever. Claudia is just as infatuated with Kolya, who is
flattered by her attentions, though she is obviously too young and
silly for him. These relationships unfold pleasantly as they walk and
sing on the first day, then as they ride and joke on the second day in
Karp's wagon. The old man has overtaken them on his way to
another market, and his return brings some badly needed humor
back to the movie.

However, the mood of the film quickly shifts as the road is
bombed by German aircraft. The war on the Eastern Front has
begun. Milestone handles this first bombing sequence with admira-
ble technical mastery, particularly in terms of sound. Kolya stops
the group's singing and joking to listen for something; there is
absolute silence. Slowly the sound of approaching aircraft is heard.
All the characters strain to see the planes, and Milestone quickly
cuts between them and the horizon, which is now filled with

approaching aircraft. Then he cuts between the extreme angles of
the characters searching the skies and the airmen looking down at a
depersonalized landscape Only Kolya realizes what is happening;
he pushes the others out of the wagon and toward the ditch. Before
he can empty the other wagons the bombs begin to rain down on
them for a fearful few seconds. Then there is absolute quiet once
more as the director pans the smoking wreckage strewn along the
road. Human casualties are mixed in debris; the injured and the
dead, men and women, old people and infants. The sequence
momentarily recalls the power of *All Quiet on the Western Front;*
Karp says that the young people have seen the face of war for the
first time, and that they are no longer children.

Immediately afterward the commune is also bombed by the
German planes. With similar skill, Milestone presents the shock of
war enveloping these peaceful people. His focus here is on the
families the young people left behind in the village. Marina's little
sister is killed while playing in the yard, and other children are
injured and crying. Again this is the reality of war, war as announced
by Commander Petrov of the Border Army over the town's loudspeaker system. These war sequences have the power of documentary, of Ivens's *Spanish Earth* or the Soviet news footage assembled
in *Our Russian Front.*

Unfortunately, from this point on the picture becomes unreal, a
Hollywood vision of war. Rodian, the commune manager, makes an
impassioned speech in which he calls on the men to form a guerrilla
force and the women, children, and old people to stay behind,
scorch the earth, and deny any help to the enemy. The men are
soon assembled on horseback as Rodian administers an oath in
which the group swears not to lay down their arms until "the last
Fascist is driven from the land." In a fine pullback shot followed by
a long pan the camera presents the galloping horsemen riding from
the square to the outskirts of the village; the Eastern Front has been
reduced to the dynamics of the screen Western. Meanwhile, Boris,
the boys' father, has gotten through to Petrov's headquarters and
cajoled a truckload of rifles and ammunition for the villagers. When
he starts back with it, the German Stukas strafe his truck just as it
approaches the point in the road where Karp's wagon was attacked.
The young people are able to save the supplies and comfort the
dying father. After he is buried the sons vow to do their duty in
driving out the aggressors; Kolya leaves for the nearest airbase,
while Damian, with the other youngsters and Karp, loads the

Two of Milestone's epic landscape shots in *The North Star*: (top) circles of dancers at the festive supper; (bottom) the peasants burn their commune and retreat to the hills.

munitions in two wagons and sets off for the village. Meanwhile, back at the commune, the villagers are preparing to burn their homes under Dr. Kurin's orders. Here Milestone creates some fine moments as the women linger over their homes before putting them to the torch. Marina's mother hesitates over her daughters' picture; another woman lights a lamp and sadly contemplates a wall clock, obviously a family heirloom.

The genre changes, once more, from Western to Gothic, as the plot moves from the Russian defenders to the Nazi attackers. The German columns are moving inexorably across the landscape; one of their goals is the strategic crossroad of the North Star commune. In their mechanical fury the Nazis are the same monsters who appear in dozens of war films. Yet among them Hellman's script places one multi-dimensional character, another doctor, obviously intended as a foil for Dr. Kurin. Dr. Otto von Harden, admirably played by Erich von Stroheim, is a famous surgeon impressed into the Nazi army. Like Kurin he is an intellectual and man of great skill. Unlike the Russian doctor, von Harden is a decadent aristocrat, a man ready to make compromises with his conscience in order to preserve his position in the world.

As the Nazis approach the commune they see the smoke from the fires set by the women and old people left behind when the men had taken to the hills. Rushing into the village, the troops shoot everyone in sight and quickly extinguish the flames. After the survivors are corralled in the town square before the hospital the inevitable confrontation scene begins. Rodian's wife is seized and tortured for information about her husband. Here Milestone makes effective use of silence once more, as the woman disappears through multiple doorways into the hospital while the crowd waits in breathless quiet, finally punctuated by her agonizing scream. Kurin and von Harden exchange words, with the German doctor insisting that he does not countenance such inhuman conduct.

However, von Harden proves directly responsible for an even worse atrocity, the bleeding of the children. Evidently the Nazi armies did take transfusions for their wounded from conquered peoples, including children. The image was perfect for propaganda purposes, and it forms the central metaphor of the film. The cruel Nazis, like vampires, bleed the innocent in order to accomplish their evil purposes, and they perform this abomination through the cooperation of men who should morally defy them. Here von Harden is such a man. When Kurin confronts him and tries to stab him, he answers calmly that he is only obeying orders. This terrible revelation scene is handled in still another style, that of German Expressionism, recalling von Stroheim's early direction. Sharply angled and harshly lighted close-ups of the villainous doctors and the innocent children are mirrored in the windows of the room. The climax of horror occurs as one little boy dies in Kurin's arms.

Bearing the body of the child, Kurin escapes to find the guerrillas in the hills. In the meantime Kolya has commandeered a Russian bomber and made several attacks on the enemy. In a final raid the plane is hit by antiaircraft fire, and in true World War II movie fashion Kolya pilots the burning wreck into a column of enemy tanks. Damian and his group have also been exterminating Nazis as they make their way toward the village with the load of precious weapons. At first they escape unscathed, but in a vicious shootout poor little Claudia is killed just as she finds her courage; then Damian is blinded by a grenade explosion. Karp guides them back, however, arriving just in time to arm the men for the attack planned to save the children from von Harden's scientific butchery.

The attack on the German garrison proves an action movie set piece, complete with garroted sentries, blazing gasoline drums, cavalry charges, and hand-to-hand fighting. Occasionally the warfare is savagely captured, as in the hospital corridor, a tracking shot which recalls the trench fighting of *All Quiet on the Western Front*. But for the most part, it is presented with only professional competence. The melodramatic climax occurs when the Russians finally storm the hospital, the garrison's last stronghold. Kurin is now leading the fight along with Rodian, and the doctor has his long-awaited confrontation with von Harden, after accusing him of letting the evil of Nazism triumph in Germany, Kurin shoots him down to save the world from this scourge. This denouement provides the single surprise of the script and the film, as the shooting of unarmed prisoners generally did not take place in Hollywood back lots no matter how often it occurred in real combat situations. The death of von Harden ends the fighting, and soon the villagers are marching out of the burning commune, singing once again and vowing with Marina in her final speech to fight "to make a free world for all men."

Dr. Kurin's action also symbolizes the ideological climate that spawned *The North Star*. Singleminded hatred of Fascist evil countenanced any action, shooting a prisoner or shooting a mindless melodrama. Finally the blame for the film's failure is hard to assign specifically. Lillian Hellman in her autobiographical volume *An Unfinished Woman* relates the evolution of the film through her association with Sam Goldwyn and William Wyler, and then describes how she walked out halfway through the filming. She asserts: "It could have been a good picture instead of the big-time, sentimental, badly directed, badly acted mess it turned out to be." [10] Yet after reading the screenplay it is hard for the writer to see how the movie could have been much else. The film follows the screenplay exactly, with the excision of a few lines praising life under the commissars and the addition of the dancing and singing. [11] The screenplay itself exhibits the one-dimensional characterization, melodramatic plotting, and ingenuous leftism which weakens all but the very best of Hellman's work. Goldwyn bankrolled a lavish production, Milestone directed competently, and the cast does well enough with what it has. [12] Aaron Copland's music, James Wong Howe's cinematography, and William Cameron Menzies's sets also prove more than adequate. Yet the film finally sinks under the weight of wartime hysteria and patriotic assertion; like so many other commercial war movies, *The North Star* is a casualty in the battle between reality and fantasy constantly refought on the back lots in Hollywood. [13]

The Purple Heart (1944)

In Milestone's next film, *The Purple Heart,* the setting switched from the European to the Pacific Theater of the Second World War. The movie was made at 20th Century–Fox for Daryl Zanuck, who also provided the basic story under the pen name Melville Crossman. (Zanuck evidently did not want to reveal himself as the source of story ideas, and he used several pen names to conceal his inspiration of his own productions.) [14] The story was based on the bare facts of an incident which occurred after the famous Doolittle raid on Tokyo, April 18, 1942. The Japanese homeland was bombed for the first time by carrier-based B-25 bombers, which overflew their target to American bases in China. Two American planes, typically named *Mrs. Murphy* and *Leaping Lena,* were damaged in the raid and forced down in occupied China. Their crews were taken back to Japan for a show trial, after which they were executed for deliberately bombing civilian targets. Some evidence exists to indicate that the eight Americans were tortured in an attempt to extract confessions from them before their executions. [15] Until 1944 the War Department played down stories of Japanese atrocities in fear of further reprisals against American prisoners. Thus Zanuck began the film without government cooperation, and it was shot under great secrecy on a closed set.

With the aid of screenwriter Jerry Cady, Milestone fashioned a terse melodrama from the few historical details at their disposal. The director tried to maintain a documentary tone, but the lack of substantial facts encouraged melodramatic speculation, which in turn soon became overindulgence. Milestone admits that he used a technical advisor, ". . . to prevent our *ersatz* Tokyo from becoming too wild."[16] More than any of his war films, *The Purple Heart* was overpowered by patriotism and propaganda; what emerges is not a documentary but a morality play which divides the world into honest Yanks and evil Japs. At the same time the tight story line, the confined settings, and the natural drama of the confrontation inspired Milestone, his production crew, and his cast to a rather high level of accomplishment. In a technical sense *The Purple Heart* is a much better movie than the two melodramas on the theme of Nazi occupation which preceded it. As usual, the movie also proved to be exciting entertainment and excellent propaganda; even today it is hard to view the film without feeling outrage at the perpetrators of these vile deeds.

This emotional overkill proves to be the film's major fault. It reduces the potentially high drama of the courtroom scenes to mere histrionics, while it vitiates the thematic power of the confrontation. As Mary McCarthy observes in her review, the case, underplayed, could have stood on its own merits. It was ". . . a violation of international law so flagrant that no script writer could possibly have improved on it." Yet Zanuck, Cady, and Milestone attempted to do just that, creating, McCarthy says, ". . . unquestionably the worst war movie I have seen, the apotheosis of a type in which the world conflict becomes a struggle between five or six Oriental character actors . . . and seven or eight recurrent American actors representing the forces of Democracy."[17] In a thoughtful review published in the *New Republic*, Manny Farber went beyond the accusations of overplaying to point out that the film itself does exactly what it accuses the barbaric Japanese of doing in the trial—fabricating fact to fit bias.[18] In its vilification of the Japanese, the film exhibits an inhumanity which matches the inhumane conduct of the Japanese prosecutors. The "one dimensional portrayal of Japanese brutality might help to solidify hatred of a group of people (The Japanese Warlords) into hatred of a whole people."[19] Indeed, from this historical perspective, it is hard not to assign some responsibility for the adamant American attitudes which motivated the later atomic raids to movies like *The Purple Heart.*

In fact, the McCarthy and Farber statements represented the minority viewpoint even among the critics. Most reviewers thought it excellent fare, with only the more astute even mentioning the melodrama which mars the work. For example, Bosley Crowther, in the *New York Times*, stated: "Here is a film which hammers the deep chords of a symphony."[20] *Life* labeled it "A Ringing Indictment of Jap Atrocity"; *Time* hailed it as Milestone's best since *All Quiet on the Western Front.* Even an astute critic like James Agee could find it ". . . well organized, unusually edged, and solidly acted under Lewis Milestone's direction, his best in years."[21] Clearly *The Purple Heart* fits the American mood in 1944, a mood of militant hatred for the "Japs." The Japanese were inscrutable, implacable foes, a nation of Samurai and snipers. Dozens of Hollywood efforts would replicate this public vision, fitting the Pacific war into generic patterns already created by the Western.

However, *The Purple Heart* proves more a Gothic than a Western. The action is limited, the sets are confining, the characters are extremes of innocence and insidiousness. The wounds which here merit the Purple Heart, the national decoration for injuries received in the line of duty, are inflicted by sadistic torture, not thrilling combat. Milestone's dark scenes in the crowded prisoners' cell recall the shadows of German Expressionism more than the bright landscapes of adventure movies. In general, the style proves somewhat Expressionistic, more so than the director's European war efforts. Even in the courtroom there are many close-ups on symbolic details as well as of the faces of the characters. This mixture of styles perfectly complements the subject matter—part documentation, part fantasy.

The Purple Heart medal itself serves as a backdrop for the title, establishing the heroic, medal-winning nature of the enterprise. The opening evokes atmosphere as the camera wanders through an empty, claustrophobic courtroom, finally fixing on the Rising Sun flag. Then Milestone moves quickly and efficiently through the details of the raid and its immediate aftermath by both reminiscence and flashback. Things drag a bit until the Americans enter to the tune of the Air Force Hymn ("Off we go, into the wild blue yonder"). Here the real psychological tensions start to build. For the most part Milestone's cast performs quite well in their one-dimensional roles. The Japanese are all portrayed by veteran Chinese character types, many familiar from Charlie Chan movies, with Richard Loo as the most despicable, General Mitsubi. The Americans include Dana Andrews and Farley Granger, just arrived from the Russian Front of *The North Star,* as Capt. Ross, the group's leader, and Sgt. Clinton, the archetypal frightened but game kid. Both are a good deal better than in their previous effort for Milestone, perhaps more comfortable as Americans than as Russians. Other above-average performances are given by Richard Conte as Lt. Canelli, Sam Levene as Lt. Greenbaum, and Donald Barry as Lt. Vincent. Barely adequate are Charles O'Shea as Sgt. Skoznik, the requisite All-American football player, John Craven as Sgt. Stoner, and Charles Russel as Lt. Bayforth.

The group at first seems bewildered by the charges against them, but they quickly resolve to stand together against this Japanese propaganda effort. It seems the High Command has been severely embarrassed by the raid on the homeland, and the various service branches are trying to pin the blame for the raid on each other. The Americans are ready scapegoats, but they will be even better ones if they confess and reveal their home base. The brave Americans resist these suggestions and, led by Capt. Ross and Lt. Greenbaum, a natural barracks lawyer, they bring the trial to a standstill. Greenbaum cites the Geneva Convention, in a speech reminiscent of Clifford Odets's dialogue, while Ross exposes the fakery of the filmic evidence of their bombing of civilian targets. The film within the film adds to the documentary sense, but it unfortunately suggests the phoniness of the whole proceeding to the thoughtful viewer.

The day's events are cut short by a disturbance and a death in the courtroom, and the Americans are herded off to their cage-like prison. Here Milestone achieves some striking visual effects to accompany the cat-and-mouse game played by the Japanese. The fliers are all tortured sooner or later, but each is tortured in a different manner, increasing the tension of those awaiting their turn. Capt. Ross faces the psychological torture of responsibility for the other men's sufferings. Skoznik suffers the greatest physical torture, which his strong body bears, though not his mind as he snaps under the horror of what is done to him. Milestone wisely does not show the actual torture scenes, but only their results. Lt. Canelli returns with broken wrists, Lt. Bayforth with mutilated hands, Lt. Vincent with a twisted mind. Young Sgt. Clinton appears unscathed at first glance, but when he cannot answer his comrade's questions they realize his tongue has been cut out.

Still the Americans won't break, and in desperation the General offers them their freedom if they will meet his conditions of confession and information. Of course, they refuse. They dramatically vote by dropping their Air Force insignia one by one in a vase; one pair of broken wings will be a signal for them all to accede to the Japanese demands. None are broken, and the fliers return to the courtroom to face their sentences of death. In the film's best scene, Milestone closeups each man at the moment of the verdict; small smiles of pride and triumph cross their faces. Then they all walk out and down a long confining hall toward certain death while the Air Force hymn resounds once more. The symbolism is heavy but effective. These downed airmen are flying higher than ever by facing death with dignity and honor.

If the film stayed with this moving theme, it would be effective, if simplistic. Rather, it sinks into Gothic melodrama in the depiction of the brutal efforts of the oriental villains to torture information out of their brave prisoners. Milestone's altered attitudes can be somewhat justified by realizing that he is essentially condemning warlords, sophisticated Japanese versions of General Yang from his earlier Chinese film of 1936. Yet the simplistic identification of all good with America, all evil with Japan, ultimately renders the film both false and dangerous. A good cause could justify a good deal of melodrama and propaganda, but even the best of causes cannot countenance paranoia and hatred. The Purple Heart remains the most successful of Milestone's World War II films in a purely technical sense; it is both effective entertainment and propaganda, but it is finally bad art. As Milestone himself has said, "We didn't hesitate to make this kind of film during the war."[22]

A Walk in the Sun (1945)

After he completed The Purple Heart, Milestone was granted some respite from the rigors of war in the direction of a psychological thriller, A Guest in the House, for Kurt Stromberg at United Artists. In this Hitchcockian piece Anne Baxter plays a demented young lady who moves in with a sympathetic family and soon has them all at each other's throats. Again the film was a new direction for Milestone, and it might have proved interesting if he had been able to finish it. Before he was very far into it, his appendix ruptured and he had to have it removed. John Brahm finished the picture,

Two doomed groups of American soldiers in Milestone's formally orchestrated shots: (top) the captured B-25 bomber crew in *The Purple Heart*; (bottom) the reduced platoon pursuing its mission in *A Walk in the Sun*.

which received rather mixed reviews. Evidently even the parts that Milestone shot were changed considerably, so it seems best to regard the movie as another unrealized project.

The last film Milestone made during World War II proved to be the best. *A Walk in the Sun* repeats some of the clichés encountered in *Edge of Darkness, The North Star,* and *The Purple Heart,* problems of patriotism and pat characterization, but, all in all, the later film genuinely merits the inevitable comparisons with *All Quiet on the Western Front.* Like his earlier masterpiece, *A Walk in the Sun* realistically portrays the effects of war on a small group of ordinary soldiers. Undoubtedly, Milestone was attracted to Harry Brown's novel of the same title, published in 1944, by its clear connections with Remarque's classic war story, as well as with other classics of the genre, such as Stephen Crane's *The Red Badge of Courage.* Milestone helped finance the independent production of *A Walk in the Sun* with $30,000 of his own money, a clear indication that the film was another labor of love.[23] As usual, the director tried to realize the values of his literary property. "The book was my script," he told one reviewer.[24] Robert Rossen again served as screenwriter, helping to fashion a literate screenplay from Brown's successful novel. With the aid of cinematographer Russell Harlan, Milestone then realized the work in strong visual terms. His all-male cast was for the most part excellent also. Thus *A Walk in the Sun* became a very fine film indeed, perhaps the best Hollywood war story to be made during the Second World War.

This assertion of praise also sets the limits of the film's artistic success, for, as outlined above, Hollywood's wartime vision was extremely limited. Fine American war movies were few, not more than half a dozen at most. For that matter, the literary war effort was meager also; Harry Brown's little novel might well have been the best American book to be published during the war, as its publishers and reviewers claimed in 1944 when it appeared. Brown's novel and Milestone's film were products of the war years, and both exhibit some of the simplifying and propagandistic tendencies of the period. In both works, characters tend to be one-dimensional, plot is overly simple, and clichés are all too evident as themes. Although very good for what they are, both the literary and cinematic versions of *A Walk in the Sun* prove limited in their final success as works of art.

The comparison of book and movie versions proves enlightening, not only because Rossen and Milestone relied heavily on the novel, but because the two versions present both similar and contrasting strengths and weaknesses. Most contemporary reviewers found the movie fine but not quite as strong as the novel. A generation later, the present critic finds the film much more interesting than its literary source. The difference of opinion exists not in terms of basic characterization or plotting, but in the symbolic extension of the central action as a metaphor of a world at war. Neither novel nor film manages to keep the short walk in the sun in proper artistic perspective; in both, the ultimate implications of this one small story are neglected. *All Quiet on the Western Front,* both novel and film, used the microcosm of one platoon to make a major thematic statement about the macrocosm of war; *A Walk in the Sun's* thematic statement is muted by the demands of propaganda in the novel and the studio system in the film.

In Harry Brown's novel this difficulty exists in the frequent, pseudoprofound statements uttered by an intrusive authorial voice. These statements seem intended to present the long view, the universal vision of war, yet they are often flat, simplistic, even sophomoric. The technique seems modeled on Stephen Crane's in *The Red Badge of Courage,* but Brown lacks Crane's sense of ironic distance. Neither Crane nor Brown had ever seen combat, but Crane as literary artist could evoke both the feeling and the idea of war, while Brown could not. For example, when Crane uses metaphors of sports and games in his descriptions of battle he creates ironies which emphasize both the horror and the childishness of war. When Brown tells us that "in its way war is like a lethal game of football" (p. 140)[25] he only blurs his vision. The platoon, like many others in war movies, often acts as if they were involved in some lethal football scrimmage, and the individuals do not exhibit much more sense of what is going on around them. They are rather unperturbed by war, death, or the enemy.

The funny thing was that they were not very much concerned with what was facing them ahead. Each had his own problems, his own desires and wishes. They kept these personal things uppermost in their minds, as they had always done ever since they came into the Army. The war was incidental to a man's thoughts. It entered into them, of course, but it did not take them over bodily. There had been too many years of life, too many memories, before the war had come along. A man could withdraw into them, he could construct them into an unpierceable shell. They were his defence against the violence of the world. Every man in the platoon had his own thoughts as he walked along, and they hovered unseen over the little

group, an indefinable armor, a protection against fate, an indestructible
essence. (p. 148)

This may well be the American civilian attitude toward war, one
partially created by war movies, but one doubts that it could be
supported through the North African, Sicilian, and Italian cam-
paigns. At some point this innocence becomes merely simple-
minded, and the story becomes another propaganda piece.

Certainly Brown does present some of the terror, chaos, and
alienation of war. Essentially he tells the tale of one small operation,
a walk of six miles from the beach at Salerno to a German-held
bridge and farmhouse. The platoon must blow up the bridge and
secure the house, seemingly a simple task. Then difficulties begin to
thwart them. Their officer is killed by a random shell splinter before
they even hit the beach; then their noncommissioned officers are
eliminated one after another by death, wounds, and nervous exhaustion. They are strafed by enemy aircraft, attacked by an enemy
armored car, and raked by enemy machine guns from within the
farmhouse. Through all of this the platoon coheres as a team, and a
corporal emerges as a natural leader. The novel ends with Corporal
Tyne leading a confident charge on the final objective. Thus the
random violence of war is subsumed in patterns of evolution and
accomplishment, and fear is transmuted into a sort of nervous joy.

Still, Brown's novel has its strong points. His characters are
believable, if one-dimensional; his action is underplayed; his setting
is used to create symbolic value. In fact, the narrative voice often
contrasts the reality of this walk in the sun with the melodramatics
of most war movies. When the platoon seems lost, Corporal Tyne
worries that the operation is turning into *The Lost Patrol* (1934),
but he knows that "This wasn't the movies" (p. 118). The fact that
Brown later wrote screenplays for war epics such as *The Sands of
Iwo Jima* (1949) and *D-Day, The Sixth of June* (1956) does not
negate the refreshing realism with which he generally tells this
story.[26]

By sticking close to the novel, Milestone also manages to avoid
the melodramatics and clichés of the typical Hollywood war movie.
His largely unknown cast realizes the characters capably enough;
Rossen's screenplay skillfully pares down the dialogue and action;
and Russell Harlan's camera work helps create a generally convincing visual style. However, Milestone's movie, like the novel, foun-
ders in terms of larger thematic issues. His work preserves the

evolutionary pattern of leadership and even extends the pattern of accomplishment by depicting the platoon actually taking the farmhouse. In addition, some of the overblown statements of the narrative voice in the novel are transposed to the mouths of the characters in the film, where they seem even more out of place. Finally, Milestone attempts to open out the vision of the work by means of a ballad which counterpoints the action with the story.

Milestone claims that his ballad was the first use of this device, which would become a cliché by the 1950s; perhaps it is. He also insists it works like a charm, though it does not. Milestone attributes the idea to his childhood memory of war veterans who sang military ballads on streetcorners of Czarist Russia.[27] Of course, such ballads present a romantic and sentimental view of war, war as adventure and melodrama. In his cinematic style, Milestone tried to capture the realism of the wartime documentaries, such as John Huston's *The Battle of San Pietro* (1944). But onto this visual realism Milestone imposes the romanticism of four ballads by Millard Lampell and Earl Robinson which archly tell of "coming across the sea / to Sunny Italy" or portentously compare this road with "the road out from Stalingrad." Instead of avoiding Brown's weaknesses, Milestone only exacerbates them.

The film version also labors under other difficulties which detract from the crisp documentary effect which might have made the film great. Although his cast was uniformly solid, just enough of studio casting exists to remind the audience of a hundred other platoons with the requisite Texans and Brooklynites, Italians and Jews. And though the cast was relatively unknown in 1945, the later careers of many, especially Dana Andrews, Lloyd Bridges, John Ireland, in the platoon create an overlay of typecasting which makes the film much less fresh for today's viewer. Likewise the pattern of desultory conversation counterpointed by violent action seems quite familiar after thirty-five years. Even Milestone's distinctive style contributes to the problems as he often is tempted into stylistic overstatement when understatement would be the better artistic strategy. As in *All Quiet on the Western Front,* expressionistic effects often contradict the realism of the work by calling attention to themselves as devices. Examples include the frequent use of close-ups in the conversational interludes and the bravura stylistics of the battles. James Agee, reviewing the film for *Nation,* perhaps summed up these weaknesses by calling *A Walk in the Sun* ". . . an embarrassing movie . . . more related to ballet than to war."[28] However, other critics had nothing but praise for the film and, compared with most of its genre, including Milestone' own efforts during the war years, it does seem a minor masterpiece.

The film begins with the timeworn device of a titled book cover which opens to reveal the production credits printed as text and the cast presented through still pictures.[29] Here the balladeer's voice also characterizes each individual, perhaps a good idea as they all tend to merge together in their GI uniforms. The first shot duplicates the opening of the novel as the audience sees a fleet of landing barges circling in the dark, waiting for the operation to start. Milestone cuts to a watch face which shows the time as 6 A.M.; the landing is to take place at first dawn. He then moves his camera carefully through the crowded landing barge, capturing darkened medium shots and close-ups of the same group identified in the titles. The director and screenwriter also introduce another narrative device. A minor character named Craven in the novel wrote mental letters to his sister to pass the time more quickly; in the film he becomes a major character, Windy (recreated by John Ireland in his first screen role) who is introduced much earlier so that his spoken letters become a sort of ironic narration to accompany the action. Of course, Milestone does not hesitate to use voice-over narration, in addition to the narrative ballads. This proliferation of narrative devices seems to indicate an imperfect hold on the story and its themes; Milestone seems vainly searching for some way to force his story to yield profound meanings it really does not contain.

The opening dramatic sequence in the landing barge works well enough without all of this forced additional commentary. The men are figuratively as well as literally in the dark; they do not know where they are landing in Italy nor do they know their mission. Their leader, Lt. Rand, is new to his job, and he seems somewhat lost. He strains to see something as an artillery duel begins between the escort ships and the shore batteries. Milestone's camera looks up at him, a tall figure above his platoon, who are hugging the deck of the barge. But leadership and curiosity both mean exposure in war, and the officer is smashed down by a random shell fragment which tears away most of his face. In the dark, his subordinates can only feel his wounds and hope that they can get him ashore before he dies. The camera works its way back through the barge for a number of reaction shots which are counterpointed by the compulsive verbal motifs which characterize the individuals, in particular, the ironic motto, "Nobody dies!" The sequence could easily stand on its own for its careful evocation of the murderous chaos of war; unfortunately, Milestone must reinforce it with voice-over narration, plus Windy's dreary ironies and additional verses of the deplorable ballad.

The next sequence follows the platoon onto the beach, as the director pans the landing craft sweeping in to unload their human cargo. Strangely, all is silent ashore, and the men easily race over the horizon, where they are outlined against the dawn sky. Now Sgt. Halverson has assumed command; he orders the platoon to stay put in a small hollow while he searches out the company commander to confirm their orders. The men are left digging into their hiding place, strangely disconcerted by the quiet and dark which surround them.

Once they are settled, the inevitable dialogue, punctuated by the compulsive verbal motifs, begins in earnest. Sgt. Porter (Herbert Rudley), left temporarily in command, keeps asking when Halverson will return. Sgt. Tyne (Dana Andrews), for some reason promoted from a corporal's rank in the novel, quietly reassures him. Windy (John Ireland) composes another letter to his sister. Rivera (Richard Conte), the machine gunner, keeps demanding cigarettes from his buddy Friedman (George Tyne). Archimbeau (Norman Lloyd) complains cynically how he will probably be fighting in the Battle of Tibet in a few years more. Rankin (Chris Drake) talks about his "baby," his submachine gun. Sgt. Ward (Lloyd Bridges) reminisces about farm life in the States and wishes he had an apple.

These verbal motifs are accompanied by visual ones also: Porter moves nervously; Tyne sits quietly; Windy slumps and tilts his helmet far back on his head; Rivera and Friedman punch at each other; while Archimbeau sulks, Rankin flexes his muscles and Ward draws thoughtfully on his pipe. Other visual symbols become prominent. Hands and touching are important; when Rivera and Friedman exchange cigarettes only their hands and arms fill the frame. In contrast are the hard, inhuman shapes of weapons; Rivera and Friedman loaf on either side of the heavy machine gun; then a three-shot shows Archimbeau resting under its murderous barrel. These motifs are obviously reminiscent of *All Quiet on the Western Front*, and they increase the visual complexity of *A Walk in the Sun* much as they did in the earlier film.

Sgt. Porter soon becomes too nervous to wait in the exposed hollow, and he moves the platoon to a nearby wood which will provide more cover; Tyne is left behind in the hollow to meet

Halverson. Instead the medical aid man, McWilliams (Sterling Holloway), arrives with the news that both Lt. Rand and Sgt. Halverson are dead. All of these movements are outlined against the lightening sky and counterpointed by the sound of explosions in the background. Soon dark clouds of smoke are billowing over the rise which separates the platoon from the beach. They are lost, isolated without a clear sense of where they are or what they are to do. When McWilliams climbs the hill to reconnoiter he is cut down by an enemy fighter plane. In war it seems best to huddle close to mother earth and try to save oneself alone, the advice old Kat gave the young recruits in *All Quiet on the Western Front*.

The attacking planes have also strafed the woods, and several of the platoon are killed or badly wounded. Sgt. Porter neurotically blames himself, clearly exhibiting signs of his rapidly approaching crack-up. Tyne manages to get Porter and the platoon moving toward the vaguely defined road and farmhouse. Now it is full light as the platoon stretches out in columns along a ridge and then across a wide, flat plain. In the distance shells explode, but the men press inexorably onward. Another plane strafes them, and they take cover in a ditch. But two soldiers are caught in the field, and one is killed and the other wounded. The dead man's limp hand hangs over the edge of the ditch to fill Milestone's frame. Even this reminder of their precarious position does not daunt the platoon; the enemy plane is shot down by American P-38s, and the men are soon moving forward again.

The next sequence involves a pair of Italian soldiers who surrender to the platoon. They turn out to be deserters, not defenders, who claim they have turned against the Nazis. The prisoners realistically do not speak English, and Sgt. Porter must call on Tranella (Richard Benedict) to translate, creating a good deal of subtle humor. The whole interlude is like something imported from Italian Neorealism which depicts the pathetic futility of fascism and the war. The prisoners insist on staying with their captors, but Sgt. Porter leaves them behind with some rations. As the platoon marches away a tracking camera leaves them even smaller and more pathetic in the distance, as Tyne comments on how they were sold "a bill of goods" by the Fascists.

When they stop to let a reconnaissance patrol scout ahead, Sgt. Porter finally cracks. He falls and weeps and simply cannot go on. Herbert Rudley handles this difficult scene very capably, projecting a sense of utter battle exhaustion. This collapse seems almost exhilarating after the heroic posturing of most war movies; it is a human touch like the ones which gave *All Quiet on the Western Front* its mood of humane reality. However, like the death of Lt. Rand, Sgt. Porter's collapse does not disturb the platoon; the men take it in stride and prepare to finish their mission. The conversations continue much as before. Archimbeau asks what country comes after Tibet. Rivera demands another cigarette while recalling trips to Coney Island. Sgt. Ward studies the soil around him, concluding that it has been worn out by the tread of too many soldiers in too many wars. The sterility of the soil represents the moral failure of the Old World for these yeomen of the New World.

Suddenly the quiet is broken by the approach of a German armored car. Tyne hides the platoon until it passes, and then prepares to destroy it when it returns from its reconnaissance mission. This ambush becomes the first real battle scene of the film, and Milestone presents it in his best bravura style. First he lets tension build as the men wait with clutched grenades along the road. Then as the armored car slowly approaches Sgt. Tyne silently counts down from ten to one and loudly blows his whistle. Grenades rain from all sides but they do not stop the enemy vehicle. Milestone tracks the car, first from the lower angle of the ditch and then from the upper angle of its own gun turret, creating a 180-degree reversal of direction. Intercut with these three long tracking shots are inserted shots of Rivera's pounding machine gun and disintegrating parts of the car. A final grenade sends it toppling into the ditch, where Rankin finishes the crew with a burst of submachine-gun fire into the driver's slit. This finale is also powerfully presented as a hand pushes open a hatch, only to drop when Rankin opens fire, and dangles from the slit. Even the faceless enemies are human, as the motif of hands illustrates.

Moving forward, Tyne discovers that the American reconnaissance patrol has knocked out two tanks with its bazooka. Soon they are marching past the burning hulks, still wondering about their final objective. The men sweat in the heat of the day and grumble about the marching. The conversational motifs are heard once more until the platoon breaks into the clearing which surrounds the farm. Its house appears impassive and mysterious; they are not even sure if it is occupied. The platoon takes cover behind a stone wall, while Tyne tries to decide on a plan of action. Sgt. Ward volunteers to take a patrol across the field to investigate, but before they are halfway across the enemy opens fire with several machine guns.

Rankin and Tinker are killed; Tinker dies atop the wall, his hand hanging down to fill another frame. Windy finally comes up with a plan to bypass the farm and blow the bridge; so Tyne sends Ward to attack the bridge, after which they will all charge the farmhouse.

Again tension builds as they wait for the bridge to be blown. Watch faces are again closed up as they synchronize their operations; by contrast Milestone cuts up to the high noon sun beating down on them. Then the explosion rips the quiet air; Tyne leads his squad over the wall, while Ward and Windy bring theirs up from the river. This final charge at the farmhouse proves to be a wonderful battle scene, again recalling the tracking shots of charges in *All Quiet on the Western Front*. The camera tracks across the charging soldiers and then pans out on them along the barrels of the enemy machine guns. Men tumble and fall like dead bundles; Archimbeau, for example, dies whining "Tibet." Inside the house Milestone cuts among four different openings as he shows the attack progressing from four sides. Then the Americans are close enough to fire in and hurl grenades; quickly they leap through windows and fill the frames of doors. In a minute all is quiet; once again the farmhouse is secured. To the tune of the "Army Hymn" ("As the caissons go rolling along") the survivors emerge into the bright sunshine, fondling weapons, eating apples, drinking wine. Those left alive fall into their visual motifs; their walk in the sun completed, they can rest before beginning the march to ultimate victory. The film ends with the ballad summing up the story and drawing the moral—this six-mile walk was the shortest way home for men "who would fight to be free."

If this ending reeks of other Hollywood visions of successful American feats of arms, most of the film does not. The documentary passages, such as the night landing, the walk across the plain, and the tense breaks in the ditch, are all excellent. Many of the dramatic scenes, such as McWilliams's death or Sgt. Porter's collapse, are also well handled. The battles, though overly exciting and expressionistic, are expert in Milestone's usual manner. The cast, aside from disconcerting presences such as Huntz Hall, is uniformly good, with fine performances from Dana Andrews, Richard Conte, John Ireland, Lloyd Bridges, and Norman Lloyd.

Like the literary property from which it was drawn, Milestone's *A Walk in the Sun* suffers from stylistic and thematic confusion. The film cannot quite make up its mind whether it is a low-key documentary or a high-action adventure, and, more importantly, it cannot meaningfully relate the short walk to the larger world of war. Like almost all Hollywood products of the war years, certainly like Milestone's other efforts during this period, *A Walk in the Sun* is a product of its place and time. (It was not released, incidentally, until after the war had ended.) It certainly has its own excellences but they are balanced by its faults. Finally, it is a good movie which somewhat redeems the excesses of *Edge of Darkness*, *The North Star*, and *The Purple Heart*, but it does not recapture, in spite of the opinions of contemporary reviewers, the greatness of *All Quiet on the Western Front*.

5

The Postwar Period

A Reprise

WHEN THE Second World War ended in 1945, Lewis Milestone was fifty years old. His film career, which began directly after the First World War, had developed through several distinct cycles during an important quarter-century of Hollywood history. After an apprenticeship period, Milestone had achieved modest success as a director of silent features, even winning one of the first Academy Awards. However, it was the brilliant use of the new technology of sound, especially in *All Quiet on the Western Front* (1930), which made Milestone an important figure on the Hollywood scene. During the 1930s he had two periods of achievement, the early sound years and later the fulfillment of his liberal Realism in *Of Mice and Men* (1939). World War II marked a new cycle as Milestone returned to war movies, directing five distinctive, if not entirely effective, examples. Milestone's last film would be *Mutiny on the Bounty* in 1962; in the seventeen intervening years he would direct thirteen more features.

Essentially these thirteen films fall into two different groups. In the immediate postwar period, Milestone, still near the height of his powers, created several interesting movies: *The Strange Love of Martha Ivers*, from a strong script by Robert Rossen; *Arch of Triumph*, from another novel by Erich Maria Remarque; *The Red Pony*, with a script by John Steinbeck from his own short story sequence; and *Halls of Montezuma*, a reprise of his World War II films. In the 1950s and 1960s Milestone drifted between works, directing a series of weak efforts abroad, doing several television programs, and leaving several projects unrealized. This chapter will unify the immediate post-war period as a modestly successful reprise of some of his best earlier efforts, while the next chapter will chronicle the later, less successful pictures.

Charles Boyer and Ingrid Bergman during a tense moment in
Arch of Triumph (1948).

Once again, Milestone's career essentially parallels Hollywood history. The postwar years were the last flowering of the Hollywood studios. In the 1950s and 1960s the economic demise of the studio system found Hollywood reeling, stunned by the competition of burgeoning television in the entertainment sphere and of resurgent foreign film in the artistic world. Another factor in Hollywood's loss of confidence was the hysterical reaction to the Red Scare of the McCarthy era. Russian-born Milestone, always a liberal intellectual of Leftist inclination, was a natural target for the witchhunters of the House Un-American Activities Committee. As early as November of 1946, Milestone appeared before the committee as an "unfriendly" witness; in other words, he claimed his Constitutional privilege not to testify.[1] In 1948, the anti-Communist writer Myron Fagan implied that Milestone was a Red sympathizer, an implication made more blatant by Hedda Hopper (a bit player in Milestone's *The Caveman* [1926]) in her nationally syndicated Hollywood column.[2] Unlike the Hollywood Ten and many others, Milestone was able to keep working through these tense times, but the film critic must wonder how much these tensions affected the director's creativity. Did guilt by association block the financial backing necessary for truly creative projects, or did pressure make him opt for "safe" subjects in *Arch of Triumph, The Red Pony,* and *Halls of Montezuma*? In any case, Milestone refused to comment on this side of his life: evidently he always found it very painful.[3]

The Strange Love of Martha Ivers (1946)

Producer Hal Wallis liked Milestone's war film, *A Walk in the Sun,* so much that he insisted the director do a film for him.[4] In turn, Milestone had been sufficiently impressed with Robert Rossen's screenwriting in *Edge of Darkness* and *A Walk in the Sun* to solicit the writer's help on the film commissioned by the producer. When the writer-director team could not find anything worth filming among the six properties Wallis offered them, Rossen suggested that they use the prologue of a story idea by John Patrick, writing a new script for it while giving Wallis the impression that his property was being filmed.[5] Between them the writer and the director created a taut, harsh tale of American moral corruption which became a classic example of the postwar Hollywood style known as *film noir*. Because the film resembles nothing else in the Milestone canon, the critic must suspect the strong influence of Rossen's screenplay and of the cinematic style of *film noir*. In spite of these obvious influences, however, the movie is still Milestone's, and it proves to be one of his best. *The Strange Love of Martha Ivers* is a somewhat neglected classic of the postwar period, a tribute to the director's eclectic interests and diverse talents.

Film noir is a rather ambiguous term coined by French critics to describe the cynical melodramas which proliferated in Hollywood during the late 1940s and early 1950s. These works are "dark films" in the sense of both subject matter and cinematic style. Most often they are urban in setting, revealing the seamy underside of the city in an America which has lost its older, traditional value systems derived from nature, the frontier, the farm, and the small town. In Hollywood the traditional genres of gangster, mystery, political, and social protest films were transformed into something much more cynical, violent, and brutal. Pop psychoanalysis was employed to probe the aberrant psyches of mad-dog killers, sadistic detectives, and crooked politicians. Complex plots revealed corruption as the norm of contemporary society, a condition beyond the amelioration of social protest. Stylistically these dark themes were realized in a fascinating amalgam of Realistic and Expressionistic devices, particularly in the chiaroscuro (use of light and shadow) which recalled the work of the German Expressionists.[6] The nightmare world is captured in surrealistic cityscapes, dark labyrinths of streets lit only by flashes of neon, or in the muted shadows of the claustrophobic interiors ranging from seedy one-night hotels to Hollywood mansions.

The style had been anticipated in the prewar period in films like Raoul Walsh's *High Sierra,* John Huston's *The Maltese Falcon,* and Orson Welles's *Citizen Kane* (all 1941); it was established in films like Billy Wilder's *Double Indemnity* (1944), Michael Curtiz's *Mildred Pierce* (1945), and Howard Hawks's *The Big Sleep* (1946); and it continued to influence both film and television productions even into the 1960s. The stylistic elements of *film noir* demonstrate an obvious affinity for Milestone's creative talents. His heightened sense of cinema Realism was almost always balanced by a predilection for the devices of Expressionism. Robert Rossen seems even more akin to the leading practitioners of *film noir* such as Billy Wilder, Robert Siodmak, or Edward Dmytryk. Several of Rosen's screenplays as well as his early films as director demonstrate the *film noir* emphasis on compulsive, often perverse, psychoanalytic drives played out in a larger social world. *Johnny O'Clock* (1947) depicts the greed of the gambling set; *Body and Soul* (1948) exposes the brutality of the boxing ring; while *All the King's Men* (1949), from the novel by Robert Penn Warren, reveals the corruption of the political world. In these works and in films as late as *The Hustler* (1961), an unstable, tragic protagonist wreaks havoc on the people and the institutions around him. Martha Ivers proves a female version of Rossen's corrupted gamblers, boxers, and politicians, and it seems as if his fine screenplay became the strong literary vehicle Milestone always needed to create a successful film.

Aside from Rossen's screenwriting, Milestone received considerable support from a solid production group. Victor Milner's cinematography renders the requisite stylistic effects of *film noir*, while Archie Marshak's editing helps create two of the most memorable montage sequences in the Milestone canon. In addition to these visual effects, the sound track is enhanced by Miklos Rozsa's brilliant original score. Milestone had worked with Aaron Copland and other fine musicians in many films, and he clearly demonstrates an awareness of the importance of music in establishing mood. In *The Strange Love of Martha Ivers,* Rozsa presents themes for each of the characters and then skillfully intertwines and contrasts them in an almost perfect counterpoint to the visual images.[7] Only one member of the production staff really hindered Milestone—producer Hal Wallis. The producer didn't bully the director or cut the film; rather he insisted on inserting a number of pointless close-ups of his latest starlet, Lizabeth Scott, in Milestone's finished director's print.[8] These inserts stand out in the final version like so many sore thumbs, as the rest of the film is as faultless in its visual rhythms as everything Milestone ever did.

Milestone was also assisted by an excellent cast. Barbara Stanwyck was at her best in the title role, a part that reminded many critics of her performance in Wilder's *Double Indemnity*, a classic of *film noir*. Martha Ivers is actually a more difficult role. A complex character twisted by dark, sublimated forces and driven to the cruel exploitation of those around her, Martha must remain basically understandable, human, and sympathetic. Stanwyck manages all of this in what must be one of her finest screen perforances. Van Heflin turns in a good performance as Martha's major antagonist, but his part is not so complicated. Sam Masterton is a tough kid from the wrong side of the tracks who grows up to be both a war hero and a cynical, perhaps crooked, gambler. Even aside from the period clichés involved in the part, Heflin always seems to be "playing" Sam.[9] Much better is Kirk Douglas in his screen debut, in the role of Martha's alcoholic husband, Walter O'Neil. Although Douglas's strong personality—which we recall today from later films—somewhat submerges Walter's weak identity, Douglas admirably portrays a person destroyed by a haunting sense of the past. The fourth major role, that of Toni Maracek, Heflin's love interest, is played by newcomer Lizabeth Scott, working, as one contemporary critic put it, "from Lauren Bacall's scrapbook." Scott, like Bacall a former model, generally seems to pose rather than act, though she is adequate for her somewhat limited characterization. The minor parts are handled by a host of familiar Hollywood faces, many remembered from other Milestone films. Worth mentioning are Judith Anderson and Roman Bohnen, Milestone regulars, in the small but important roles of Mrs. Ivers, Martha's hateful aunt, and Mr. O'Neil, Walter's destructive father. Darryl Hickman leads a trio of child actors who portray the principals in a prologue set eighteen years before the main action. Although their performances prove only adequate, they seem well cast in terms of an uncanny physical resemblance to the adult characters.

The prologue, the only action retained from John Patrick's original story, served as the germ of Rossen's screenplay.[10] Patrick had a group of children witness a murder committed by one of their number; in later years their relationships are affected by this guilty knowledge. Essentially, Rossen has taken this central action and from it generated a tortuous plot typical of *film noir*. The writer is fascinated by the multiple effects of the childhood crime on both the individuals and the social order. He makes the young murderess the heiress of the powerful Ivers family, the ruling house of Iverstown, evidently a small city in the Northeast. However, Rossen makes the city representative of modern industrial America. In fact, his screenplay becomes both a clinical case history (hence the title) and an allegorical tale describing the generic American experience. In both facets the story turns on the power of the past to influence the present, a constant theme in serious American art; perhaps this theme proves so pervasive because it is so often ignored in ordinary American life.

Martha proves the most twisted psychologically of the characters. Because she is the representative of the Ivers dynasty she must forget her real identity as Martha Smith, the love child of an Ivers heiress and a working man from the Ivers mill. Her aunt, the sadistically cruel Mrs. Ivers, insists on the destructive transformation to Martha Ivers, a change which becomes complicated by the young girl's developing sexuality. In reaction to her aunt's bullying Martha yearns to run away with Sam Masterton, the son of another Ivers mill worker. When her aunt frustrates this plan and later tries to kill Martha's beloved pet cat (in some rather obvious Freudian symbolism), Martha causes the old lady's death. The only witness to her deed is little Walter O'Neil, the son of Martha's ambitious tutor, who, guessing the real story, forces Martha to adopt him as a surrogate father. In turn, he engineers Martha's marriage to Walter, and Walter's prosecution, some years later, when he has become Assistant District Attorney, of an innocent man for the death of Mrs. Ivers. Thus Martha's adult life is shaped by impulses and frustrations of her youth, as she is tied to Walter by their guilty knowledge of their crimes.

Rossen has removed Sam from the scene until the present, some eighteen years after the prologue. Sam ran away with the circus shortly before the death of Martha's aunt, thinking he would be sent to reform school for his part in Martha's attempted escape. In the present (1946), Sam is driving across the country, seemingly to his home on the West Coast, after his discharge from the army as a war hero. When he swings by Iverstown, a minor accident smashes his radiator, and he is forced to spend the night in his old hometown, which now boasts on its signboard "Iverstown—America's Fastest Growing Industrial City." The place clearly represents a changing America, a once pastoral scene transformed into a small town dominated by the repressive Ivers family, and then into an industrial wasteland created by the willfullness of the twisted Ivers heiress, Martha.

On his return Sam soon meets Toni, a working-class girl from nearby Ridgeville who has just been released from a jail term for petty theft. Toni takes to the handsome gambler when he offers her a ride to the West Coast, which still retains something of the frontier image of freedom. Complications ensue when the police, motivated by District Attorney Walter O'Neil's election-year crackdown on vice, grab Toni for a minor parole violation. Now Sam is forced to contact Walter and later Martha. Both of the O'Neils suspect that Sam has returned to blackmail them, though Sam is oblivious to their suspicions as he really does not know about the crime. However, Martha cares little about Sam's motivation because she sees his return as a way to escape Walter's deadly hold on her. Walter hates and fears Sam, and he conspires with the crooked police chief to have the gambler run out of town.

Sam is too much the Bogart-style tough guy to be run off by

Walter or his hired thugs, and eventually Toni promises to stay with him. He decides to stay and to fight corruption in Iverstown as he has in Europe. Matters becomes even more complicated when Sam guesses the cause of the O'Neils' fears and tries to panic Martha by means of a blackmail threat. Martha willingly offers him half of her widespread interests if he will only remove Walter from the scene. Again playing along, Sam visits the Ivers mansion and confronts Walter. The district attorney is too drunk to handle the situation, so Sam deals with Martha instead. In a final confrontation, Martha entreats Sam to kill Walter who has collapsed down the stairs. Sam refuses, and, in turn, Walter refuses to kill Sam. Facing the prospect of Sam's revelation of their crimes both of the O'Neils commit suicide. A final coda shows Sam returning to Toni at the hotel, and finally the happy twosome, driving off for the fabled West, discussing marriage.

Neither this stock happy ending nor the bright love plot which supports it balances off the dark doings in the house of Ivers. Martha's natural development is frustrated by the destructive family pride, while Walter is destroyed by his father's, and his own, greed. Sam and Toni are nearly corrupted by this world, flirting with petty crime and amoral cynicism before emerging as the hopeful couple of the conclusion. Almost everyone else in the picture seems corrupted, perverted, or destroyed by the wasteland world of the modern city. Thus postwar malaise and cynicism become evident even in Hollywood melodrama; Iverstown becomes a microcosm of the American macrocosm despoiled by its own history.

Since Milestone generally collaborated with his screenwriters it seems likely that at least part of the cynical vision evident in *The Strange Love of Martha Ivers* emerged from his artistic consciousness. Milestone was always a man of his times, both emotionally and intellectually, so he would have felt the disappointments of the postwar years much as any other American. In fact, a director who had made four war movies depicting the heroic fight to overcome Fascism might have been doubly disappointed by the problems of the peace, a peace poisoned by the tensions of the Cold War. Certainly Milestone ably combines the talents of his crew and cast to realize fully the thematic implications of Robert Rossen's screenplay. In particular, Milestone finds the perfect visual style to express graphically these abstract themes. Undoubtedly, the director was influenced by other examples of *film noir*, but his own well-developed sense of cinematic style could shade the visual Realism of

Hollywood storytelling with the emphatic and symbolic devices of Expressionism.

The film opens with the visual image of the Ivers mansion and the aural images of Rozsa's overture as backdrops to the credits. The house of Ivers is shown during a heavy, depressing rainstorm, symbolic of the emotional climate evident in the story. After the credits, a title announces the scene as "Iverstown—1928." Near the E. P. Ivers factory building a boy stealthily enters a boxcar in the railroad yards on the night of the storm. Inside the darkened car he lights a candle, revealing a young girl huddled in the corner. In whispered conversation accompanied by shadowed movement they discuss their situation until they are surprised by the police. The girl, thirteen-year-old Martha Ivers, is captured, but the boy, Sam Masterton, escapes into the stormy night. Martha is returned to the Ivers mansion to confront her aunt, against the backdrop of the lightning storm. At his father's urging Walter O'Neil has betrayed his young friends, and now Walter accompanies Martha to her room while the adults remain below to discuss the girl's reaction. The storm knocks out the electrical system, plunging the house into total darkness.

Martha lights a candle, and, in a perfect match cut, Milestone moves to her aunt performing the same action in the library below with Mr. O'Neil. When Sam returns and climbs in through the window the scene is set for the aunt's death. Sam slips downstairs to find Martha's cat, but Mrs. Ivers hears him and starts upstairs to investigate. The setting here is a long spiral staircase which realistically represents the opulence of the mansion but also symbolically suggests the convolutions of its inhabitants' twisted psyches. In a scene lit only sporadically by flashes of lightning, Milestone deftly plays up and down the staircase in balletlike action which perfectly captures the relationships of the participants. Sam panics and runs out the downstairs door, while Walter stands frozen with fear; Martha and Mrs. Ivers move inexorably up and down the staircase, ever closer to final confrontation. Seeing the cat, the aunt begins to strike it with her heavy walkingstick. The hand and stick are seen in close-up in the frame, until another hand intrudes and wrestles the stick away. Next the stick alone is shown in an upward angle, and then the camera angles down as Martha brings down the stick again and again. Mrs. Ivers stumbles and falls down the steps into a crumpled heap, as Martha's vision follows her from above, emphasizing her fearful victory. Martha, trailed by Walter, creeps down the stairs toward the body, only to be startled by Mr. O'Neil. He looks up to see her, and his gaze fixes on the stick, the Freudian symbol of Martha's awful power. She quickly creates a story about a prowler, claiming she has just picked up the stick. Mr. O'Neil sees a way out and coaches the children in the story; then, in a careful three-shot, Milestone shows the tutor taking each of the children by the hand and promising to keep them all together for as long as they live. This dark murder scene is powerfully handled in an expressionistic montage as effective as any in Milestone's work.

After a brief sequence which shows Sam jumping aboard the circus train, another title identifies the scene as "Iverstown—1946." Sam is driving into town in the opposite direction from which the train departed. Strangely, he seems unaware that he is near Iverstown until he sees the aforementioned billboard. The sign distracts him, causing the accident which forces him to stay overnight. In Dempsey's Garage he hears with interest a radio announcement about Walter O'Neil's campaign speech and later listens intently as the garage owner fills him in on Walter's career—and Martha's. In an arresting shot Sam walks up to look at a campaign poster above a mirror, so that the contrasting images of Walter and himself are quickly juxtaposed. However, Sam, the gambler, has little interest in looking up Walter, the district attorney, so he walks downtown to the old apartment house where his parents had lived. He finds no trace of them; instead he discovers Toni waiting for a cab on the porch of the building. Shooting up and down the porch steps in a reprise of the staircase scene, Milestone quickly establishes the relationship between the two characters as they come to the same level to share a cigarette. Inserts of Lizabeth Scott's long legs look suspiciously like an afterthought here, a problem which is repeated whenever Toni appears.

Toni is bound for the bus station, and she offers Sam a lift in her taxi when it arrives. On the way, a train blocks a crossway, causing her to miss her bus and necessitating a drink with him at a local bar. Both the bus station and cocktail lounge scenes are neatly and unobtrusively handled, with the only close-ups on the neon signs identifying the settings. After some talk they decide to drive West together the following day, and then they start back to Sam's hotel. On the street another lightning storm has blown up, forcing them to seek shelter in a doorway where they see another poster adorned with Walter's picture.

Here Milestone cuts to the Ivers mansion, looking exactly as it did behind the credits. A limousine pulls up in the drive, and the front door opens to admit Barbara Stanwyck as the adult Martha. Her grand entrance through the door, past the butler (and the camera) and up the spiral staircase, recalls the drama of the earlier scenes in the Ivers mansion. Now coming into her room and switching on the light, Martha again discovers Walter, this time slumped in a chair hugging a bottle of Scotch. The lamp serves as a spotlight emphasizing Walter's pathetic weakness. Angles are also effectively used as she looks down on him, and Walter, awakening slowly, looks up at her. When Martha demands an explanation for his neglected campaign speech Walter explains that it is the fourth anniversary of his father's death. He is only drinking in memory of the dead father, who lived to see all his dreams come true—"his son a successful and famous man, married to a beautiful and wealthy woman." Later he elaborates on this dream turned into nightmare by the death of an innocent man to establish his own career. These haunting visions silence him before any audience and drive him to the anodyne of alcohol. The camera holds the couple together in the middle of the room, catching Martha's rigid rejection when Walter embraces her. Swilling the last drink from the bottle, Walter leaves for his own room.

Meanwhile Toni and Sam have returned to the hotel, where they are arranged in adjoining rooms connected by a bath. Milestone makes the most of this physical and dramatic setting by using the multiple doors as symbolic framing devices. Each is hesitant to enter across the threshold of the other's room, so they very decorously take their showers and don modest bathrobes. (There are a few inserts of Scott wrapped in a towel.) Finally she enters his room, and they talk about their checkered pasts, resolving their plan to drive West the next morning. But morning is announced by a newspaper pushed under the door, one whose headlines proclaim a vice crackdown by the incumbent district attorney. Alerted by the desk clerk, two detectives force their way into Sam's room; they have just arrested Toni at the bus station. By turning in her ticket to Ridgeville she has violated the terms of her parole, and she is now in the city jail. Sam refuses to be intimidated and resolves to see his old friend Walter O'Neil.

The scene in Walter's office is also very smoothly handled in terms of inner and outer doors, symbolic details (a hidden bar, for example), and neat two shots. Walter is immediately frightened by Sam's reappearance, but Martha seems delighted when she arrives.

At first she hesitates in Walter's office doorway, not recognizing her girlhood lover; then she rushes in to embrace him much more warmly than she had Walter in the earlier scene. After Sam leaves, Martha advises her husband to release Toni and get Sam out of town. Later, Walter finds out that she had quickly called Dempsey's Garage and had Sam's repair delayed. In the meantime she has invited Sam to the Ivers house, and here they are reunited at the site of their last meeting. Milestone replays earlier scenes and motifs as Martha guides Sam on a house tour showing the rooms she has redecorated. Rooms, doorways, and the spiral staircase provide the visual analogues for their reminiscences. Martha nervously pumps Sam for some sign of his motivation, but he simply announces that he is heading West as soon as Toni is released from jail. After one last kiss, "for old time's sake," Sam departs to meet Toni.

Toni, however, is in Walter's office being grilled by the police chief. Walter now knows that Martha is trying to keep Sam around, so he forces Toni to set him up for a beating by hired thugs. Afraid of going back to jail, Toni agrees, though she tries to warn Sam when they have dinner in an Italian restaurant. Sam does not heed her warning, and he is given a terrific beating and left half dead on the outskirts of Iverstown. He at last crawls out of a ditch and flags a bus for a ride back into town, arriving just as Toni is departing on the bus to Ridgeville. Milestone does some nice boom work in this scene, establishing the relationship of the two buses in the same shot and then showing Sam intercepting Toni. When Sam hears her story, he forgives her, and she decides to stay and help him fight the O'Neils.

Milestone returns to the Ivers mansion for the confrontation between Sam and Walter, which is dramatically highlighted by Walter's attempt to pull a pistol from his desk drawer. Sam smashes the drawer on the other man's hand in a series of tight close-ups and then knocks him unconscious. Martha arrives and tries to smooth things over, but Walter not only admits the beating but talks too much about the blackmail issue. Sam then heads back to town, where he talks with Toni and checks out the story of Mrs. Ivers's death and the resulting trial of the innocent dupe at the *Iverstown Register*. Armed with this information, Sam is ready to confront Martha at her office the next morning. Here she is the boss, the lady executive of E. P. Ivers Industries, which she has expanded from 3,000 to 30,000 workers. The scene is neatly presented in terms of dramatic cutting and the symbolic byplay between a window

overlooking the plant and a mural depicting the plant on the office
wall. The sense of Martha's compulsive dynamism pervades the
scene, which ends when Martha offers Sam "a partnership" if he
will get rid of Walter.

Sam takes her offer under advisement as he heads back to the
hotel to apprise Toni of his plans, though his attitude toward Toni
seems to change as he is tempted by Martha's offer. When Martha
arrives at the hotel (she owns it also) a confrontation between the
women takes place. Unfortunately this scene becomes more of a
mid-1940s fashion show, with Toni in her new "sun outfit," a
cheesecake combination of halter and shorts, and Martha in a
flowing cape and snood. After dinner at a local nightclub, Sam and
Martha drive to the old lovers' lane on the hill above town. In this
temptation scene, she offers him all she sees below if he will return
her love and rid both of them of Walter. At first Sam resists the
temptation, but when they struggle after an argument, they kiss and
their passion is rekindled. They have come upon a campfire left by
some teenagers, and sitting before it Martha confesses the killing of
her aunt, even reenacting it with a firebrand. When Sam seizes the
burning stick from her, the camera closes on the fire. In the next
shot the fire is cold, indicating, in Production-Code symbolism, the
consummation of their passion.

Yet when she returns to the hotel Sam is drawn to the more
innocent Toni once more. Toni has seen him kiss Martha goodbye,
and she wants to leave until Sam asks her to stay so that he can sort
out his emotions. This does not take long as Walter calls almost
immediately, demanding a final confrontation. Returning to the
Ivers mansion Sam finds Walter drunk and raving, with Martha
making no attempt to stifle him. Clearly, Sam must make some
quick decisions. Again Milestone plays the symbolic motif of doors,
rooms, and staircases. Moving from the front door, up to Martha's
room, and from outer to inner doors, Walter makes his ugly
revelation to Sam. He is only the most current of many lovers
Martha has taken in her attempt to rid herself of her husband.
Slumping in a chair, Walter makes his harshest accusation: "She'll
get you to kill me." Then in a nice three-shot Walter rises between
Sam and Martha, who are staring into each other's eyes. "It will be
you or me," Walter cries. Racing out the door and downstairs to get
his gun, Walter tumbles down the spiral staircase. As Martha and
Sam look down on him in an obvious replay of the earlier crime, she
urges him to do away with her husband. A blow on the head would

The climactic moment in *The Strange Love of Martha Ivers*: Martha (Barbara Stanwyck) and Sam (Van Heflin) plot what to do about her unconscious husband (Kirk Douglas).

never be suspected. As Sam walks slowly and purposefully down the staircase, Martha retreats a step ahead of him, hissing her schemes. Then Sam brushes past her, picks up Walter, and carries him to a couch in the library.

Now as Sam and Walter talk, Martha pulls the gun from the desk drawer. If she can get either man to side with her, then she can murder the other. But neither man will play her game. Sam turns his back and walks out, daring her to shoot, saying, as he goes, "I feel sorry for both of you." As the front door closes, the gun falls from her hand to the floor. She runs to the window to call Sam back once more, and Walter goes to her side, after picking up the pistol. Milestone presents the dramatic climax in another brilliant montage. As Walter begs her to reconsider, the camera cuts between the two of them, also showing Sam walking down the front path. Close-ups show the gun in Walter's hand, and then Martha's hand as she guides it toward her body. A final close-up shows her holding it almost lovingly, as if this were erotic foreplay; her thumb covers

Walter's finger on the trigger, and Sam turns back toward the house at the sound of the shot. In the window, he sees Martha go limp in Walter's embrace, and then watches horrified as Walter turns the gun on himself. From here Sam hurries back to the hotel and reconciliation with Toni, which is confirmed as they drive out of town the next day, headed West toward a new American Dream.

Yet this Hollywood happy ending cannot balance the thematic thrust of the nightmare world represented by Iverstown. Finally Milestone's *The Strange Love of Martha Ivers* proves a perfect example of *film noir*, a dark revelation of a corrupt and corrupting urban America. From Robert Rossen's literate and intelligent screenplay, a work which recalls literary sources as diverse as Eugene O'Neill and John O'Hara, Milestone, his cast, and his crew fashioned an excellent movie. Not only one of the best of its type, the *film noir*, *The Strange Love of Martha Ivers* remains one of Milestone's best films, a dramatic confirmation of the director's diverse and generous talents.

Arch of Triumph (1948)

Arch of Triumph should have been a much better film than it turned out to be. It was based on a solid literary property, Erich Maria Remarque's novel of the same title published in 1945. The book is probably the German writer's best after *All Quiet on the Western Front*. Following the success of his autobiographical anti-war novel, Remarque was forced to leave Germany, and he became the sort of new "world citizen" described in his later novel. During those years, Remarque published another autobiographical work, the story of his return from the war, *The Road Back* (1931, filmed in 1937), a melodrama about the war, *Three Comrades* (1937, filmed in 1938 with a screenplay by F. Scott Fitzgerald), and a story of refugees in the years before World War II, *Flotsam* (1941, filmed as *The Other Love* in 1947). *Arch of Triumph* continued his depiction of the human wreckage created by the displacements of modern history.

Set in Paris during 1939, *Arch of Triumph* centers on the relationship between Ravic, a brilliant surgeon forced to flee Nazi Germany, and Joan Madou, a neurotic cabaret singer. During the course of the novel the characters reverse roles. A displaced person without passport, Ravic is forced to do "ghost" surgery for other physicians at cut-rate prices; soon he is sinking into a *demimonde* of alcoholism, prostitution, and abortion. His loss of identity is most

fully symbolized by the major subplot, his revenge on Haake, a
German agent who had tortured him and killed his mistress in
Germany years before. Ravic finally strangles Haake in one of the
most terrifying murders in modern fiction. Joan, though she loves
Ravic in her own ambiguous way, takes a successful actor as her
protector and rises into the fashionable world of fancy restaurants
and plush apartments. At the conclusion Joan is shot by the jealous
actor, and Ravic mercifully lets her die when he realizes that she
will live as a vegetable if she recovers at all. This final ironic reversal
mirrors the central irony of the title; there is no triumph in the
fallen world of modern Europe. Although the relationship of Ravic
and Joan is central, the book is populated by a number of well-
drawn minor characters who complement the pair of lovers in the
dramatization of this tragic malaise. The book ends on September 1,
1939, at the opening of World War II.

Like his earlier novel, *All Quiet on the Western Front*, Remarque's
Arch of Triumph is in the realistic mode. The later novel has more
literary polish and less raw power than the earlier work, but it also
presents a sordid, destructive universe where the rhythms of life
have become rhythms of death. In his adaptation of *All Quiet on the
Western Front*, Milestone brilliantly succeeded in capturing the
harsh vision of the novel; in *Arch of Triumph*, he fails almost
completely. A great part of this failure was beyond Milestone's
control. The Production Code would not allow an unpunished
strangulation (even of a Nazi) or a mercy killing, so the conclusion
is changed. Of course, all of the sordid details from the bars,
brothels, and operating rooms were also excised from the screenplay.
His producers saw the adaptation of the bestselling novel as a
blockbuster on the scale of *Gone With the Wind* (1939), which had
just been reissued, and they opted for a lavish production with
major stars in the central roles. Milestone was stuck with Charles
Boyer and Ingrid Bergman as Ravic and Joan. Both were badly
miscast; Boyer is, as usual, a matinee idol rather than a refugee
doctor, while Bergman, as one critic put it, portrayed an international tart about as convincingly as Boyer would have played an All-
American fullback. The minor parts, particularly Charles Laughton
as Haake and Louis Calhern as Morosow, a White Russian refugee,
are almost laughable. Milestone himself has commented on this
central difficulty: "One thing wrong was that it was supposed to be
a realistic piece and it had two major stars in the leads. If you have

two major stars like that, then half your reality goes out the window."[11]

The screenplay was pushed by the producers toward glamorous romance, so that the result becomes a sort of second-rate *Casablanca* (1943) rather than the Hemingwayesque tale the original had been.[12] The second major difficulty was that at the last moment the producers opted against the long version of the film and it was cut from about four hours to a more conventional two. Obviously, such drastic cutting destroyed the continuity of the work. Major characters were completely eliminated, loose ends of plot abound, and the movie romance of Boyer and Bergman becomes even more central. Needless to say, the final product was both an artistic and a financial disaster; it grossed $1.5 million, while it cost almost $4 million to make.[13]

Although much of the blame can be attributed elsewhere, Milestone cannot be completely absolved of responsibility for the disaster. Even given the fragmentary state of the final print, the film seems strangely inert and lifeless. Mainly studio shot, the careful *mise-en-scène* of earlier Milestone films is missing from *Arch of Triumph*. Aside from two or three sequences the compositions are dull, the camera is static, and the editing predictable, in particular in the inevitable reaction shots of the Boyer-Bergman scenes. The only arresting sequences are Ravic's memories of Haake's torture, a clear throwback to German Expressionism, and the single operating-room scene left in the final print. Both are carefully composed and lit with quick juxtaposition of extreme angles. Both scenes also come early on in the film; after them Milestone seems almost to have given up. Perhaps he did, as in later years he has practically disowned the film. Wherever the blame is placed, *Arch of Triumph*, is a clear failure, a bad film made from a good book.

After he completed *Arch of Triumph,* Milestone reverted to the weak, semisophisticated comedy of his Paramount and RKO pictures of the 1930s in *No Minor Vices* (1949). In particular the movie seems a reprise of *My Life with Caroline* as a jealous husband must thwart his wife's phony suiters. In this case, the husband is Dana Andrews, somewhat more mature than in the war movies, as a self-satisfied doctor. His wandering wife-receptionist is Lilli Palmer, and the artist-gigolo type is Louis Jourdan. Perhaps reflecting the change in attitudes since the earlier film, the marriage does seem in doubt for a few moments. However, the inevitable reconciliation finally takes place and all live happily thereafter. Milestone labored to make the film interesting with stream-of-consciousness soliloquies and deft pans moving between characters, but most reviewers found it dull stuff, too labored and slow for comedy. In general, it seems the kind of programmer that the director might have better avoided.

The Red Pony (1949)

Milestone's next film was a screen adaptation of John Steinbeck's story sequence "The Red Pony." The director had been interested in adapting the story sequence since it had appeared in the author's 1938 collection of stories, *The Long Valley.*[14] The valley of the title is the Salinas Valley in California, the setting for much of the writer's most successful fiction, including *Of Mice and Men.* Steinbeck and Milestone became good friends during the making of the earlier film, and they discussed the possibility of bringing "The Red Pony" to the screen as early as 1940.[15] However, various other projects kept both men from advancing the idea until 1946 when the author and the director went into partnership with Republic Studios to make the film version. Steinbeck served as screenwriter, his only adaptation of one of his own works, while Milestone took credit as both producer and director. The film is also notable as Milestone's first color effort. Assisted by a capable production team and a fair cast, the writer and the director created a competent screen version of a fine fictional work, a movie which proved a moderate success, both critically and financially.

Unfortunately, the artistic climate of the Hollywood studio system in the postwar period prevented even the author himself from scripting a fully realized film version of "The Red Pony." *Of Mice and Men,* though an artistic success, had failed commercially because it fitted no generic box-office formula; in desperation, the Roach studios even tried to peddle it as a sex shocker. In a similar fashion, "The Red Pony" could not be produced simply as a fine narrative; rather it had to be pigeonholed as a children's picture, a kind of a kids' Western about a boy and his horse, before Republic, essentially a studio devoted to Westerns, would make it. The film's conclusion, altered to a stock happy ending, represents the general transformation of plot, character, and theme in the screen version of "The Red Pony," one of Steinbeck's finest works of fiction.

Steinbeck evidently began "The Red Pony" fairly early in his career; his letters indicate he was working on "a pony story" as early as 1933, and the first two sections of the story sequence, "The Gift" and "The Great Mountains," were published in the *North American*

Review for November and December of that year. "The Promise" did not appear in *Harper's* until 1937, and "The Leader of the People" was not added until the publication of *The Long Valley* in 1938, and even here it was a sort of postscript. However, manuscript and textual evidence indicates that the later sections were written some time before their publication, not very long after the first two stories.[16] The sequence was finally unified in a volume under the title *The Red Pony* in 1945. The four separate tales are connected by common characters, settings, and themes.

All four stories involve the maturation of Jody Tiflin, a boy of about ten when the action opens. The stories are set about 1910 on the Tiflin ranch in the Salinas Valley, where Jody lives with his father, Carl, his mother, Ruth, and the hired hand, a middle-aged cowboy named Billy Buck. From time to time they are visited by Ruth's father, a venerable old man who led one of the first wagon trains across the continent to California. The stories seem somewhat autobiographical, having a sense of careful observation. "The Gift," the first story in the sequence, concerns Jody's red pony, which he names Gabilan Mountains. The pony soon becomes symbolic of the boy's growing maturity and his developing knowledge of the natural world. Later he carelessly leaves the pony out in the rain, and it takes cold and dies, in spite of Billy Buck's promises to save it. Thus Jody learns of nature's cruel indifference to human desires. In the second story, "The Great Mountains," the Tiflin ranch is visited by a former resident, Gitano, an aged Chicano laborer who was raised in the now decayed hacienda. Gitano has come home to die. In a debate reminiscent of Robert Frost's "The Death of the Hired Man," Carl persuades Ruth that they cannot take Gitano in, but as in the poem their dialogue proves pointless; the old man steals a broken-down nag significantly named Easter and makes off into the mountains to die in dignity. Again, Jody has discovered some of the complex, harsh reality of adult life.

In "The Promise," the third story, Jody learns more of nature's ambiguous promises when his father has one of the mares put to stud to procure the boy another colt. However, the birth is complicated, and Billy Buck must kill the mare to save the colt, demonstrating that life and death are inextricably intertwined. The final story, "The Leader of the People," ends the sequence with another vision of death and change. Jody's grandfather comes to visit, repeating his time-worn stories of the great adventures of Westering. Carl Tiflin cruelly hurts the old man by revealing that no one is really interested in these repetitious tales. The grandfather realizes that Carl is right, but asserts to Jody that the adventurous stories were not the point. Rather his message was "Westering" itself. For the grandfather, Westering was a force like Turner's frontier, the source of American identity; now with the close of the frontier, Westering has ended. The pioneers have degenerated into petty landholders like Carl Tiflin and aging cowboys like Billy Buck. Yet, in his grandfather's ramblings, Jody discovers some sense of mature purpose, and by the conclusion of the sequence he too can hope to be a leader of the people someday.

This story sequence, along with the other tales unified by the setting of the long valley in the volume of the same name, are among Steinbeck's finest work. "The Red Pony" traces Jody's initiation into adult life with both realism and sensitivity, a balance which Steinbeck did not always achieve. The sense of the characters caught up in nature is balanced by their deep human concerns and commitments. The evocation of the ranch setting in all its vital beauty is matched only in the author's finest works, such as *Of Mice and Men*. Steinbeck's symbols grow naturally out of this setting, and nothing in the story sequence seems forced into a symbolic pattern. In its depiction of an American variation of a universal experience, "The Red Pony" deserves comparison with the finest of modern American fiction, especially initiation stories like Faulkner's *The Bear* or Hemingway's Nick Adams stories.

Obviously, such a fine work of fiction had much to offer as a film, but it also presented some inherent difficulties. Steinbeck's story sequence was episodic, unified only by continuities of character, setting, and theme. These subtle variations on the theme of initiation had to be woven together and considerably cut for a screenplay. The exigencies of production forced Steinbeck to cut out completely one of the four stories in the sequence, "The Great Mountains," and to cut severely another one, "The Promise." The two remaining stories were then spliced to form a sequential narrative which limits the complexity of the adaptation. Finally Steinbeck concluded his screenplay with a Hollywood happy ending which completely distorts the meaning of the original.

The characters, particulary Jody and his grandfather, are types, albeit complex ones, and, therefore, rather hard to realize. In the cast only Robert Mitchum as the ranchhand Billy Buck really remains convincing throughout the movie. Even Mitchum is not exactly Steinbeck's Billy, as he proves too youthful, too vital, and too ideal. In many ways he seems a variation of another idealized screen character created by Alan Ladd a few years later in *Shane* (1953). As in George Stevens's film, though not in Steinbeck's story, a romance between the ranch wife and the friend becomes a confusing issue in Milestone's movie. In fact, Myrna Loy and Mitchum were given the star billing for the film, creating a sense of romance between the characters they portray. Perhaps trying to escape her role as William Powell's sophisticated spouse in the Thin Man series, Miss Loy, who made her screen debut in Milestone's *The Cave Man* (1926), seems straining to be sweet in her role as Alice Tiflin. (For some reason, Steinbeck changed the name of all three Tiflins from novel to screenplay.)[17] Fred Tiflin is weaker and less interesting than in the story sequence, and he is made even less so by Shepperd Strudwick's hangdog interpretation. Louis Calhern, fresh from Milestone's *Arch of Triumph*, is adequate though not inspired as the grandfather; he seems a strange amalgam of Will Geer's Grandpa Walton and Joel McCrea's Buffalo Bill. The major casting problem, however, is with the protagonist, Tom Tiflin, as portrayed by Peter Miles. Perhaps no child star could capture the complexity of this role, as it is much easier for an adult to write about sensitive children than for a child to play one. Young Miles's sensitivity often seems rather sugary and his anger at the world more or less a tantrum.[18] The only other characters of note are a group of Tom's schoolmates, who make Peter Miles's performance seem peerless by comparison with their "Our Gang" antics.

Aside from casting other production values are good. The film was shot on location at a Salinas Valley ranch, one that looks very much like the ranch used in *Of Mice and Men*. As in the earlier film *mise-en-scène* is very well handled, with realistic interiors and natural exteriors. Tony Gaudio's color cinematography records the setting in natural, muted tones which often suggest the best of regional American painting. Perhaps the best single feature of the film is the powerful score by Aaron Copland, who had also scored *Of Mice and Men;* both scores became concert favorites, among the finest pieces of music created for Hollywood. As in his earlier work with Milestone, Copland's score perfectly matches the mood of the visuals, and in this case often surpasses them in evoking the lyric naturalism of Steinbeck's original work.

Milestone opens the film with a pretitle sequence which clearly recalls *Of Mice and Men* in both visual and aural imagery. As in the earlier film, this sequence establishes a complex relationship between the human characters and the natural world. First the camera pans left over a scenic shot of the dark mountains, at last establishing the ranch house and outbuildings nestled in a hollow. A narrative voice-over establishes time and place:

In central California many small ranches sit in the hollows of the skirts of the Coast Range Mountains. Some, the remnants of the old and gradually disintegrating homesteads; some the remains of Spanish grants. To one of them in the foothills to the west of Salinas Valley, the dawn comes, as it comes to a thousand others.[19]

The natural cycle of day begins earlier for the animal than the human inhabitants of the ranch. In quick sequence Milestone shows close-ups of a crowing rooster on a post, a gobbling turkey in a tree, two dogs waking slowly from sleep, a softly hooting owl in another tree, and finally a rabbit. The dogs and the owl respond to the presence of the rabbit; by implication it seems the owl sweeps down on the hapless rabbit just beyond camera range. The natural world presents a complex beauty, marked by rhythms of life and death, of beginnings and endings, of ever repeated cycles. This sequence ends when Billy Buck walks out of the bunkhouse and into the barn, lighting a lantern to see to the horses. The light falls on the cover of the novel, which in turn opens to present the production data. Like many Milestone films, *The Red Pony* opens quite well, but unfortunately, like many others, it does not sustain the artistic intensity of the beginning.

After the titles fade out, Billy whistles and calls his mare, Rosie; the horse enters through a door and walks toward the camera; then Billy fondles her and begins a morning ritual of feeding and currying. Milestone cuts to the farmhouse, where Alice Tiflin is preparing breakfast; she stops and walks out on the porch to ring the triangle which calls the rest of the characters to meals. Two quick close-ups show the awakening Fred Tiflin and his son, Tommy. Billy arrives at the kitchen first, but he waits for the others to enter before him, subtly establishing the relationship of owner and hired hand, as well as the equation of Tommy and Fred as the immature members of the family and of Alice and Billy as the really mature. Inside the kitchen some homey bits are done with the close-ups of cooking ham and eggs, the boy washing behind his ears, and the father kidding Billy about going into town. The screenplay includes a long conversation here not included in the final print, about Billy's mare, Rosie, who is expecting a colt in a few months. Probably Milestone felt the discussion slowed the development of the story, even though it foreshadowed the symbolic birth of Rosie's colt at the conclusion. However, the film does add scenes to the story at this point. After Billy and Tom leave, Alice and Fred Tiflin talk about Tom's attachment for the ranchhand, clearly indicating the father's sense of inadequacy and his resulting jealousy of his hired man. The reason for his anxiety is revealed in the next sequence, where Tom asks Billy to show him the newspaper clipping reporting Rosie's victory in the Sacramento Stock Show. As the best hand with horses in the area, Billy is nature's nobleman for young Tom, an extension of his grandfather's days of glory in the Old West.

Milestone dramatizes these feelings as Tom sets off for school, fantasizing that he and Billy are knights leading a troop of splendid soldiery. This interpolated sequence includes an animated background which seems right out of a Disney production. Of course, it is intended to visualize the boy's fantasy life, but all it establishes is a kids'-picture undertone which would have been best avoided. This mood is reinforced by the next scene when Tom's reverie is disturbed by the other schoolchildren. As indicated above Peter Miles is only barely capable of the complexity of his role, while the rest of the kids are refugees from a Little Rascals Comedy. (For example, one schoolchild is called Little Brown Jug, which the credits also list as his real name.) In his story Steinbeck handles both of these sequences in a single sentence: "At the crossroads over the bridge he met two friends and the three of them walked to school together, making ridiculous strides and being rather silly." When this sentence is translated into a combination of Disney and Our Gang, the film quickly loses much of the power promised by the literary source and anticipated in the strong opening sequence. Milestone does handle the scene well by having the other children chase Tom until they surround him before a great oak tree (a scene reminiscent of the park chases in *Hallelujah, I'm a Bum*). The camera pans the group in a semicircle and then closes on Tom, who produces the clipping and boasts that Billy may give him Rosie's colt.

Back at the ranch, Alice and Fred talk about the expected arrival of the grandfather, introducing the themes of "The Leader of the People." In the film the grandfather owns the ranch and lives with the Tiflin family, establishing a much different relationship from

Fantasy and reality in *The Red Pony*: (top) Tom (Peter Miles) dreams of himself as a knight in armor; (bottom) under the watchful eye of Billy Buck (Robert Mitchum), he inspects the red pony.

that which existed in the story. Once again Fred is made a childish
dependent, much like his son, Tom. In this conversation it becomes
apparent that he doesn't even like ranch life and longs to return to
town life in San Jose. Alice is more thoroughly identified with her
father as a symbol of a natural tradition also represented by Billy
Buck. However, when Tom returns from school in the next sequence
Alice remembers Fred's complaint about the boy's neglect of his
schoolwork while knocking about with Billy. She even repeats her
husband's very words. "There are other things to know besides
ranching." But her heart is not in her admonition and she soon
allows Tom to leave his books and go off to prowl the ranch yard.
Here he feeds the chickens, among other chores performed in Tom
Sawyer or Huck Finn fashion, while Milestone makes a nice over-
head shot of the boy circled by the clucking hens. However,
animation changes the fowl to white circus horses prancing around
a ring while Tom directs them with a long ringmaster's whip. The
screenplay indicates that both of these animated fantasy sequences
were to have been longer, but wisely Milestone cut them down; he
would have been even wiser to cut them completely.

This time Tom is pulled from his reverie by the call of his arriving
grandfather. The arrival scene and the dinner which follows are
taken almost verbatim from "The Leader of the People" and
intertwined with the themes of "The Gift." Although this process
creates some dislocations, it does make the grandfather's story seem
less of a digression from the process of Tom's maturation. When
Tom tells the grandfather that he plans a mouse hunt after the
haystacks are leveled, the grandfather compares the hunt to the
troopers' slaughter of the Indians on the frontier, and Tom learns
that the frontier experience was not entirely like the heroics of dime
novels. His initiation into the complex realities of adult life continues at dinner when his father harshly slights his grandfather at every
opportunity, clearly demonstrating the immaturity hinted at in
earlier scenes.

After dinner, the red pony is presented. Billy and Fred bought
the animal in town, where it was left stranded by the collapse of a
traveling show. Both the rancher and the hired hand agree that
raising a pony will be a maturing responsibility for the boy. Tom, of
course, is ecstatic both with his pony and its show saddle. He
promises to take the best possible care of the animal and to perform
all of his other chores faithfully in repayment for the gift. Fred soon
leaves with a threat to sell the pony off if he ever finds it hungry or

dirty. Billy Buck takes over as the real father surrogate, promising to help Tom raise the best horse in the region. The pony will be trained well enough to ride by Thanksgiving, Billy assures the boy. Clearly Gabilan, the red pony, represents a link with primal nature within the natural process of a boy's maturation.

The next day, the childish side of Tom's gift is revealed when he brings his school friends home to see the pony. Once again the film falls to the level of *My Friend Flicka* (1943) as the kids cut some cute capers only briefly mentioned in Steinbeck's original work. Better scenes are created when Milestone shows Billy and Tom working with the animal. In many of these ranch scenes the director achieves the naturalistic poetry he created from California ranch life in *Of Mice and Men*. In *The Red Pony* the color illustrations by Wesley Dennis for the 1945 special edition of the story also seem visual sources. When Tom trains the horse with a rope and halter, the camera pans for 180 degrees on the resulting circle of movement and then rises for a down-shot, a composition which clearly duplicates the frontispiece of this illustrated edition.

The following two sequences combine the climactic actions of both "The Leader of the People" and "The Gift." At breakfast, after Tom has shown how well he has trained his horse, his father reacts by bullying both the boy and the grandfather. Thinking that the old man can't hear him, Fred complains bitterly about the grandfather's repetitious tales of his days as wagonmaster. However, the old man overhears him from behind the doorway, embarrassing the whole group who have gathered for breakfast. Milestone handles this scene very nicely in terms of quick, close-up reaction shots capturing the drama of the scene. Fred apologizes and prepares to retreat to his parent's home in San Jose, a clear desertion of his responsibility to his family and the ranch. The grandfather must also reassess his relationships and his attitudes, concluding that he has indeed bored everyone with his tales. Yet he insists that his purpose was right, he wanted not to tell of wild adventures, but to capture the essence of the Westward movement in his talk.

. . . We carried life out here and set it down and planted it the way ants carry eggs and I was the leader. The westerin' was big as God and the slow stops that made up the movement piled up . . . and piled up until the continent was crossed. . . . Then we come down to the sea and it was done. . . . Well, that's what I oughtta be tellin' instead a' the stories. The stories ain't what I want to say.[20]

Tom intuitively understands what his grandfather means, and his sympathy for the old man indicates his developing maturity. Yet he is not ready to be a leader of the people himself. First he must mature further through the experiences of love and death. Partially because of his own carelessness, partially because of Billy Buck's, his beloved pony is left in the corral through a long, cold, rainy afternoon. When Tom returns from school the pony is shivering and sneezing. (The school scene has been more Disney, with byplay between the kids and the teacher played by Margaret Hamilton, the Wicked Witch of the West from *The Wizard of Oz*.) In his own guilt feeling Tom accuses Billy Buck of failing in his responsibility: "You said it wouldn't rain," he whines in protest. The boy has learned another lesson: all of the adults in his world are fallible. As the pony sickens, he learns more of nature's indifference to human wishes. He may fantasize all he wants about his "trick pony," but nature plays the final trick. Billy is unable to save the weakening animal in spite of a promise to pull the pony through. Finally Billy opens a hole in the animal's windpipe in a futile, last attempt to save its life. In a discreet reaction shot Milestone captures the boy's sensitive response to blood and pain. Of course, this scene is more powerfully depicted in the story, but the film must avoid the shocking symbolic gore out of respect for its young audience. Some contemporary reviews complained that this scene and that of the pony's death were too harsh for children.

A couple of sentimental scenes intrude before the pony's death and Tom's fight with buzzards. The mother recalls the father from San Jose, and he pledges his love for her, the boy, and the ranch. On Thanksgiving, the other kids come to see Tom ride the pony for the first time, and he is forced to put them off with a story about the pony being shod in town. His pride won't allow him to share the hurt he feels for his dying pony. Later in the same evening, Tom beds down in the pony's stall but the animal wanders from the barn, seeking the hills to die in nature. Waking from his fitful sleep, Tom follows the pony's footprints up into the scrubby forest. Looking up, Tom sees a circle of buzzards, scavenging on some dead creature. Tom runs along the crest of a bare hill as the camera follows him in a long tracking shot. Then in a down angle it catches Tom's running reflection in the pool of a stream; suddenly he stops, and then reverses his direction. The camera looks at the dead pony through Tom's eyes. A buzzard has come down on the body, and as Tom watches another lands near the head. The boy races back down the bank, screaming, chasing the buzzards; then the camera follows him past the pony as he grabs a thrashing bird. The camera cuts quickly between the boy and the buzzard, as the frantic bird pecks at him wildly. The bird's beak and claws cut Tom in several places, and blood soaks his ripped shirt. He finds a piece of sharp stone and smashes the bird with it. Billy and Fred come running in just as the boy strangles the bird in one final burst of rage. Following the dialogue of the story, Fred tells Tom that the buzzard hasn't killed his pony; and Billy, more perceptive in this crisis, snaps at the father, "Of course he knows it. Use your head, man, can't you see how he'd feel about it?"

It is Billy, not Fred, who carries Tom back to the ranchhouse. As they retrace the muddy tracks left by the dying pony, Billy feels he must make some act of expiation to the disillusioned boy so he promises to give him Rosie's colt when it is born. This development is taken from the third story in Steinbeck's sequence, "The Promise," where the events take place about a year after the red pony's death. Here the action is shortened as Billy's mare is already nearing the end of her gestation cycle. At first Tom refuses to take any interest in Billy's promise. He has been too badly hurt by the loss of the red pony to chance his feelings on another horse. Instead he rejects Billy, accusing him with the words, "You let him die!" Tom turns away from everyone, his family and his friends at school, when they try to comfort him. In one fine scene he sits reading, reflected in the stream seen earlier in the death of the pony; Rosie, coming to drink, nuzzles him gently, but he rejects her also.

Yet as spring opens out, the sense of life overpowers the memory of death. Tom again talks to his family and his friends; he begins to play with his dogs and Rosie; finally he asks Billy for the colt. Billy promises that the mare will drop a fine colt with no complications. But again nature ignores human desires. In a scene recalling the earlier unsuccessful operation on the red pony, Billy encounters unexpected problems with Rosie's colt. Evidently it is turned the wrong way in the mother's womb, and the horseman must choose between killing the mother or the colt. In the story the boy watches horrified as Billy brutally fulfills his promise by killing poor Rosie in the process of delivering a beautiful colt. The screenplay, probably under studio pressure, opts for an easier conclusion.

Billy makes the decision to kill Rosie, but Tom takes his knife and runs off to the house. By the time the ranchhand has caught up with him, the rest of the family are able to prevail on him to spare the

mother animal. The central group is seen through the doors of
Tom's room, then of the house, then of the barn, as they go back to
the birth scene. Suddenly, they all stop in amazement as the camera
pans them in row along the side of the stall. Next a point-of-view
shot reveals the surprise; somehow in the few moments she was left
alone, Rosie has discreetly and antiseptically brought a perfect colt
into the world. The pan of the characters is repeated as they all
laugh in happy reaction to the bounty of nature. The film's final
shots are of Tom riding the mature colt, one which bears a decided
resemblance to the original red pony, across the beautiful foothills
of the Gabilan mountains.

Of course, this conclusion alters the thematic thrust of Steinbeck's
story sequence. The author himself included it in his screenplay,
and it seems likely that he felt this final compromise was justified by
the realistic presentation of the earlier death of the red pony. Yet
this last alteration only typifies the general change in mood wrought
in the film version of the story sequence. Generally, Steinbeck's
grimly naturalistic yet hauntingly beautiful Salinas Valley is too
often transformed to the pastoral dreamland of *National Velvet*
(1944) or *The Yearling* (1947), of *Lassie Come Home* (1943) or *So
Dear to My Heart* (1949), or even of a 1973 television version of *The
Red Pony*.[21] Some of the characters, particularly Mitchum's Billy
Buck, some of the scenes, particularly the death of the red pony,
some of the settings, particularly the barn, and some of the themes
are still very much Steinbeck's. In its best places the film adds
Milestone's graceful visual touch and Copland's powerful musical
score to the author's naturalistic yet lyrical vision. Although Milestone's *The Red Pony* is not as artistically successful as Steinbeck's
story sequence of the same title, it remains a sincere film adaptation,
one much better than most in its generic pattern.

A made-for-television film version of *The Red Pony* was directed
by Robert Totten in 1973. In spite of a strong cast featuring Henry
Fonda, Maureen O'Hara, Ben Johnson, Jack Elam, and Clint
Howard, this version proves considerably weaker than Milestone's.
The script wanders far from Steinbeck's story sequence and is
further weakened by indifferent direction. As with the later version
of *All Quiet on the Western Front*, this later version of *The Red
Pony* points out strengths in Milestone's earlier adaptation.

Halls of Montezuma (1951)

Halls of Montezuma is one of Lewis Milestone's most underrated
efforts. The movie is rarely discussed, and, when it is mentioned at

all, it serves critics as an example of either the declining powers or the commercial cooption of the director during the 1950s. In particular, the film is negatively contrasted with *All Quiet on the Western Front*, as the critics shake their heads in amazement.[22] Even Milestone himself dismisses it as a potboiler; "I was collecting some money I needed very badly," he told one interviewer.[23] Although he liked certain things in it; "it was really just a job, not a true opportunity to state my personal beliefs about war." However, even if Milestone was not "crazy about the whole idea,"[24] he managed to take a stock Hollywood genre piece and to turn it into something both entertaining and thoughtful. Finally, *Halls of Montezuma* proves a very interesting little movie, one that neatly fits into the succession of war films Milestone made from *All Quiet on the Western Front* to *Pork Chop Hill;* it is most clearly a reprise of his World War II efforts, and the last film in his postwar cycle.

Milestone's great antiwar film was made in 1930, more than a decade after World War I, and it reflected the prevailing intellectual currents of its day, pacificism and isolationism. In contrast, the five war movies the director created during the Second World War reflected changed attitudes, both personal and national, as the intellectual commmunity recognized that armed resistance was the only response to Totalitarianism. After the documentary he edited from Russian newsreel footage, Milestone made three extremely melodramatic features presenting the evils of our enemies. Finally, with *A Walk in the Sun*, he redeemed himself by returning to the understanding of war first seen in his 1930 classic. After this spate of war films, Milestone did not turn again to the war genre until he made *Halls of Montezuma* in 1951. The film's chronology proves quite interesting. It concerns a Marine landing on a Pacific island, probably intended to be the Okinawa attack of 1945, but it was produced during the Korean War. In turn, Milestone would not make his Korean War film, *Pork Chop Hill*, until almost a decade later in 1959.

The Korean involvement was not popular in 1951. Most Americans perceived it as no-win situation, where lives would be lost without the hope of ultimate victory, a kind of preview of Vietnam. At the same time, most Americans felt that some involvement was necessary. Although opposition to the Korean involvement existed on both the political left and the right, the organized antiwar effort of the Vietnam years did not emerge. Probably the difference lay in the acceptance of Cold War rhetoric as part of the heritage of the Second World War. In the 1950s Americans generally entertained a much more simplistic world view than they would in the next decade. Unable to accept a sophisticated vision of a pluralistic Communism, Americans felt compelled to resist local incursions, such as the Korean situation, yet they could not face the grim prospect of a global showdown. Hence the stalemate of Korea, and the popular fantasies of total victory embodied in the adulation of General MacArthur. The popularity of the Pacific hero of World War II was mirrored in a new wave of Hollywood war movies, for the most part mindless efforts concerned with the successful battles of the Pacific.

Milestone's *Halls of Montezuma* certainly seems part of this general development, at least at first glance. The story of two or three days of Pacific island fighting, the film is filled with rousing action and war-movie clichés. The central plot revolves around the destruction of a Japanese rocket-launching facility which is imped-ing the American advance. The enemy is foiled, and the Leather-necks move forward to the tune of the title song, "The Marine Hymn." Shortly before this climactic battle, the letter of a dead soldier was read to the central platoon, accompanied by the soft strains of "My Country 'Tis of Thee." The letter itself contains the film's thematic core. The marines are witnesses to the horrors of war: "War is too horrible for human beings." Still the world must remain free, and weakness will lead to defeat and slavery. Finally, the marines fight because they are on the side of right, ". . . on God's side." Certainly this is the Cold War vision of the American position; we must be strong, and we must fight if necessary to preserve right and freedom. In its ultimate thematic thrust and in its action plot Milestone's film obviously resembles many of the mindlessly self-congratulatory war films of the 1950s.

Yet *Halls of Montezuma*, for all its disconcertingly patriotic entertainment values, also has moments of real insight into the horrors of war. For the most part the characters are complex and believable, not the cardboard stereotypes of similar films. Although the marines have the plot situation well in hand by the film's conclusion, the real story is of a small group, one platoon, involved in an unheroic patrol action, a short "walk" in the Pacific sun recalling Milestone's best film of World War II. The setting is a wasteland of war, recalling Milestone's earlier recreation of the Western Front. In all, Milestone's "Marine Hymn" is not so much a tribute to American military bravado as an American retelling of *All Quiet on the Western Front*, a salute to the courage of men who must bear this horror. As Bosley Crowther put it in the *New York Times* review, the film finally is "a remarkably real and agonizing demonstration of the horribleness of war," all the more surprising coming as it did, in the midst of the Korean conflict.[25]

The movie is based on an original story by Michael Blankfort, who developed it into a screenplay. During the 1950s Blankfort was the screenwriter for a number of films which combined solid entertainment values with liberal ideology.[26] Milestone generally worked with his screenwriter, and it seems likely that his own brand of liberal realism also influenced the work. In particular, there are many interesting correspondences with *All Quiet on the Western Front*. Aside from the overall situation of men lost in the horrors of war, specific characters and actions recall the earlier film. The marines are divided into the toughened veterans and the raw, green recruits. The hardening of characters like Coffman (Robert Wagner) and Conroy (Richard Hylton) recalls the situation of Paul Baumer and his comrades in the earlier film. Slattery (Bert Freed), the oldest private in the corps, is intent only on brewing homemade whiskey, yet tough Sgt. Zelenko (Neville Brand) tells the new recruits to stick with him like glue in combat. Slattery's shepherding of his young charges recreates the tough side of "Kat" Katczinsky, while Doc (Karl Malden) represents the nurturing side of Paul's father figure. The central character, Lt. Anderson (Richard Widmark), becomes a sort of complicated version of Paul's Lt. Bertinck, and a flashback establishes the teacher-student relationship between Anderson and Conroy. The American teacher is the antithesis of the petty disciplinarian Kantorek, while Richard Boone as Col. Gilfillan is a down-to-earth soldier who is nothing like the Prussian martinets of *All Quiet on the Western Front*. All of the cast does quite well, including infantrymen Jack Palance and Martin Milner. Although these actors are quite well known today, they were relative newcomers in 1951, so that Milestone's casting recalls his use of realistic unknowns in *All Quiet on the Western Front*.

The plot also resembles Milestone's classic in that *Halls of Montezuma* moves immediately into battle, opening on the attacking task force only a few moments before the landing operation is to commence. The troops are addressed over the loudspeaker system by Col. Gilfillan, who assures them that their fight is necessary and that they will eventually triumph. The camera studies the group as they listen to their orders and as they board a smaller landing craft, establishing the gallery of types who will be more fully developed

later in the film. A problem ensues when Anderson learns that
Conroy is in sick bay, claiming that he is too ill to go ashore. A
flashback establishes their earlier relationship and in the present,
Anderson gently helps the younger man overcome his fears. The
sick-bay setting also establishes another potential difficulty: Anderson suffers from psychosomatic headaches which he alleviates with
large doses of painkillers supplied by the kindly Doc. Meanwhile,
Slattery is distributing the parts of his still among the members so
that he can set up his moonshining operation as soon as he gets on
dry land. Obviously, this is no group of John Wayne heroes waiting
to wade ashore and whip the Nips.

The landing itself is beautifully handled. Milestone shot the scene
with the cooperation of the Marine Corps at Fort Pendleton, and
the production values are first class. He also edited in some news
footage from actual Pacific battles to create a montage of considerable power. In particular, Milestone cuts in on an action-reaction
basis in showing the discharge of a weapon and the final effects.
One of the most arresting images occurs when the first sea doors
open in the bow of the transport ship and the smaller landing craft
float out as if from some great womb. As the platoon looks longingly
back to the safety of the mother ship, they seem like children lost in
a world of war they never made. The fighting on the shore
particularly recalls *All Quiet on the Western Front* as the landing
marines must dislodge the stubborn Japanese from their entrench-
ments. Similar compositions (especially around machine-gun em-
placements) angles, distances are employed, and once again Milestone favors long tracking shots interspersed with close-ups. Huge
tanks roll over the camera, metallic monsters which dramatize the
crushing power of war. The enemy pillboxes spout machine-gun
fire, while the American tanks pour liquid fire in response; men are
smashed by bullets and run from fortifications enveloped in flames.
Clearly war is no child's play. . . .

After a tense night sequence, again reminiscent of *All Quiet on
the Western Front* in its use of flares, the marines are ordered to
take a strategic ridge. But as they begin their long walk across the
plain before the ridge, they are suddenly pinned down by the
enemy rocket attack. Naval and air fire are unable to locate and
destroy the rocket launchers, and the attackers are stymied. The
colonel in desperation orders Anderson to lead a hand-picked patrol
behind enemy lines and take some captives who can be sweated for
information about the rockets. Anderson sets out with most of his

platoon and the British interpreter, Sgt. Johnson, colorfully played by the veteran Reginald Gardiner, and a young writer, Dickerman, stoically portrayed by Jack Webb. This nightmare patrol forms the spine of the story, and it seems harsh stuff indeed. One by one, the marines are killed and wounded, maimed and blinded. The Japanese employ snipers and deceitful ambushes to frustrate their mission, but finally the patrol captures several prisoners who have holed up in a cave. Now they must get back with the prisoners through the enemy lines and across rough terrain. Finally they make it back after enduring heavy casualties, including one soldier killed when he tries to attack the prisoners in his rage at the enemy.

Unfortunately, at this point, or for about the final half-hour, the film deteriorates into a rather standard adventure movie, with a mystery to solve. The Americans fight a battle of wits with the captured Japanese officers (who are presented as human and fallible), finally solving the mystery of the rockets in the nick of time. Marine aircraft pinpoint their positions on the key ridge and soon they are put out of action in a blaze of napalm bombs. The surviving marines, led by Lt. Anderson, are now free to advance, inspired by the words of a letter the dying Doc left with Dickerman, and Martin Milner's recitation of the Lord's Prayer. Widmark yells, "Give 'em hell," and the movie ends to the strains of the "Marine Hymn."

Yet this obligatory Hollywood ending should not blind the critic to the film's real strengths. In spite of action set pieces, the adventure plot, and the Cold War rhetoric concealed in Doc's dying message, *Halls of Montezuma* captures the outrage and despair of modern war. True it says that this horror is sometimes necessary, a position many would see as contradictory, but the film dramatically presents the individual tragedies of men at war. The underrated *Halls of Montezuma* must rank with *A Walk in the Sun* as a marred but interesting film, only a cut below Milestone's classic of the genre, *All Quiet on the Western Front*. The reprise of his Second World War movies in *Halls of Montezuma* also brings to a close the first cycle of Milestone's postwar films.

6

The Later Years

AS THE PREVIOUS chapter indicates, the immediate postwar years proved to be the last distinctive period in Lewis Milestone's long career. In the decade following *Halls of Montezuma* (1951) he would direct another eight films, concluding with *Mutiny on the Bounty* in 1962. However, this group of films, with the exception of *Pork Chop Hill* (1959), seem less a reprise of the director's earlier achievements than several desperate efforts to keep working. Even more markedly than in his earlier career, Milestone moved frenetically between pictures which varied widely in setting, style, and accomplishment. Again the director's development paralleled Hollywood history as he tried his hand at television, foreign productions, and remakes of earlier classics. None of these films really requires close analysis; therefore, the present chapter will survey them briefly in connection with the other developments of Milestone's later career.

Kangaroo (1952) was evidently a pragmatic project created by 20th Century–Fox to make use of·funds frozen in Australia, while cashing in on the popularity of location-shot, Technicolor adventure epics, such as *King Solomon's Mines* (1950). Milestone was packed off to Australia with a screenplay, his principal cast members, and a skeleton production crew. In Sydney he filled out the cast and crew with local talent, scouted locations, and soaked up local color. As always, he tried to make the best of a bad job by pleading with the studio to scrap the uttrely ridiculous script, a collection of Western clichés transposed from the American plains to the Australian outback, and give him a chance to do something serious with the setting. As he anticipated, the studio replied in the negative, and the director then·tried to shoot his way around the story as best he could.

etropolitan Opera star Patrice Munsel makes her film debut
Dame Nellie Melba in Melba (1953).

The result of Milestone's efforts is a curiously divided work, about half formula Western and half fictionalized travelogue. The plot, such as it is, involves Peter Lawford and Richard Boone as a pair of amiable rogues set adrift in nineteenth-century Australia. After some preliminary crimes, including a killing committed by Boone in the course of a holdup, they try to swindle an alcoholic rancher (Finlay Currie) by convincing him that Lawford is his long lost son. The stockman and his beautiful daughter (Maureen O'Hara) are easily convinced that the prodigal boy has come home, but the scheme unravels when Lawford predictably falls in love with O'Hara, kills Boone, and then surrenders to the long arm of the law (Chips Rafferty).

Among these inanities, Milestone manages to capture the feeling of the harsh Australian bush, particularly in a long cattle-drive sequence, which proves as good as anything in Ford's or Hawks's Westerns. Also notable are a range fire, a rain dance by the local aborigines, and a nice fight atop a wind tower. Cinematographer Charles G. Clarke proved capable of capturing the landscape, flora, and fauna of Australia in poetic documentary style.[1] Clarke created some beautiful Technicolor effects within the familiar Milestone patterns of pans and tracking shots. In particular, the ranch scenes seem very close to the compositions he employed in *Of Mice and Men* and *The Red Pony*. If the studio had provided any sort of a literary vehicle, *Kangaroo* might have become a fine film; as it is, the film proves to be only another interesting failure, "an antipodal Western," as one reviewer called it.[2]

Later in 1952 Milestone completed another film for 20th Century–Fox, the sixteenth screen adaptation of Victor Hugo's *Les Miserables* (1862). That he did little better with this literary and cinematic classic than with the hapless plot of *Kangaroo* seems to indicate the waning of the director's creative energies. In Milestone's defense, it should be said that Richard Murphy's screenplay telescopes all the novel's famous set-pieces into the cliché-ridden 104 minutes. Thus the director was forced to recreate the well-known episode of the Bishop's Candlesticks yet once more, in a seeming reprise of Richard Boleslawski's 1935 version. On the other hand, inherently exciting material like the famous chase through the Paris sewers also remains strangely inert. Casting does not aid Milestone's effort; Michael Rennie plays Jean Valjean like a British schoolmaster, and Robert Newton is a strangely subdued Inspector Javert, perhaps in reaction to what Milestone considered a hammy performance by Charles Laughton in 1935. The rest of the cast includes a number of

Hollywood types doing weak impersonations: Sylvia Sidney is an adequate Fantine, Debra Paget is a nubile Cosette, and Cameron Mitchell is a doughty Marius, Cosette's lover. Milestone once again pleaded to change the scripting, to add new things like the adventures of Gavorche, the street urchin, during the Revolution, but again studio management turned him down. His reaction was natural enough: "Oh, for Chrissake, its just a job; I'll do it and get it over with."[3] The final print bears every evidence of this attitude, and both the 1935 Hollywood version and the 1979 television adaptation were much livelier.

Milestone again ventured abroad in 1953, this time for United Artists, to film a biography of famous coloratura soprano Dame Nellie Melba. A number of musical biographies such as *The Great Caruso* (1951) and *The Great Gilbert and Sullivan* (1953) convinced studio management to launch the screen career of Metropolitan Opera star Patrice Munsel in an appropriate vehicle. Miss Munsel, possessed of a fine voice and fair presence, proved equal to the challenge, but the vehicle turned out to be another Hollywood travesty on the career of a struggling artist, retaining only the creation of a dessert called Peach Melba from the soprano's real life. As Milestone puts it: "My biopic of Dame Nellie Melba should have been called *Melba* like I should have been christened Napoleon."[4] Again stuck with a worthless script and an insipid cast (aside from Miss Munsel), Milestone opted for a documentary use of setting. Able to shoot on the Walton-on-Thames soundstage for only two weeks, Milestone filmed his ersatz biography at actual locations around London. The result is a visually striking anthology of "Great Moments from Music," with Patrice Munsel's efforts ranging from "Comin' Through the Rye" to the mad scene from *Lucia*.

After finishing *Melba*, Milestone stayed on in England to film another war story for the British Mayflower Studio. *They Who Dare* (1953, United States release in 1955) bears little resemblance to the usual Milestone war film. The final product is perhaps more influenced by Robert Westerby's screenplay from a true account of a commando-style raid on a German airfield in Rhodes. The accomplishment of the single objective recalls *A Walk in the Sun* and *Halls of Montezuma*, but Milestone's melodrama and action are missing. The military details are vague, and the characterization seems shallow. Bits of action and suspense recall the old Milestone, but too much time is wasted in dull talk or unmotivated histrionics. A very young-looking Dirk Bogarde changes unconvincingly from scared kid to a battle leader, while Denholm Eliot seems as little

178

LEWIS MILESTONE

motivated as a sniveling shirker. Milestone veteran Akim Tamiroff
and British actor Gerard Oury are much better as the Greek officers
who guide the Britishers to the Nazi base. The rousing action finale
seems more the old Milestone, but its flashy five minutes cannot
redeem the prolonged boredom of the long buildup.

Continuing to work abroad, Milestone next directed a joint
British-Italian venture, *La Vedova/The Widow* (1954), for a company called Venturini-Express. This little-seen effort seems to have
had limited release in the United States in 1957. It starred Patricia
Roc in a soap opera–ish love-triangle story from a novel by Susan
York with a screenplay by Louis Stevens. Roc is a wealthy widow in
love with a dashing race driver (Massimo Serato) who loses him to
the younger, prettier Anna Maria Ferrero. Akim Tamiroff again
appears in a supporting role. The triangle and its consequences are
predictable, and Milestone's part in the proceedings seems to be
simply to record the inevitable tragedy on film.

After this minor project it would be five years until Milestone
made another feature film, *Pork Chop Hill* (1959). During this
period the director worked on several unrealized projects, notably
King Kelly (1956–1957), a story reminiscent of *Citizen Kane*, with
Kirk Douglas (who made his film debut in *The Strange Love of
Martha Ivers* for Milestone in 1946).[5] In 1957 he also tried his hand
at television production, directing two programs in the series
"Alfred Hitchcock Presents," two for "Schlitz Playhouse," and one
for "Suspicion." The following year, the director also completed
two programs in the "Have Gun, Will Travel" series, which starred
Richard Boone (who made his screen debut in Milestone's
Kangaroo). Milestone did not find television direction to his liking,
and he has characterized it as a form of wage slavery.[6]

Pork Chop Hill (1959) proves the strongest of Milestone's late
films, and without the studio interference which considerably weakened its impact the movie might well rank with *A Walk in the Sun*.
It was produced by Sy Bartlett for the Melville Company and
released by United Artists. The film's star, Gregory Peck, also was
one of the movie's backers and thus exercised a great deal of control
over the production. Finally, it seems that Peck more than anyone
else interfered with Milestone's artistic vision in *Pork Chop Hill*.

The film fits neatly into the pattern of Milestone's war movies, as
his attempt to view the Korean conflict within the perspectives
created in his earlier efforts concerned with the First and Second
World Wars. Although the director's basic position on the necessity
of defensive wars seems unchanged from *Halls of Montezuma*,

why certain view pork chop hill as anti-war

made in 1951 during the Korean conflict, *Pork Chop Hill* perhaps recalls the antiwar attitudes of *All Quiet on the Western Front* more fully than any of his World War II movies. Six years after the Korean truce of 1953 restored the status quo of 1950, it would have been natural to emphasize the futility of the entire "police action." The battle for Pork Chop Hill seems especially absurd as it was fought essentially to provide psychological support for the American position at the truce talks then taking place less than a hundred miles away. At the time of the truce the site of bloody attack and counterattack became a sort of no-man's land, and the Americans retreated from their hard-won positions on Pork Chop Hill.

The screenplay by James R. Webb from General S. L. A. Marshall's factual account of the conflict (1956) provided Milestone with a realistic literary vehicle which he in turn translated to the effective film language he had learned in his earlier war movies. Of course, the screenplay prettied up the factual account. The lieutenant of King Company seems a rather confused individual in Marshall's book, a greenhorn officer who makes some rather funda- *clemons* mental military errors. In the Webb-Milestone version he is tougher and more efficient, perhaps because the real lieutenant was serving as a technical advisor for the film. It was Peck's conception of the part which doomed Milestone's vision; Peck converted the role into the more or less standard superman of World War II vintage and along the way also cut much of Milestone's careful development of other characters, his artistic counterpointing of the opposing forces, and his bitterly ironic conclusion.

The film's plot recalls *A Walk in the Sun* or *Halls of Montezuma;* an infantry company is sent to perform a dangerous mission. In this case, King Company must take and hold Pork Chop Hill, a rocky elevation of little strategic value, because it seems the enemy wants it. The general staff feels they must respond to this challenge or lose ground at the truce table. Peck as company commander leads a group which includes the various types found in American war films and played here by Harry Guardino, George Shibata, James Edwards, Woody Strode, Rip Torn, George Peppard, and Robert Blake in his first adult role. These fighting men and Lewis Gallo as a comic-relief information officer are all fine in their parts, though, as with *A Walk in the Sun,* the overlay of later roles somewhat vitiates our appreciation today of the effective casting of relative unknowns.

After a fierce assault which Milestone presents in near-documentary fashion, the weakened company digs in to hold the hilltop. The enemy reacts with "human wave" counterassaults and constant psychological pressure created by searchlights and loudspeakers. The sound track thus matches the visuals as a disembodied voice proclaims the ultimate futility of the company's sacrifices. Characteristically, Milestone also presents the confusion of combat; reinforcements fail to arrive, and the general staff procrastinates, unable to decide if the hill is really worth the cost of its defense. Finally King Company withdraws, bloodied but unbowed.

As the company is depicted in a series of longshots, Peck's voice provides the background narration. "So Pork Chop Hill was held, bought and paid for at the same price we commemorate in monuments at Bunker Hill and Gettysburg. . . . Millions live in freedom today because of what they did." Milestone's ending would have refocused on the hill, a neutralized no-man's land, with the simpler voice-over, "the men who fought here know what they did and the meaning of it." This message would prove appropriate for any of Milestone's war movies. Only the fighting men can know the full horror of war, and only they can judge the price of victory. These men, fighting and dying together, learn human lessons which escape most people. By implication, Milestone seems to say that the lesson of Pork Chop Hill was the futility of war.

However, the changes made in the director's version of the film weaken the harsh irony of this message. The careful counterpointing of the company with the enemy, with the general staff, with the truce talks, is all gone. As Milestone puts it, "*Pork Chop Hill* became a picture I am not proud of," because it looked as if it were "cut with a dull axe." All that remained was "Gregory Peck and a gun." Milestone undoubtedly overstated his position, as much excellent dramatic and visual work still exists in the final version. Even the near absurdity of the central situation still persists in spite of Peck's Hollywood heroics throughout and his rationalizing speech at the conclusion. Yet without the larger vision *Pork Chop Hill* does tend to become, in the director's words, "one more war movie."[7]

Pork Chop Hill must have impressed someone at Warner Brothers, however, as the following year Milestone was given the direction of *Ocean's Eleven* (1960), a comedy vehicle for Frank Sinatra and his "Rat Pack." The plot involves a gang of old army buddies out to heist the biggest casinos in Las Vegas under the leadership of Danny Ocean (Sinatra), the group's former combat leader. Perhaps Warners felt Milestone could orchestrate both the military operation of the plot and the comic turns of the cast. Given what he had to work with—a preposterous screenplay by Harry Brown and Charles

"Gregory Peck and a gun," all that Milestone thought was left of *Pork Chop Hill*.

Lederer and a cast including Dean Martin, Sammy Davis, Jr., Peter Lawford, Joey Bishop, and Buddy Lester—he did a fair job. But the movie never quite decides if it is being played straight or as a spoof; if it is an amoral satire of American values or a silly television variety show. It turns out as much a Las Vegas travelogue as anything else, a lightweight bit of fluff, in spite of fair performances by Angie Dickinson, Richard Conte, Cesar Romero, Ilka Chase, Akim Tamiroff, and Henry Silva, as well as guest spots by Red Skelton, Shirley MacLaine, and George Raft. Sinatra and his cohorts cut off the power and rob the five big casinos on New Year's Eve, but in an unmotivated twist of plot they are deprived of their ill-gotten gains. As entertainment the movie made money, but it proves completely forgettable as a film.

Milestone's next project also proved to be his last completed feature. This is the ill-starred *Mutiny on the Bounty* (1962). The story of this Hollywood disaster is long and complex, but the central figure in every sense is Marlon Brando, not Lewis Milestone.[8] By the end of the 1950s Hollywood had decided it could lure audiences away from their television sets only with the combination of "Big Name Stars" and "Spectacular Productions." Producer Aaron Rosenberg, working through MGM, came up with a plan to remake the 1935 classic *Mutiny on the Bounty* with Marlon Brando in the Clark Gable role. Brando resisted the idea for some time, but finally signed a contract early in 1960. Shooting was to have started on October 15 of the same year, but delays in the construction of a larger-than-life reproduction of the *Bounty* forced the starting date back to December 4. By this time the monsoon season had begun in the South Pacific, forcing the production back to Hollywood, where Brando soon chafed under the direction of British veteran Carol Reed. Reed quickly and sensibly abandoned ship.

Milestone came on board in February of 1961, perhaps chosen by the studio because of his earlier reputation as a film doctor. He expected to find the film near completion but instead discovered only a few usable scenes. In March Milestone and the rest of the production company again set sail for Tahiti, where the new director experienced the same rebellion from his star which had greeted Carol Reed earlier. Soon, as Milestone says "I wasn't directing Brando, just the rest of the cast. He was directing himself and ignoring everyone else. It was as if we were making two different pictures." (His remark foreshadows comments on Brando's performance in Francis Coppola's *Apocalypse Now*.) Work went very slowly, and later production virtually ceased when the scene switched to Pitcairn Island. This sequence was later reshot in Hollywood, with Milestone sitting in a dressing room, reading the newspaper, as Brando directed himself. The film was finally released for the holiday trade at the end of 1962; it proved a financial disaster, recouping less than half of its costs of $20 million plus. Milestone claims that Brando cost the production at least $6 million, and commented: "They deserve what they get when they give a ham actor, a petulant child, complete control of an expensive picture."

Blame is difficult to assess in this complicated scenario. Brando undoubtedly was a stubborn and petulant performer, but even Milestone admits that the star was promised many things which the producer did not deliver. Brando probably took on the project much as Milestone did, with the hope of making a fine film. Brando's vision depended on revising the 1935 screenplay and improvising his own part. Finally the studio would not let him do either, and they brought in Milestone, a careful craftsman and a hard taskmaster, to direct the mercurial Brando. Quite naturally the two men clashed almost immediately.

The result of their conflict was a very expensive production of strangely flawed film. The basic flaw, however, may have been with producer Rosenberg's original idea. Charles Nordhoff and James Hall's "H.M.S. Bounty" novels are not complex literary works, nor is *Mutiny on the Bounty*, in Frank Lloyd's 1935 screen version, a cinematic work of art. They are rousing adventure stories, the latter carried by bravura performances from Clark Gable and Charles Laughton. In many ways the Brando-Milestone version seems the best of all, though it is weakened by the very scope of the production. The basic vehicle simply seems incapable of bearing the weight of its 20 million dollar production or its three-hour running time.

Some elements of the film are excellent. For example, many of the performances prove superior to the earlier version. Brando is a darker, more complex Fletcher Christian than Clark Gable, while Trevor Howard creates a much better motivated Bligh than Charles Laughton. The supporting crew, in particular Richard Harris, Hugh Griffith, Richard Hadyn, and Gordon Jackson, brings a British authenticity to their smaller parts. Robert Surtees's brilliant color photography captures the incredible beauty of the Tahitian land- and seascapes, while Bronislau Kaper's symphonic score proves highly chromatic and affecting. The second-unit work, especially on the storms at sea, is especially good.

Yet the project never coheres into a film for the reasons outlined above; rather, it remains a big Hollywood production of a traditional property, which never lets the viewer forget he is watching a movie. As such, it is every bit as boring as critics found it, then and now. Though Milestone tried his best to save the sinking production, he deserves his share of the blame for its ultimate failure. However, Marlon Brando is more culpable than the aging director, as he became the actual *auteur*. Probably it was a project which never should have been begun.

Mutiny on the Bounty proved to be Milestone's final completed

[Overleaf] Two generations of matinee idols play Fletcher Christian in *Mutiny on the Bounty*: (left) Clark Gable with Mamo in Frank Lloyd's 1935 classic; (right) Marlon Brando with Tarita in Lewis Milestone's 1962 disaster.

film. In 1963 he began work on a film version of *PT 109*, Robert Donovan's 1961 factual book about President John F. Kennedy's experiences as a patrol-torpedo boat commander during World War II. Jack L. Warner personally handled the production for Warner Brothers because of his long friendship with Kennedy. The controversial nature of the project (Kennedy would have run for reelection in 1964) caused Warner to opt for a rather simplistic script by Richard Breen which combines the worst of service-comedy and combat-adventure genres. According to Lewis Gallo, assistant director on the film, Milestone saw the book as a potentially fine vehicle centered on the maturation of a young man in combat experience.[9] Milestone carefully prepared his production and shot for twenty-four days before Warner removed him, ostensibly because "satisfactory progress was not being made."[10] The real reason seemed a fear of any political controversy over the picture. The movie was safely finished by Leslie Martison; and, in spite of a fair performance by Cliff Robertson as Kennedy, it proved a mediocre effort.

In 1963 Milestone also directed two more television programs, one for the series "Arrest and Trial," another for "The Richard Boone Show." Over the following years he contemplated several unrealized projects, including a comedy from a story about a lady burglar by Gelett Burgess.[11] In 1965 Milestone contracted to direct an episode in a joint British-Italian-American production, *La Guera Seno—The Dirty Game*, for American International. The director's declining health prevented the completion of this assignment, and he was replaced by Terence Young, director of several James Bond movies. Health problems of several sorts have plagued Milestone in later years, though he continued to keep up with the Hollywood scene. One personal project was an uncompleted autobiography, tentatively entitled *Milestones*.

In 1978 the director was shocked by the death of his wife and by a serious stroke which has impaired his movement. He lived in his modest Beverly Hills home of forty years, surrounded by his collection of books and paintings, often visited by his many friends from every era of Hollywood history. As Milestone approached his eight-fifth birthday, the Directors Guild honored him with a Pioneer Tribute on July 28, 1979. No Hollywood pioneer better deserved such recognition and respect than the director of *All Quiet on the Western Front* and *Of Mice and Men,* a dozen other fine films, and twenty-four other entertaining movies. After a succession of illnesses Lewis Milestone died on September 25, 1980, at the UCLA Medical Center, five days before his eighty-fifth birthday.

7

The Quiet Craftsman

FROM THE OUTSET the present study has stressed Lewis Milestone's place as an important figure in the Hollywood studio period, that cinematic peak which began shortly after World War I and lasted until sometime after World War II. Over these years the studio system brought together myriad talents for the creation of movie entertainment and film art which set the standards for the world. Arriving in 1919, Milestone soon became one of the more successful directors on the Hollywood scene in terms of both entertainment and art. Between 1925 and 1962 he created thirty-eight features: most of them are entertaining pictures; at least a dozen are interesting movies, about half a dozen are good films, and two, *All Quiet on the Western Front* and *Of Mice and Men,* are classics. Several of his films, particularly his antiwar classic, were influential in terms of technical and artistic developments. Even his less successful efforts reflect the general developments of Hollywood history during this era. Thus Lewis Milestone proves one of the more important directors, both historically and artistically, of the Hollywood studio period.

Milestone's creativity was rooted in the studio system. Both his best and his worst movies resulted from his pragmatic commitment to the cinematic transformation of literary properties presented by the production system. This commitment to his literary sources provided Milestone with a careful working method which facilitated the success of his stronger efforts; at the same time, it limited his creative transformation of weaker properties, resulting in a number of mediocre program fillers. However, the technical expertise he acquired from years of editing evolved into an eclectic cinema style which enlivened even his dullest efforts and made possible the filmic artistry of his classic works. This complex yet efficient style was

189

The climactic moments of Lewis Milestone's greatest films: (top) the death of Sergeant Katczinsky in All Quiet on the Western Front *(1930); (bottom), just before Curly's wife is murdered in* Of Mice and Men *(1939).*

blended from the Expressionism of the silent screen and the Realism which evolved with sound. Milestone's films prove very diverse in subject and theme, very eclectic in style and mode, and very uneven in quality. Essentially, Milestone was an intelligent, literate, and creative director working within the studio system; both his strong points and his corresponding limitations were generated by that Hollywood system.

As this study has demonstrated, Milestone's career provides consistent parallels with Hollywood history between 1919 and 1962. Arriving in the early 1920s he grew up with Hollywood and achieved his first success within the contexts provided by the golden years of the silent screen. He directed his first feature, *Seven Sinners*, in 1925, and by 1927 he had earned the Academy Award for Best Comedy Director with *Two Arabian Knights*, a rough-and-ready comedy in the style of *What Price Glory?* His two films of 1928, *The Garden of Eden*, a sophisticated comedy in the Lubitsch manner, and *The Racket*, a tough gangster classic perhaps influenced by von Sternberg, also won wide acclaim.

However, it was not until the introduction of sound that Milestone found his stride as a cinematic artist. The inherent realism of sound balanced the devices of Expressionism he learned from the masters of silent film in the creation of his first classic, *All Quiet on the Western Front*, in 1930. This brilliant antiwar film, from the harshly realistic novel by Erich Maria Remarque, established Milestone as a leading young director, earning him another academy award for Best Direction. *All Quiet on the Western Front* also helped to free the early sound film from the constrictions of recording technology and a theatrical point of view. His succeeding sound films, *The Front Page* (1931) and *Rain* (1932), from two successful stage vehicles, confirmed his importance on the Hollywood scene and remain somewhat neglected movies of the early sound era. The unsuccessful *Hallelujah, I'm a Bum* (1933) unfortunately prefigured a succession of studio programmers that Milestone made in the middle 1930s for Paramount.

Milestone regained his artistic pace with *The General Died at Dawn* in 1936, an exciting adventure story with a provocative script by leftist playwright Clifford Odets which dramatized the growing tensions between democracy and totalitarianism. After this film, however, Milestone's career was again stalled with a succession of uncompleted projects and legal tangles. Finally, in 1939, he returned to direction with his second masterpiece, the filmic adaptation of John Steinbeck's *Of Mice and Men*. In many ways *Of Mice and Men* proves to be the director's most fully satisfying film, one in which his developing liberal realism fully captures the essence of Steinbeck's harsh vision. Again the director failed to maintain this high standard of artistry as he fell back to grinding out light comedies for RKO.

A new cycle in his career began with Pearl Harbor and Hollywood's return to the war movie. During the war Milestone made five films in the genre, including *Edge of Darkness* (1943), concerned with the Nazi occupation of Norway, *The North Star* (1943), from a Lillian Hellman script about civilian resistance on the Eastern Front, and *The Purple Heart* (1944), about the show trial of American airmen following the first bombing raid on Japan. However, it was *A Walk in the Sun* (1945), from the understated, realistic novel by Harry Brown, which proved Milestone's best war effort after *All Quiet on the Western Front*. Although Milestone had changed his intellectual position from pacificism to a conviction that democracy had to be defended with force, *A Walk in the Sun* partially recreates the thoughtful, poignant, and ironic vision of his earlier war classic.

The postwar period proved a reprise of some of Milestone's more successful earlier efforts. *The Strange Love of Martha Ivers* (1946), with a strong screenplay by Robert Rossen, was an interesting melodrama in the mode of *film noir*. *Arch of Triumph* (1948) failed despite the fact it was adapted from another fine novel by Erich Maria Remarque. However, another Steinbeck adaptation, *The Red Pony* (1949), with a screenplay by the author, recaptured at least partially the artistic integrity displayed in *Of Mice and Men*. Finally, *Halls of Montezuma* (1951) the story of a Marine landing in the Pacific, recreated the patterns of his more successful World War II movies. The films of Milestone's later career, aside from *Pork Chop Hill* (1959), a realistic Korean War story, seem less a reprise of earlier efforts than desperate attempts to stay in the business during the years when Hollywood was reeling from the collapse of the studio system. His final work includes several foreign-made films, several television programs, and several unrealized or uncompleted projects. The ill-starred *Mutiny on the Bounty* (1962) marked the end of Milestone's active career.

Yet for all the high points and low spots of his very uneven career, Milestone directed more good films than many directors awarded higher places in the critical pantheon of Hollywood. Some of the so-called *auteurs* command attention out of all proportion to their cinematic achievements in comparison with a literate, intelligent, and creative director like Milestone; the continual reevaluation of Hollywood history will no doubt correct some of these balances of critical reputation. When this reevaluation occurs Lewis Milestone will be recognized as one of the more important directors of the Hollywood studio period. Milestone's films deserve reviewing and will repay critical reexamination; this study hopes to encourage such reconsideration. If it does, it will have rendered some critical justice to its subject, Lewis Milestone, an important director and a fine man.

Notes and References

Preface

1. Andrew Sarris, *The American Film* (New York: Dutton, 1968), pp. 162–63.

Chapter One

1. All quotations from Charles Higham and Joel Greenberg, "Lewis Milestone," in *The Celluloid Muse: Hollywood Directors Speak* (Chicago, 1969), pp. 158, 162, 168, 166.
2. Unpublished article, written about 1949, located by the author among Milestone's papers.
3. Higham and Greenberg, p. 171.
4. Charles Shibuk, *An Index to the Films of Lewis Milestone* (Theodore Huff Memorial Film Society, 1958), p. 3.
5. Located by the author in Milestone's papers, undated.
6. Higham and Greenberg, p. 171.
7. Unpublished reminiscence of Milestone, made available to the author by Mr. Gallo.
8. Ibid.
9. Barry Freidkin, unpublished interview with Lewis Milestone, UCLA, 1966.
10. Shibuk, p. 3.
11. Unpublished article, written about 1949, located by the author among Milestone's papers.
12. Unpublished, undated article, located by the author among Milestone's papers.
13. Author's unpublished interview with Lewis Milestone, Beverly Hills, May 15, 1979.
14. "The Reign of the Director," *New Theatre and Film*, March 1937.
15. Freidkin interview, 1966.
16. Ibid.
17. Freidkin interview, 1966: author's interview, 1979.
18. David L. Parker and Burton J. Shapiro, "Lewis Milestone," in *Close Up: The Contract Director,* ed. Jon Tuska (Metuchen, N.J.: Scarecrow, 1976), p. 299.
19. Author's interview, 1979.
20. Unpublished autobiographical fragment by Lewis Milestone.

21. Parker and Shapiro, p. 299.

22. Unpublished autobiographical fragment by Lewis Milestone.

23. Author's interview, 1979.

24. Ibid.

25. Parker and Shapiro, p. 299.

26. Higham and Greenberg, p. 145.

27. Parker and Shapiro, p. 300.

28. Mark Lambert, unpublished interview with Lewis Milestone, UCLA, 1968.

29. Higham and Greenberg, p. 145.

30. Lambert interview, 1968.

31. Author's interview, 1979.

32. Parker and Shapiro, p. 300.

33. Lambert interview, 1968.

34. Ibid.

35. Parker and Shapiro, p. 301.

36. Author's interview, 1979.

37. Parker and Shapiro, p. 301.

38. Ibid., p. 303

39. Higham and Greenberg, pp. 146–47.

40. Parker and Shapiro, pp. 304–305.

41. Ibid., p. 304

42. See Gerald M. Perry, "*The Racket:* A 'Lost' Gangster Classic," *Velvet Light Trap* 14 (Winter 1975): 6–9. Howard Hughes evidently liked the picture: he remade it in 1951 with John Cromwell directing.

43. Higham and Greenburg, p. 149.

Chapter Two

1. Higham and Greenberg, p. 150.

2. Ibid., p. 151.

3. Ibid., p. 171.

4. Ibid., p. 150.

5. The quotation is from the Fawcett-Crest edition of the novel (1979), the most readily available; all page references to this edition are in the text.

6. In the interview with the author in 1979, Milestone said that he thought about superimposing a typewriter spelling out the ironic message.

7. Higham and Greenberg, p. 154.

8. Milestone says that the final shot was suggested by someone from the studio (Author's interview, 1979).

9. Suzanne Howes, *Wilhelm Meister and His English Kinsmen* (New York: AMS Press, 1966) p. 4.

10. Milestone used the dugout as a backup set when bad weather prevented outdoor shooting (Author's interview, 1979).

11. Digby Diehl, "An Interview with Lewis Milestone," *Action* 7 (July-August 1972): 6.

12. Of course, it could have been much worse. Milestone says that the studio wanted a "happy ending," a request he squelched by suggesting that they could have the Germans win the war (Author's interview, 1979).

13. Higham and Greenberg, p. 136.

14. Ben Hecht and Charles MacArthur, *The Front Page* (New York: Covici, Friede, 1928), "Epilogue," pp. 191–92.

15. Herbert Feinstein, "An Interview with Lewis Milestone," *Film Culture* 34 (September 1964): 25.

16. Higham and Greenberg, p. 136.

17. Authors interview, 1979.

18. Parker and Shapiro, p. 309

19. Rudy Behlmer, ed., *Memo From David O. Selznick* (New York: Avon, 1972), pp. 72–73.

20. Higham and Greenberg, p. 156.

21. A scene from *Rain* is the only interesting sequence in *Jeanne Eagels* (1957), directed by George Sidney and starring an inept Kim Novak as the ill-fated actress.

22. As well as to the real woman, if *Momie Dearest*, her daughter's autobiography, is to be believed.

23. Author's interview, 1979.

24. Parker and Shapiro, p. 312.

25. A long, rambling essay by Jon Tuska provides much additional information about the multiple versions of Maugham's story: "Rain: A Cinematograph," *Views and Reviews* 3 (Spring 1972): 4–14; 4 (Fall 1972): 20–31.

26. Parker and Shapiro, p. 313.

27. Higham and Greenberg, p. 157. However, in his article "*Hallelujah, I'm a Bum:* A Reappraisal," *Film Collector* 48 (Fall 1975): 37–38, Edward Watz claims d'Arrast quit.

28. Higham and Greenberg, p. 157.

29. Richard Rodgers, *Musical Stages* (New York: Random House, 1975), p. 155.

30. Watz, p. 37.

Chapter Three

1. Shibuk, p. 16.

2. Kingsley Canham, "Milestone: The Unpredictable Fundamentalist," in *The Hollywood Professionals* (Cranbury, N.J., 1974), II, 118.

3. Bob Thomas, *King Cohn* (New York: Doubleday 1967), p. 100.

4. Ibid., p. 101.

5. *New York Times*, November 29, 1934, p. 33.

6. See John Baxter, *Hollywood in the Thirties* (New York, 1968).

7. Higham and Greenberg, p. 158.

8. See Thomas Bohn and Richard Stromgren, *Light and Shadows* (Sherman Oaks, California: Alfred, 1978), pp. 205–207, on the importance of Hans Dreier's sets in creating the Paramount look.

9. Baxter, p. 98.

10. For the complicated history of the remark as well as a fine summation of Odets's career see Gerald Weales, *Clifford Odets: Playwright* (New York: Pegasus, 1971), p. 112. Excerpts from the screenplay appeared in *New Masses* 20 (July 28, 1936): 12–13; a clear indication of 1930s radical chic.

11. Milestone discusses some of the censorship problems, including the appearance on the set of a real Chinese general, in an article on the film in *Stage* 14: 1 (October 1936): 42.

12. *New York Times* review by Frank S. Nugent, September 3, 1936, p. 17.

13. Parker and Shapiro, p. 318.

14. Ibid. The film finally was released in 1941 by Roach.

15. Ibid., p. 319.

16. Author's interview, 1979.

17. Quentin Reynolds, "That's How Pictures Are Born: *Of Mice and Men*," *Collier's*, January 1940, pp. 14–15.

18. William K. Everson, *The Films of Hal Roach* (New York: Museum of Modern Art, 1971), p. 77.

19. *John Steinbeck: A Life In Letters*, ed. Elaine Steinbeck and Robert Wallsten (New York: Viking, 1975), p. 195.

20. Steinbeck had several other works adapted as films, and he wrote several screenplays, the most important of which was *Viva Zapata!* for Elia Kazan in 1952. Robert E. Morsberger has edited the screenplay (New York: Viking, 1975).

21. Page references are to the Bantam Pathfinder edition (New York, 1971), which is the most widely available.

22. The opening is very reminiscent of that of Pare Lorentz's documentary *The River* (1937), which had a wide influence on Hollywood directors of a serious bent. (John Steinbeck later worked with Lorentz.)

23. The picture can be found in *Years of Protest*, edited by Jack Salzman and Barry Wallenstein (New York: Pegasus 1967), p. 73.

24. Peter Lisca, *The Wide World of John Steinbeck* (New Brunswick, N.J.: Rutgers University Press, 1958), p. 140. Professor Lisca cites a letter of Steinbeck to his literary agent dated March 1938 as the source of this statement.

25. George is not handcuffed as Andrew Sarris states in his essay "Toward a Theory of Film History," which prefaces *The American Cinema* (New York: Dutton, 1968), p. 20.

26. Higham and Greenberg, p. 162.

Chapter Four

1. Ezra Goodman, "Directed by Lewis Milestone," *Theater Arts*, February 1943, p. 111.

2. Bosley Crowther, *New York Times*, April 10, 1943, p. 12.

3. Higham and Greenberg, p. 162.

4. Unsigned review in *Newsweek*, April 19, 1943, p. 74.

5. *New York Times*, April 10, 1943, p. 10.

6. *New York Times*, November 5, 1943, 23.

7. *Mission to Moscow*, a filmed version of former American Ambassador Davies's Russian diary, proved particularly controversial, as it whitewashed Stalinism and the purge trials of the 1930s. Interestingly enough, the film featured Walter Huston and Ann Harding as Mr. and Mrs. Davies; as they also play Kurin and Sophia in *The North Star*, Mary McCarthy wondered in a review if the American couple decided to retire to a farm commune. See "Mary McCarthy Goes to the Movies," *Film Comment*, January-February 1976, p. 33. The Hearst papers even attacked *The North Star* as Red propaganda; see the *Los Angeles Examiner*, December 27, 1943, p. 23.

8. *Nation* 157 (October 30, 1943): 509.

9. *Film Comment*, January-February 1976, p. 33.

10. Lillian Hellman, *An Unfinished Woman* Boston: Little, Brown, 1969), p. 125.

11. Lillian Hellman, *The North Star* (New York: Viking, 1943)

12. Milestone does complain about Goldwyn's interference in the production, so perhaps some of the schmaltz came from the producer. See Higham and Greenberg, p. 162.

13. *The North Star* was reissued as *Armored Attack* in the late 1950s, with voiceover narration indicating that the Russian people were fine folks, but their leaders could not be trusted.

14. *Newsweek*, March 20, 1944, pp. 90–91, quotes a Walter Winchell radio broadcast as the source of this information.

15. Ibid.

16. Higham and Greenberg, p. 163.

17. *Film Comment*, January-February, 1976, p. 34.

18. *New Republic* 110 (May 27, 1944): 407.

19. Ibid.

20. *New York Times*, March 9, 1944, p. 15.

21. Quoted in Parker and Shapiro, p. 326.

22. Feinstein: interview, p. 26.

23. Richard MacCann: interview, 1950.

24. Bosley Crowther, *New York Times*: January 12, 1946, 10

25. *A Walk in the Sun* (New York: Knopf, 1944).

26. Brown wrote several more novels, as well as screenplays including *A Place in the Sun* (1951) (From Theodore Dreiser's *An American Tragedy*,

1925), which won him an Academy Award, and two failures for Milestone—
Arch of Triumph (1948) and *Ocean's Eleven* (1960).

27. Higham and Greenberg, p. 163.

28. *Nation* 162 (January 5, 1946): 24.

29. Perhaps these are the freeze frames Milestone claims he pioneered in
the movie (Freidkin interview, 1966); the present writer did not find any in
the prints he viewed. Of course, the freeze frame had been developed long
before; it probably was first used in an artistically significant manner by D.
W. Griffith in *A Corner in Wheat* (1908), an important film made from a
Frank Norris story.

Chapter Five

1. Parker and Shapiro, p. 332.

2. Ibid., p. 333.

3. Author's interview, 1979.

4. Higham and Greenberg, p. 164.

5. Ibid.

6. The development of *film noir* was undoubtedly influenced by the
influx of many European exiles in the 1930s and 1940s. Filmmakers like
Fritz Lang, Otto Preminger, and Alfred Hitchcock helped create a revival
of German Expressionism in Hollywood during this period.

7. Frederick W. Sternfield's article "The Strange Music of Martha
Ivers," *Hollywood Quarterly* 2 (1947): 242–51, provides an excellent musical
analysis of Rozsa's score.

8. Higham and Greenberg, p. 465.

9. Heflin and Stanwyck were also paired in *B. F.'s Daughter* (1948) and
East Side, West Side (1949).

10. Patrick was a prolific though somewhat less than serious screenwriter,
as his credits indicate; they include *Battle of Broadway* (1938), *Enchant-
ment* (1948), *Three Coins in the Fountain* (1954), and *High Society* (1956).

11. Higham and Greenberg, p. 165.

12. Perhaps some of these problems are inherent in the novel itself.
Literary critic Diana Trilling talked about "a certain Humphrey Bogart-
esque cynicism" in the book (*Nation* 162 [February 16, 1946]: 203). But
novelist Hamilton Basso, who compares the book with Hemingway's major
works, insists that it seems a novel written without a thought of Hollywood
(*New Yorker*, [January 26, 1946], p. 78).

13. Parker and Shapiro, p. 352.

14. Author's interview, 1979.

15. Ibid. Steinbeck also discussed the project with Victor Fleming and
Spencer Tracy. See *Steinbeck: A Life in Letters*, ed. Elaine Steinbeck and
Robert Wallsten (New York: Viking Press, 1975), pp. 195–96.

16. Lisca, p. 93.

17. Perhaps because of the use of the name Jody in *The Yearling* (1947), a very similar story.

18. Peter Miles, brother of Gigi, Gerald, and Janine Perreau, appeared in eight films between 1947 and 1951, none of any importance other than *The Red Pony*.

19. *The Red Pony, A Cutting Continuity* (Republic Studios, 1949), p. 1.

20. Ibid., p. 40 (this key passage follows closely the wording of Steinbeck's original story).

21. In an unpublished paper read at the Popular Culture Association Convention in 1975, Warren French argues quite persuasively that Steinbeck's changes in the screenplay can be attributed to his mellowing attitudes in a successful middle age.

22. In particular, see Karel Reisz, "Milestone and War," *Sequence*, 1950.

23. MacCann interview, 1959.

24. Higham and Greenberg, p. 166.

25. *New York Times*, January 6, 1951, 9.

26. His other screenwriting credits include *Broken Arrow* (1950), *My Six Convicts* (1952), and *The Juggler* (1953).

Chapter Six

1. Clarke provides a good bit of background on the film in his article "We Filmed *Kangaroo* Entirely in Australia," *American Cinematographer* 33 (July 1952): 292–93, 315–17.

2. Bosley Crowther, *New York Times*, May 17, 1952, p. 22.

3. Higham and Greenberg, p. 168.

4. Ibid.

5. Parker and Shapiro, p. 341.

6. Higham and Greenberg, p. 172.

7. Dale Mackey interview, 1959.

8. The best account of production problems is provided by Bill Davidson, "The Mutiny of Marlon Brando," *Saturday Evening Post*, June 16, 1962, pp. 18–23. Also see Darin Scot, "Photographing Mutiny on the Bounty, *American Cinematographer* 44 (February 1963): 90–91, 114–15.

9. Unpublished reminiscence about Lewis Milestone, made available to the writer by Mr. Gallo.

10. Parker and Shapiro, p. 344.

11. Higham and Greenberg, p. 171.

Selected Bibliography

The following bibliography lists only those works which contribute significantly to an understanding of Lewis Milestone and his films; many other studies which yield less important insights are mentioned in the "Notes and References."

Primary Sources

MILESTONE, LEWIS. "First Aid for a Sick Giant." from *New Republic*, January 31, 1949. Reprinted in *Hollywood Directors: 1941–1976*, ed. Richard Koszarski. New York: Oxford University Press, 1977, pp. 149–54. An accurate estimate of Hollywood in the post-war period.

————. "The Reign of the Director," from *New Theatre and Film*, March 1937. Reprinted in *Hollywood Directors: 1914–1940*, ed. Richard Koszarski. New York: Oxford University Press, 1976, pp. 318–20. Interesting short article about the decline of the Hollywood director.

Secondary Sources

BAXTER, JOHN. *Hollywood in the Thirties*. New York: A. S. Barnes, 1968, pp. 96–100. A short, insightful, laudatory estimate of Milestone's work during the Depression decade.

CANHAM, KINGSLEY. "Milestone: The Unpredictable Fundamentalist," in *The Hollywood Professionals*, Cranberry, N.J.: 69–119. A thorough discussion of the career and the major films, somewhat subjective in its approach.

CLARKE, CHARLES G. "We Filmed *Kangaroo* Entirely in Australia," *American Cinematographer* 33 (1952): 292–93, 315–17. A short account of the difficulties of location shooting.

DAVIDSON, BILL. "The Mutiny of Marlon Brando," *Saturday Evening Post*, June 16, 1962, pp. 18–23. The best source of information on the controversial remake of *Mutiny on the Bounty*.

DIEHL, DIGBY. "An Interview with Lewis Milestone," *Action*, July-August 1972, pp. 4–11. This important interview focuses on *All Quiet on the Western Front*.

EVERSON, WILLIAM K. "Thoughts on a Great Adaptation," in *The Modern American Novel and the Movies*, ed. Gerald Peary and Roger Shatzkin. New York: Ungar, 1978, pp. 63–69. A fine essay on *Of Mice and Men* by a veteran film historian.

FEINSTEIN, HERBERT. "An Interview with Lewis Milestone," *Film Culture*, September 1964, pp. 25–27. This short interview contains several interesting points.

GOODMAN, EZRA. "Directed by Lewis Milestone," *Theater Arts*, February 1943, pp. 111–19. An interesting discussion of the director's technique, which focuses on *Edge of Darkness*.

HIGHAM, CHARLES, and GREENBERG, JOEL. "Lewis Milestone," in *The Celluloid Muse: Hollywood Directors Speak*. Chicago: Regnery, 1969, pp. 144–72. A long, thorough interview.

PARKER, DAVID L. and SHAPIRO, BURTON J. "Lewis Milestone," in *Close Up: The Contract Director*, ed. Jon Tuska. Metuchean, N.J.: Scarecrow, 1976, pp. 299–350.

PERRY, GERALD M. "The Racket: A 'Lost' Gangster Classic." *Velvet Light Trap*, Winter 1975, pp. 6–9. Interesting details on this pioneering film.

REISZ, KAREL. "Milestone and War," *Sequence*, 1950. A thoughtful article on Milestone's changing attitudes toward war by a Czech refugee film director.

REYNOLDS, QUENTIN. "That's How Pictures Are Born: *Of Mice and Men*." *Collier's*, January 6, 1940, pp. 14–15. Good background on what is perhaps the director's best film.

SCOT, DARIN. "Photographing *Mutiny on the Bounty*," *American Cinematographer*, February 1963, pp. 90–91, 114–15. Interesting insights into the production difficulties on this troublesome project.

SHIBUK, CHARLES. *An Index to the Films of Lewis Milestone*. Theodore Huff Memorial Film Society, 1958. A short introduction and filmography.

STERNFELD, FREDERICK W. "The Strange Music of Martha Ivers," *Hollywood Quarterly*, 2 (1947): 242–51. An excellent article on Miklos Rozsa's score for *The Strange Love of Martha Ivers*.

TUSKA, JON. "Rain: A Cinematograph," *Views and Reviews*, Spring 1972, pp. 4–14; Fall 1972, pp. 20–31. A thorough consideration of all the filmed versions of the famous Somerset Maugham story.

WATZ, EDWARD. "*Hallelujah, I'm a Bum*: A Reappraisal." *Classic Film Collector*, Fall 1975, pp. 37–38. Good background information on this strange Depression musical.

Filmography

SEVEN SINNERS (Warner Brothers, 1925)
Screenplay: Lewis Milestone, Darryl F. Zanuck
Photography: David Abel
Cast: Marie Prevost, Clive Brook, John Patrick, Charles Conklin
Running Time: 76 minutes
New York Preview: November 7, 1925 (all New York release dates in this
   filmography are from Karl Thiede's checklist, appended to David L.
   Parker and Burton J. Shapiro's "Lewis Milestone," in *Close Up: The
   Contract Director*)

THE CAVEMAN (Warner Brothers, 1926)
Screenplay: Darryl F. Zanuck (from a story by Gelet Burgess)
Photography: David Abel
Cast: Matt Moore, Marie Prevost, John Patick, Myrna Loy, Phillis Haver,
   Hedda Hopper
Running Time: 75 minutes
New York Preview: February 6, 1926

THE NEW KLONDIKE (Paramount, 1926)
Screenplay: Thomas J. Geraghty (from a story by Ring Lardner)
Photography: Alvin Wyckoff
Cast: Thomas Meighan, Lisa Lee, Paul Kelly, Hallie Manning, Robert
   Craig
Running Time: 83 minutes
New York Preview: March 15, 1926

TWO ARABIAN KNIGHTS (Caddo Company, United Artists, 1927)
Screenplay: James T. O'Donohue, Wallace Smith (from a story by Donald
   McGibney)

Photography: Tony Gaudio, Joseph August
Art Direction: William Cameron Menzies
Cast: William Boyd, Mary Astor, Louis Wolheim, Michael Vavitch, Ian
    Keith
Running Time; 92 minutes
New York Preview: September 23, 1927
Not currently available for sale or rental

THE GARDEN OF EDEN (United Artists, 1928)
Screenplay: Hans Kraly (from a play by Rudolf Bernauer and Rudolf
    Oesterreicher)
Photography: John Arnold
Art Direction: William Cameron Menzies
Editing: John Orlando
Cast: Corinne Griffith, Louise Dresser, Lowell Sherman, Maude George,
    Charles Ray
Running Time: 81 minutes
New York Preview: February 4, 1928
Availability: 16mm sale, Cinema 8 (Chester, Conn., also on videotape),
    Griggs Moviedrome (Nutley, N.J.), Select Films (New York); rental,
    Kit Parker Films (Carmel Valley, Calif.) and others. This is the first of
    Milestone's films to be still widely available

THE RACKET (Caddo Company/Paramount, 1928)
Screenplay: Harry Behn, Del Andrews (from a play by Bartlett Cormack)
Photography: Tony Gaudio
Editing: Tom Miranda
Cast: Thomas Meighan, Marie Prevost, Louis Wolheim, George Stone,
    John Darrow
Running Time: 85 minutes
New York Preview: June 30, 1928
Not currently available for sale or rental

BETRAYAL (Paramount, 1929)
Production: David O. Selznick
Screenplay: Hans Kraly (from a story by Victor Schertzinger, Nicholas
    Saussanin)
Photography: Henry Gerard
Art Direction: Hans Dreier
Editing: Del Andrews
Cast: Emil Jennings, Esther Ralston, Gary Cooper, Jada Weller, Douglas
    Haig

Running Time: 73 1/2 minutes
New York Preview: May 11, 1929

NEW YORK NIGHTS (United Artists, 1929)
Production: Joseph M. Schenck
Screenplay: Jules Futhman (from a play, *Tin Pan Alley*, by Hugh Stanislaus
    Strange)
Photography: Ray June
Editing: Hal Kern
Songs: Al Jolson, Ballard MacDonald, Dave Dreyer
Cast: Norma Talmadge, Gilbert Roland, John Wray, Lilyan Tashman, Mary
    Doran, Roscoe Karns
Running Time: 82 1/2 minutes
New York Preview: December 28, 1929
16mm rental: Film Classic Exchange (Los Angeles)

ALL QUIET ON THE WESTERN FRONT (Universal, 1930)
Production: Carl Laemmle, Jr.
Screenplay: Maxwell Anderson, Del Andrews, George Abbot (from a novel
    by Erich Maria Remarque)
Dialogue Direction: George Cukor
Photography: Arthur Edeson, Karl Freund, Tony Gaudio (2nd camera)
Special Effects Photography: Frank H. Booth
Art Direction: Charles D. Hall, William R. Schmidt
Editing: Edgar Adams, Milton Carruth
Music and Synchronization: David Broekman
Cast: Lew Ayres (Paul Baumer), Louis Wolheim (Katczinsky), John Wray
    (Himmelstoss), Raymond Griffith (Gerard Duval), George "Slim"
    Summerville (Tjaden)
Running Time: 138 minutes
New York Preview: April 29, 1930
Availability: 16mm rental and lease, Universal 16 (New York);
Also for rent from Swank Films and other regional distributors

THE FRONT PAGE (Caddo Company/United Artists, 1931)
Production: Howard Hughes
Screenplay: Bartlett Cormack (from a play by Ben Hecht, Charles Mac-
    Arthur)
Photography: Tony Gaudio, Hal Mohr, Glen McWilliams
Art Direction: Richard Day
Editing: W. Duncan Mansfield

Cast: Adolphe Menjou (Walter Burns), Pat O'Brien (Hildy Johnson), Mary
  Brian (Peggy), Walter Catlett (Murphy)
Running Time: 90 minutes
New York Preview: April 4, 1931
Availability: sale: 16mm and videotape, Cinema 8 (Chester, Conn.), 16mm,
  Images (Rye, N.Y.): 16mm rental, Budget Films (Los Angeles) and
  others

RAIN (United Artists, 1932)
Screenplay: Maxwell Anderson (from a play by John Colton and Clemm-
  ence Randolph from a story by Somerset Maugham)
Photography: Oliver Marsh
Art Direction: Richard Day
Editing: W. Duncan Mansfield
Cast: Joan Crawford (Sadie Thompson), Walter Huston (Reverend David-
  son), William Gargan (Sgt. O'Hara), Matt Moore (Doctor MacPhail),
  Beulah Bondi (Mrs. Davidson), Kendall Lee (Mrs. MacPhail), Guy
  Kibbee (Trader Horn)
Running Time: 85 minutes
New York Preview: October 22, 1932
Availability: 16mm sale, Learning Corporation of America (New York);
  Super-8mm and videotape sale, Cinema 8 (Chester, Conn.); 16mm
  rental, Budget Films (Los Angeles), Kit Parker Films (Carmel Valley,
  Calif.), MacMillan (Mt. Vernon, N.Y.), and others

HALLELUJAH, I'M A BUM (United Artists, 1933)
Screenplay: S. N. Behrman (from a story by Ben Hecht)
Musical Dialoguers: Richard Rodgers, Lorenz Hart
Photography: Lucien Andriot
Art Direction: Richard Day
Music Direction: Alfred Newman
Cast: Al Jolson (Bumper), Madge Evans (June Marcher), Harry Langdon
  (Egghead), Frank Morgan (Mayor Hastings), Chester Conklin (Sun-
  day)
Running Time: 82 minutes
New York Preview: February 8, 1933
Availability: for unknown reasons, the film is today being distributed under
  the title *Heart of New York,* despite the fact that this leads to confusion
  with another Warner Brothers film directed by Mervyn LeRoy that has
  borne that title since its release in 1932. Sale: 16mm, Super-8mm, and
  videotape, Cinema 8 (Chester, Conn.); 16mm sale and rental, Learning
  Corporation of America and many others

THE CAPTAIN HATES THE SEA (Columbia, 1934)
Screenplay: Wallace Smith (from his own story)
Photography: Joseph August
Editing: Gene Milford
Cast: Victor McLaglen, John Gilbert, Walter Connolly, Alison Skipworth, Wynne Gibson, Helen Vinson, The Three Stooges
Running Time: 92 minutes
New York Preview: October 22, 1934
16mm rental: Kit Parker Films (Carmel Valley, Calif.)

PARIS IN THE SPRING (Paramount, 1935)
Screenplay: Samuel Hoffenstein, Franz Schulz, Keene Thompson (from a play by Dwight Taylor)
Photography: Ted Tetzlaff
Art Direction: Hans Dreier, Ernst Fegte
Editing: Eda Warren
Music: Harry Revel
Cast: Mary Ellis, Tullio Carminati, Ida Lupino, Lynne Overman, James Blakeley
Running Time: 83 Minutes
New York Preview: July 5, 1935
Not available for sale or rental

ANYTHING GOES (Paramount, 1936)
Screenplay: Howard Lindsay, Russell Crouse, Guy Bolton, P. G. Wodehouse (from their musical comedy)
Photography: Karl Struss
Art Director: Hans Dreier, Ernst Fegte
Editing: Eda Warren
Music and Lyrics: Cole Porter (with additional songs by others)
Additional Songs: Leo Robin, Richard A. Whiting, Frederick Hollander, Hoagy Carmichael
Cast: Bing Crosby (Billy Crocker) Ethel Merman (Reno Sweeney), Charles Ruggles (Rev. Dr. Moon, Public Enemy # 13), Ida Lupino (Hope Harcourt)
Running Time: 92 minutes
New York Preview: January 24, 1936
16mm rental: Paramount Pictures Non-Theatrical Division (Hollywood)

THE GENERAL DIED AT DAWN (Paramount, 1936)
Production: William LeBaron
Screenplay: Clifford Odets (from a novel by Charles G. Booth)

Photography: Victor Milner
Art Direction: Hans Dreier, Ernst Fegte
Editing: Eda Warren
Music: Werner Janssen
Cast: Gary Cooper (O'Hara), Madeleine Carroll (Judy Perrie), Akim
    Tamiroff (General Yang), Porter Hall (Peter Perrie), William Frawley
    (Brighton), Philip Ahn (Oxford)
Running Time: 98 minutes
New York Preview: September 4, 1936
16mm rental: United Artists 16 (New York)

THE NIGHT OF NIGHTS (Paramount, 1939)
Screenplay: Donald Ogden Stewart
Photography: Leo Tover
Art Direction: Hans Dreier
Editing: Doane Harrison, Hugh Bennett
Cast:Pat O'Brien, Olympe Bradna, Roland Young, Reginald Gardiner,
    George E. Stone
Running Time: 85 minutes
New York Preview:December 1, 1939
Not available for sale or rental

OF MICE AND MEN (Hal Roach Studios/United Artists, 1939)
Production: Lewis Milestone
Screenplay: Eugene Solow (from a novel and play by John Steinbeck)
Photography: Norbert Brodine
Art Director: Nicolai Remisoff
Editing: Bert Jordan
Music: Aaron Copland
Cast: Burgess Meredith (George), Betty Field (Mae), Lon Chaney, Jr.
    (Lennie), Charles Bickford (Slim), Roman Bohnen (Candy), Bob Steele
    (Curly)
Running Time: 106 minutes
New York Preview: January 12, 1940
16mm sale and rental: Corinth Films (New York)

LUCKY PARTNERS (RKO, 1940)
Production: Harry E. Edington, George Haight
Screenplay: Allan Scott, John Van Druten (from Sacha Guitry's play and
    film *Bonne Chance*)
Photography: Robert DeGrasse
Art Direction: Van Nest Polglase

Editing: Henry Berman
Music: Dmitri Tiomkin
Cast: Ronald Colman, Ginger Rogers, Jack Carson, Spring Byington, Cecilia
    Loftus
Running Time: 101 minutes
New York Preview: August 30, 1940
16mm rental: Films, Inc. (Wilmette, Ill.)

MY LIFE WITH CAROLINE (United Producers/RKO, 1941)
Screenplay: John VanDruten, Arnold Belgard (from a play, *Train to Paris*,
    by Louis Verneuil, Georges Berr)
Photography: Victor Milner
Art Direction: Nicolai Remisoff
Editing: Henry Berman
Music: Werner Heymann
Cast: Ronald Colman, Anna Lee, Charles Winninger, Reginald Gardiner,
    Gilbert Roland
Running Time: 81 minutes
New York Preview: August 1, 1941

OUR RUSSIAN FRONT (Russian War Relief, Incorporated, 1942)
Production: Joris Ivens, Lewis Milestone
Photography: Russian Frontline Cameramen
Editing: Lewis Milestone
Commentary: Elliot Paul
Narration: Walter Huston
Music: Dmitri Tiomkin
Running Time: 40 minutes
New York Preview: February 1942

EDGE OF DARKNESS (Warner Brothers, 1943)
Production: Henry Blanke and Jack L. Warner
Screenplay: Robert Rossen (from a novel by William Woods)
Photography: Sid Hickox
Art Direction: Robert Haas
Editing: David Weisbart
Music: Franz Waxman
Cast: Errol Flynn (Gunnar Brogge), Ann Sheridan (Karen Stensgard),
    Nancy Coleman (Katja), Judith Anderson (Gerd Bjarnsen), Helmut
    Dantine (Capt. Koenig)
Running Time: 118 minutes

New York Preview: April 24. 1943
16mm rental: United Artists 16 (New York)

THE NORTH STAR (RKO, 1943)
Production: Sam Goldwyn
Screenplay: Lillian Hellman
Photography: James Wong Howe
Art Direction: Perry Ferguson
Editing: Daniel Mandell
Music: Aaron Copland
Cast: Anne Baxter (Marina), Dana Andrews (Kolya), Walter Huston (Dr. Kurin), Walter Brennan (Karp), Ann Harding (Sophia)
Running Time: 105 minutes
New York Preview: November 4, 1943
Availability: 8mm sale, Cinema 8 (Chester, Conn.); 16mm rental (82-minute version), Budget Films (Los Angeles), Ivy Films (New York); (109-minute version), Kit Parker Films (Carmel Valley, Calif.)

THE PURPLE HEART (20th Century–Fox, 1944)
Production: Darryl F. Zanuck
Screenplay: Jerome Cady (from a story by Melville Crossman, probably a pen name for Darryl F. Zanuck)
Photography: Arthur Miller
Art Direction: James Basevi, Lewis Creber
Editing: Douglas Biggs
Music: Alfred Newman
Cast: Dana Andrews (Capt. Ross), Richard Conte (Lt. Angelo Canelli), Farley Granger (Sgt. Howard Clinton), Kevin O'Shea (Sgt. Jan Skvoznik), Donald Barry (Lt. Peter Vincent), Sam Levine (Lt. Greenbaum)
Running Time: 99 minutes
New York Preview: March 1944
16mm rental: Films, Inc. (Wilmette, Ill.)

A WALK IN THE SUN (20th Century–Fox, 1945)
Production: Lewis Milestone
Screenplay: Robert Rossen (from a novel by Harry Brown)
Photography: Russell Harlan
Art Direction: Max Bertisch
Editing: W. Duncan Mansfield
Music: Frederic Efrem Rich
Cast: Dana Andrews (Sgt. Tyne), John Ireland (Windy), Richard Conte (Riviera), Sterling Holloway (McWilliams), George Tyne (Friedman), Norman Lloyd (Archimbeau), Lloyd Bridges (Sgt. Ward)

Running Time: 117 minutes
New York Preview: March 1946
Availability: 16, 8mm, and videotape sale, Cinema 8 (Chester, Conn.),
    Glenn Photo Supply (Encino, Calif.); 16mm sale and rental, Kit Parker
    Films (Carmel Valley, Calif.); 16mm rental, Budget Films (Los Ange-
    les), Images (Rye, N.Y.), MacMillan (Mt. Vernon, N.Y.), and others

THE STRANGE LOVE OF MARTHA IVERS (Paramount, 1946)
Production: Hal B. Wallis
Screenplay: Robert Rossen (from a story by John Patrick)
Photography: Victor Milner
Art Direction: Hans Dreier, John Meehan
Editing: Archie Marshek
Music: Miklos Rozsa
Cast: Barbara Stanwyck (Martha Ivers), Van Heflin (Sam Masterton), Kirk
    Douglas (Walter O'Neil), Lizabeth Scott (Toni Maracek), Judith
    Anderson (Mrs. Ivers)
Running Time: 117 minutes
New York Preview: September 13, 1946
Availability: Sale, Syndicate Films (Dallas), 16mm and Super-8mm, Reel
    Images (North Hollywood), 16mm, 16mm rental, Kit Parker Films
    (Carmel Valley, Calif.)

ARCH OF TRIUMPH (Enterprise/United Artists, 1948)
Screenplay: Lewis Milestone, Harry Brown (from a novel by Erich Maria
    Remarque)
Photography: Russell Harlan
Art Direction: William Cameron Menzies
Editing: W. Duncan Mansfield
Music: Morris Stoloff
Cast: Charles Boyer (Ravic), Ingrid Bergman (Joan Madou), Charles
    Laughton (Haake), Louis Calhern (Morosow), Roman Bohnen
    (Dr. Veher)
Running Time: 115 minutes
New York Preview: April 30, 1948
16mm rental: Ivy Films (New York)

NO MINOR VICES (Enterprise/MGM, 1948)
Production: Lewis Milestone
Screenplay: Arnold Manoff (from his own story)
Photography: George Barnes
Art Direction: Nicolai Remisoff

Editing: Robert Parrish
Music: Franz Waxman
Cast: Dana Andrews, Lilli Palmer, Louis Jourdan, Jane Wyatt, Norman Lloyd
Running Time: 96 minutes
New York Preview: November 12, 1948
16mm rental: Ivy Films (New York)

THE RED PONY (Republic, 1949)
Production: Lewis Milestone
Screenplay: John Steinbeck (from his own story sequence)
Photography: Tony Gaudio (color)
Production Design: Nicolai Remisoff
Art Direction: Victor Greene
Editing: Harry Keller
Music: Aaron Copland
Cast: Myrna Loy (Alice Tiflin), Robert Mitchum (Billy Buck), Louis Calhern (Grandfather), Shepperd Strudwick (Fred Tiflin), Peter Miles (Tom)
Running Time: 89 minutes
New York Preview: March 28, 1949
16mm rental: Budget Films (Los Angeles), Ivy Films (New York), Kit Parker Films (Carmel Valley, Calif.), and many other regional distributors

HALLS OF MONTEZUMA (20th Century–Fox, 1951)
Screenplay: Michael Blankfort (from his own story)
Photography: Winton C. Hoch, Harry Jackson (color)
Art Direction: Lyle Wheeler, Albert Hogstett
Editing: William Reynolds
Music: Sol Kaplan
Cast: Richard Widmark (Anderson), Walter Jack Palance (Pigeon Lane), Reginald Gardiner (Johnson), Robert Wagner (Coffman), Karl Malden (Doc)
Running Time: 113 minutes
New York Preview: January 1951
16mm rental: Films, Inc. (Wilmette, Ill.)

KANGAROO (20th Century–Fox, 1952)
Screenplay: Harry Kleiner (from a story by Martin Berkeley)
Photography: Charles G. Clarke (color)
Art Direction: Lyle Wheeler, Mark Lee-Kirk

Editing: Nick DeMaggio
Music: Sol Kaplan
Cast: Peter Lawford, Maureen O'Hara, Finlay Currie, Richard Boone, Chips Rafferty
Running Time: 84 minutes
New York Preview: June 1952
Not available for sale or rental

LES MISERABLES (20th Century–Fox, 1952)
Screenplay: Richard Murphy (from the novel by Victor Hugo)
Photography: Joseph LaSchelle
Art Direction: Lyle Wheeler, J. Russell Spencer
Editing: Hugh Fowler
Music: Alec North
Cast: Michael Rennie, Debra Paget, Robert Newton, Edmund Gwenn, Sylvia Sidney
Running Time: 104 minutes
New York Preview: August 1952
16mm rental: Films, Inc. (Wilmette Ill.)

MELBA (United Artists, 1953)
Production: Sam Spiegel
Screenplay: Harry Kurnitz (from his own story)
Photography: Ted Scaife (color)
Art Direction: Andre Andrejev
Editing: William J. Lewthwaite
Music: Muir Mathieson
Cast: Patrice Munsel (Nellie Melba), Robert Morley (Oscar Hammerstein), John McCallum, John Justin, Alec Clunes, Sybil Thorndyke (Queen Victoria)
Running Time: 113 minutes
New York Preview: August 7, 1953
Not available for sale or rental

THEY WHO DARE (Mayflower Pictures/British Lion, 1953)
Screenplay: Robert Westerby
Photography: Wilkie Cooper
Art Director: Don Ashton
Editing: V. Sagovsky
Music: Robert Gill
Cast: Dirk Bogarde, Denholm Elliott, Akim Tamiroff, Gerard Oury, Eric Pohlmann

Running Time: 101 minutes
Note: Released in England in 1953 and in the United States in 1955. No reviewers' preview or first-run house showing in New York. Not available for sale or rental in United States

LA VEDOVA (English Title, **THE WIDOW**) (Venturini/Express, 1954)
Screenplay: Louis Stevens (from a novel by Susan York)
Photography: Arturo Gallea
Music: Mario Nascimbene
Cast: Patricia Roc, Anna Maria Ferrero, Massimo Serato, Akim Tamiroff, Leonard Botta
Running Time: 89 minutes
New York Preview: May 1957
Not available for sale or rental

PORK CHOP HILL (Melville/United Artists, 1959)
Production: Sy Bartlett
Screenplay: James R. Webb (from a book by S. L. A. Marshall)
Photography: Sam Leavitt
Art Direction: Nicolai Remisoff
Editing: George Boemler
Music: Leonard Roseman
Cast: Gregory Peck, Harry Guardino, George Shibata, Woody Strode, Robert Blake, James Edwards, Lewis Gallo
Running Time: 97 minutes
New York Preview: May 1959
16mm rental: United Artists 16 (New York)

OCEAN'S ELEVEN (Dorchester/Warner Brothers, 1960)
Production: Lewis Milestone
Screenplay: Harry Brown, Charles Lederer (from a story by George Clayton Johnson)
Photography: William H. Daniels (color)
Art Direction: Nicolai Remisoff
Editing: Philip W. Anderson
Music: Nelson Riddle
Cast: Frank Sinatra, Dean Martin, Sammy Davis, Jr., Peter Lawford, Angie Dickinson, Richard Conte
Running Time: 128 minutes
New York Preview: August 1960
16mm rental: Budget Films (Los Angeles), MacMillan (Mt. Vernon, N.Y.),

Select Films (New York), and many other national and regional distributors

MUTINY ON THE BOUNTY (Arcola/MGM, 1962)

Production: Aaron Rosenberg

Screenplay: Charles Lederer (from books by Charles Nordhoff, James Norman Hall)

Photography: Robert L. Surtees (color)

Art Direction: George W. Davis, J. McMillan Johnson

Editing: John McSweeney, Jr.

Music: Bronislau Kaper

Cast: Marlon Brando (Fletcher Christian), Trevor Howard (Capt. William Bligh), John Mills, Richard Harris, Hugh Griffith, Richard Haydn

Running Time: 179 minutes

New York Preview: November 1962

16mm rental and lease: Films, Inc. (Wilmette, Ill.)

Index

215

DATE DUE			
DE 1 4 '93			